MY RANDOM
REFLECTIONS

MY RANDOM REFLECTIONS

G. Palanithurai

Professor, Rajiv Gandhi Chair for Panchayati Raj Studies
Department of Political Science and Development
Administration Gandhigram Rural Institute –
Deemed University, Dindigul

Chennai   Trichy   New Delhi

ISBN 978-81-949040-0-7   **MJP Publishers**

All rights reserved   New No. 44 Nallathambi
Printed and bound in India   Street, Triplicane,
Chennai 600 005

MJP 1019   © Publishers, 2021

Publisher : C. Janarthanan

Preface

I am an academic activist and a development practitioner served in a Gandhian institution for more than two decades. While I was in the higher learning institution (Gandhigram Rural Institute – Deemed to be University), I have committed myself in the outreach activities to reach out to the rustic folk in the rural areas as I was deeply influenced by M.K.Gandhi. Any work I do wherever I am I use to think of the outcome of work from the perspective of the poorest of the poor. Further, I have learnt the perspective from M.K. Gandhi to look at issues and to respect the voice of the poor. Hence, I strongly believe the power of the participation of the poor in governance and development for the emancipation and empowerment of the poor and the marginalised. When I involved myself in teaching, research and outreach activities, I found varied opportunities for immense real learning from the class room, field and research activities. I taught socially relevant academic programmes, did research on socially relevant issues and carried out impact making outreach activities. My academic life became meaningful and purposeful only when I connect myself with community. When I started connecting myself with the community in the rural areas, in that process I learnt the art of working with people. When I work with the community my language has been changed. I have learnt the language of the poor and I never use the language of the rich and the knowledgeable. Academics who are in higher learning institutions have to work with community and thereby academics can play their meaningful role in the transformative process of the society. My two and half decades experience in working with the rustic folk in the rural areas enabled me to understand the power of public opinion. Hence, I felt that it is necessary to provide needed information to the public to create public opinion for public action. In this regard, I started writing popular articles with a purpose of sharing my views and opinion on the critical issues of development of the people with the public. For a long, I have done only academic and research writings. It is only my friends insisted that I have to share my experiences and opinions to a larger audience. My learning has to be shared with many for the benefit of the society. In this context, I have been asked to write popular articles on the themes which I have taught and did research. I always believe strongly that creating public opinion will change the life of the society. To shape public opinion I have written popular articles on politics, development, governance, decentralization, administration, participation, democratization, education and so on. They are published in the newspaper Millennium Post. All the articles are compiled in the form of a monograph.

Acknowledgement

Being a student of political science, governance and public administration, I taught the students of Masters in Development Management for a period of two and half decades. While interacting with the students in the class-room and in the field, many of the students used to ask questions on many subjects not akin to the studies. I tried to give answer to all those questions, many of the questions are relating to politics, governance, leadership, development framework, development practices and participation. While giving reply to the students, many of the students asked me, why it is not taken to the public for their consumption as all the explanations are pertinent to problems of the public. Further, a few of my friends requested me to write popular articles in English for a larger audience as I have been doing this job in Tamil to reach out to the public with objective of educating the public on politics, governance, administration and development. Hence, I started writing articles for Millennium Post. All the published articles are compiled in the form of a small monograph. Any venture requires support from many fronts. First when I started writing in English my friends enthusiastically read and giving feedback to my articles. They have encouraged me to continue the exercise. I am continuing till to-day. All the articles are published in Millennium post.

First I register my sincere thanks to the editor Millennium Post for publishing all my articles which enabled me to travel in a different domain which is totally a new experience.

My friends in the university, in the Department and in public life read all the articles and shared their feedback. I register my thanks to all my friends. At family front my daughter, son in law, grandson, my son, daughter in law and granddaughter never bothered me and they are very generous in allowing me to do whatever I want to do in academic domain and they deserve my appreciations. My wife Mala is a generous and warm hearted person took pain to manage the family works without disturbing me which ultimately enabled me to devote my whole time for academic works. She is my support and force behind me for all my public and academic activities.

She deserves my appreciation. Finally, I thank the publishers for their professional work.

G. Palanithurai

Introduction

We are in democracy. True, our's is a democratic country. What it means to poor in the rural areas. It is mere election. How elections are fought? Elections are not based on the real issues of the toiling millions. The issues are being used only during election. After the elections, things are as usual. The disparities between rich and the poor, inequalities among the social groups, exclusions, and discriminations continue to haunt our democracy. The social practices continue to challenge the power of democracy. The electoral democracy gives leverage to socially dominant groups and their leaders to wield power continuously in the society despite the constitutional mandate of equality and equity. Series of enactments of legislations in National Parliament and State Legislatures to protect the poor and plethora of schemes and programmes coupled with huge outlays for the development of the poor and the marginalized have been done. They are the weapons of the oppressed and they could be used to empower the poor and the marginalized.

Even after 73 years of democratic governance and development administration in India, 80 crore people still relying on the help of the state machinery to meet their basic requirements and more specifically for their food. The political parties are able to mobilise successfully people for electoral politics, but failed to mobilise them for participation in governance and development. Still the political parties are not able to sensitize the toiling millions on the substantial issues of democracy and development and hence people have been oriented to be either voters or beneficiaries rather than the responsible citizens to discharge the responsibility and duties of citizens in a free democracy. All the democratic institutions are symbolically democratic but behaviourally otherwise. When India has achieved its economic growth to the tune of 7.5, it has not reflected in the human development aspects of the Indian society. Yet India lives in democracy. What kind of democracy India has? It is out and out institutional and not behavioural. As a result, India still lives in authoritarian mode with feudal outlook. In this context, my continuous engagement with political parties, government departments, civil society organisations, local bodies, opinion makers enabled me to move away from the conventional framework of looking at issues and ponder over the critical issues of development. All my reflections have been shared with my academic and media friends to provoke them and after getting their feedback, I put them in the form of popular articles on varied subjects. Much of the articles were on politics and governance, administration, development, public participation, public opinion, local governance, education and a few other issues. They were published in Millennium Post in New Delhi. It is meant for popular consumption. As my friends insisted that all the articles published in Millennium Post have to be compiled in the form of a monograph. Hence this book.

Contents

Section I
Politics and Governance

1. A Leader to be Cherished

Muthuvel Karunanidhi popularly called "Kalaignar" left the world with indelible mark in Tamil Nadu politics economy, literature and society through his leadership and creative politics. His contributions are unfathomable. His contributions have been highlighted by the luminaries in the respected field while remembrance meetings have been organized in different places. The meetings had been organized after his demise in different regions of Tamil Nadu by different groups representing different fields of activities. Born in a rustic family in a feudal social setting in an integrated Tanjure district M. Karunanidhi became a party leader for five decades and the chief minister of Tamil Nadu for five times and known for his adventures and achievements in politics, governance, administration, silver screen and in the world of literature. An unusual youth with an obsession to bring social transformation, he was in search of guidance and mentor devoid of personal career ambition at the age of fourteen. He was a self-educated and a self-made man. He relentlessly pursued the path of social transformatory politics negating the established social systems and orders. A revolutionary in thinking and action began his journey at the age of fourteen and ended it at the age of ninety four, Eighty years of political experience, fifty years of party leadership experience, sixty years of experience in legislative politics he lived up with a sense of purpose and left a legacy and an imprint in leadership. He is a role model for many who are interested in transformative politics. He had been shaped, groomed and sharpened as a political leader not by any individual but through a theory of "Challenge and response". He learnt only through facing and responding challenges. He was the first in using the silver screen for socio political transformation. By responding to all challenges he won many victories not in election alone but in transforming the thought process of the people and discourses in Tamil polity. His backward and forward linkages have enabled him to ground his strategy in regional politics. His understanding of social justice and social development could be seen through the schemes and programmes meant for the poor and the deprived. No other leader in the country has had such a kind of political acumen to make an in-depth social analysis of the conditions of the marginalized and the poor and to find remedy to all the social ills in Tamil Society.

His communication ability is unfathomable to reach out to the sense and emotions of the people. He used the silver screen to reach out to the masses for social transformation. He always exhibited his concern for the poor and the marginalized. Equally his organizational ability to keep the party and cadres is unusual. He strongly believed in the strength of the organization (his political party) to deliver what he wanted to deliver through politics and governance. He has integrated his party cadres in the process of implementation of many of his pet schemes which has yielded good results and thereby he succeeded in implementing many of his development programmes as he expected. At the same time he has developed his ability to contextualize the organization, strategies and activities of the party to sustain the organization with vibrancy.

His relationship with media is unique as he himself a publisher of a newspaper and a writer. He always exhibited his sobriety and tolerance which made the press comfortable with him. He always maintained a cordial relationship with media representatives. Having served in print media, he developed the art of attracking the media. He used the media to get feedback from the people about the performance of the party in power.

His commitment to democracy is demonstrated not only through his opposition to emergency but also in listening to the dissent voice. He respected the dissent voice. He has the ability to turn his worst critics towards his side only through listening the dissent voice. His scholarship in Tamil helped him to educate the masses and made the masses to evince interest in Tamil language and Tamil literature. Apart from all, his hard work and scientific management of time is the hall mark of his leadership and a role model. Since he hailed from obscurity he knows the pain of the poor. He is always conscious and sensitive towards marginalization and discrimination. Having fought in his political career as a leader of a party, a movement and government, he never declared that he has transformed everything which he wanted to achieve. Lot more to do, hence this journey has to continue till we achieve social justice and economic justice to all. This was his wish and declarations. Will the party continue his struggle in the ideological path of M. Karunanidhi is the question tinkering in the minds of the people?

2. A Mass Leader Misunderstood

Every year 30th October, a huge crowd throngs a villge 'pasumpon' in Ramnad district of Tamil Nadu to celebrate the birth anniversary of Muthuramalinga Thevar, popularly called 'Devar Thirumaganar'. He was called Tilak of South India. It is a strange event that his birth and death fell on the same date. He was with Indian National Congress till 1939 and later with Forward Block till his death. He was a freedom fighter and spent ten years in Jail. He belonged to a landlord family with justice party background. He renounced his family life by negating marriage. He was known for his spiritual approach towards politics and dedication to freedom struggle and nation building. He was attracted towards Subas Chndra Bose and hence he was in forward block till his demise. For him spirituality and patriotism are the two eyes of the Indian nation. He led a simple bachelor life with high moral standard. He had distributed his lands in thirty six villages to Dalit families of those villages. He was elected to Parliament by defeating the candidate of the justice party. He was a charismatic leader and a powerful orator with a huge following. He was a tallest leader in each indicator of the transformational leadership. He is not only fought for freedom but also waged a relentless struggle against the British to liberate a number of rustic communities from the stigma attached with them through passing the Criminal Tribes Act in the year 1920. These communities had been mobilized by him for this struggle and ultimately he won the struggle against the British. It is to be understood that he was a reformer. He was instrumental for the temple entry event conducted in Meenakshi temple where Dalits went into the Meenakshi temple. He enabled such events in other temples also. He was a factor to reckon with in Tamil Nadu politics till his demise at the age of fifty five.

It is a tradition in India and Tamil Nadu that people use to go to the places where the leaders had been laid to rest or consecrated and pay their tributes both on birth and death anniversary days. But Pasumpon Muthuramalinga Thevar memorial and remembrance activities are different from other leaders. Many may not know this and hence people and political leaders treat it as yet another leader's memorial. Unlike other leaders, he was laid to rest in a Samadhi by performing the rituals to be performed for the saints and sages. It was done by following the tradition advocated by Saint Ramalinganar. His body was laid to rest in a Samadhi and the activities connected to it were done by a saint. The whole activities were carried out by a spiritual guru not by priest or politicians. It is a place of worship not as a memorial. Memorials had been created for C.N.Annadurai, K.Kamaraj, M.Karunanidhi, M.G.R. and J.Jayalalitha. All other leaders had been laid to rest in a memorial and where there is no religious sanctity attached to it. But Muthuramalinga Thevar Samadhi is unique compared with the places where great saints and sages were laid to rest. This distinction has to be understood by everyone. The annual event is being conducted for all leaders for both birth and death day. The event is being performed as it is performed to sages and saints. It is a function for three days with full of rituals as per the tradition. Huge mobilization of people takes place every year during the event which is called "Guru Pooja". For all other leaders, it is not Gurupooja and it happened only one day but for Muthuramalinga Thevar it takes places for three days. All the three days Poojas are being performed. Spiritual significance is attached with the celebration.

On the third day of the function all political leaders with their supporters visit the Samadhi and pay their tributes by placing flowers on the feet of the statue. Here sacred ash is being distributed and every leader used to get it and add it on their forehead. Such religious sanctity is attached to it. They get sacred ash as Prasad. This is being done with the aim of drawing the support of the Thevar community. No mainstream political party stays away from this event. There is yet another group visits the shrine from the same community to give a message to the political class that Thevar community is a force to reckon with in Tamil Nadu politics. Women go to those places as they go to temples with deep religious values and sentiments. It is yet another pity that there is a social group dalits who look at this event as it is a kind of mobilization to establish the superity of a caste by using this opportunity. Clashes had been witnessed between these two communities during this period in the past in and around Pasumpon where the function held. Hence, police force has been heavily deployed every year to keep the event free from violence.

Politics perpetuated in Tamil Nadu has reduced a tall, acclaimed, spiritual, transformational and national leader with unique traits into a caste leader without knowing the contributions made by the leader and his perspective. It is a low level of politics to visit the holy place with an objective of cornering the votes of the Thevar community by the parties which are having the objectives totally against the politics practiced by Muthuramalinga Thevar. The political parties have not given the place worthy of the stature of Muthuramalinga Thevar. Thevar chairs have been created in may universities and yet there is no substantial research contribution from the chair. They also conducted meetings annually as rituals.

No other leader's Memorial Day can be compared with the "Guru Pooja" of Muthuramalinga Thevar. His contributions are unfathomable but the manner in which the parties conducted themselves during the Guru Pooja day is unacceptable to any standard as he has been converted into a caste leader. It is a politics of simplification and reductionism.

3. A New Paradigm of Politics

The victory of the BJP under the leadership of Narendra Modi and Amitshah in the 2019 Lok Sabha Election signaled the emergence of a new narrative and a paradigm called "Limited Democracy for Development". Democracy being prime engine for development through state intervention failed to deliver services to all and hence market assumed primacy to achieve the same. At the end of three decades development experience in the market era a new conclusion has been drawn that both the state and the market have failed to live up to the promises and they are to be regulated in response to the call of the people and for which a consciousness raising among the public about their role and responsibilities in the process of development and governance, is an imperative need. At this point of time the BJP has emerged in a new form with a new narrative and ultimately it becomes a new paradigm.

The new narrative comes with new belief, values and framework of actions. The new narrative believes in leadership, nation, national pride, national culture and values. It is totally based on faith and belief not on logical and scientific arguments and discourses. It does not value arguments in authoritative bodies like legislature and parliament. Because these institutions have witnessed veritable only pandimonious and acrimonious debates. Hence debates and discourses are considered as mere waste of time. If a able leader is emerging he or she will achieve development by effectively steering the government. It rests on the ability of the leadership and capacity of the organizations to follow the command of the leader. It assiduously argue for action rather than debate and discourses. For the new narrative arguments and discourses are leading nowhere and they are considered detractive forces. In this new framework consciousness of the people on the native broader culture and values have been enhanced to turn the pride of the country. Action has to be taken to deliver services and goods but it need not provide opportunity for any lengthy debate or discourses. All democratic debates and discourses would be discouraged as anti-development forces. All market strategies would be adopted to change the mindset of the people. People are emotionally turned towards the emotive issues of the nation, its pride and its security which require not money but only inflammatory speeches. This is also not in a debate mode. All democratic practices not only in policy making bodies but also in the party pushed to the background in the name of discipline and development. The BJP has brought this narrative as many of the political parties in India are feudal in character and mostly the regional political parties supposed to be democratic but in reality they are not. For vibrant debate and discourses, leaders should have honesty, integrity and soul force. Unfortunately major political parties who were in power in the era of globalization have lost their integrity. So this election is not mere a change of party in power. 2014 signalled the change of course of politics. By all means, the BJP has furthered the new paradigm of politics whereby it gives a goby to the liberal democratic values. Even the opposition parties are also not interested in bringing the liberal values. Hence it helped the BJP to bring this narrative. Roads will be laid, bridges will be constructed, electricity would be generated adequately to meet the needs of India, companies would be given permission to use liberally the natural and precious minerals to accelerate growth, new canals would be created, new ports and airports would be created. Newer four ways, six ways and eight ways long roads would be created to promote four wheeler sales and for easy transportation of goods and natural resources to different places. These are all development works and this cannot be questioned. If it is questioned, the person who raises questions would be termed as anti-development and anti-nation. Decisions would emanate from the top and they are to be followed. Democracy will take the backseat and in such a way courses are already chalked out. All liberal values have been pushed to the background.

The opposition have to chalk out a new course of action. The entire politics has to be changed to the effect that the conventional approach of politics has to be changed from electoral and legislative politics to people's movement politics. It needs unity among the opposition parties to enter into politics of struggle. This is the only way to change the nature of politics. Will the opposition ready for a new task and responsibility? We have to wait and see.

4. A New Paradigm of Sarkar

Electoral process started in India to constitute the next Lok Sabha. In this context, a controversial film in Tamil draws the attention of the Election Commission. Sarkar (Government) is a Tamil movie acted by Vijay a popular, young and leading actor in Tamil Nadu and directed by Murugadoss. It was released on the day of Deepavali. Within a few days of its release one of the Minister of the AIADMK government have criticized that the film has shown the AIADMK and it leaders in bad light and hence those scenes have to be removed. Cadres of the AIADMK have organized protest meetings in front of the cinema houses allover Tamil Nadu. Within a few days the objectionable scenes as indicated by the AIADMK government have been removed. The controversy and agitations have created curiosity among the ordinary viewers and as result the film gained much popularity. If a sensible individual views it he or she will come to a conclusion that it is an effective film to be screened in every village and in every street of towns and municipalities to create awareness among the voters about the significance of the ballot paper how it could be used for the benefit of the people. This film can be recommended by the Election Commission of India to be screened all over the country in different languages. Apart from the importance of the ballot paper it brings to the notice of the people that the centralized system of party control has to be dispensed with through evolving an alternative system of decentralized people centric evolutionary politics to bring accountability on the part of the elected representatives.

Further, how valuable citizens have been reduced as voters by the political parties, as beneficiaries by the government as petitioners by the bureaucracy and customers and consumers by the market have been emotionally explained in this film. People are the primary agents to bring transformation in society and politics but in reality they are the most disrespected individuals in the society by the political and bureaucratic class in India. The film has brought to light the decentralized model of politics to cleanse the corrupt government, administration and politics. This has been suggested in Gorwal Committee at the dawn of independence that the Indian National Congress to search for talented committed social workers for the party to contest in the general election on behalf of the party. In this film, it has been portrayed that best service minded social workers can be involved in politics by drawing them from different field and they are to be nominated to contest in the election on the party ticket. By which huge professionals could be inducted into the policy making system.

There is yet another message has been conveyed convincingly and powerfully to the people that raising question is the hallmark of democracy. In our democracy, questioning is totally prohibited in the name of discipline in all the democratic institutions. In this film, it has been highlighted that without raising question equality cannot be achieved and democracy will not mature. All these message have communicated through the actor Vijay by writing a powerful dialogue in this film.

In the electoral process of a democracy, if a party gets huge majority by weakening the opposition party in terms of its strength, it is not a victory for democracy. This aspect has been convincingly scripted and communicated through the powerful dialogue delivered by the hero. It is out and out a political movie with hard ideas communicated in a simple way. It is a highly educative movie.

The dialogues scripted for the film criticized both the Dravidian parties not only the AIADMK. Why then the AIADMK ministers alone unnecessarily raised objections and asked them to cut a few scenes in the movie. They assumed that it is a movie completely criticized the AIADMK. Really, it is not so. The film outrightly condemned both the parties as they involved in practicing cash for votes and delivering freebies. The film argues for an alternative paradigm to the existing political party framework of politics.

Deeper democratic values are highlighted in a simple way to the public. Since Sun pictures involved in production, the DMK kept quiet. Of all the fan clubs, Vijay fan clubs has got more number of youths. He has a huge following also. He takes a different line unlike Kamal and Rajinikanth. He took an open stand against the central government and the state government. When GST was welcomed by all cine actors, he was the only person opposed it. Kamal and Rajini both are old but he is young. Yet, he indicates that he will enter into politics. This creates fear among political parties. Whenever, Vijay produces films of this sort, it is being opposed by political parties and through which curiosity has been raised among the people and thereby huge advertisement is being given free of cost. This film also had the same fate but it succeeded by earning more than their expectation. This movie has to be recommended by the Election Commission to be screened all over the country in the respective regional languages for the benefit of the public. The Election Commission has repeatedly made it clear that it faces the problem of cash for votes in South India more particularly in Tamil Nadu. In this context, this film is a welcome one to create awareness among the people about the value of votes. The entire team has to be appreciated. It is an excellent movie to create voters awareness among the people. It out rightly attacks all unethical electoral political practices to cleanse body politics. It is one of the best political movies taken in the recent past in Tamil.

5. Allies are Arch Enemies in the Electoral Battle in Tamil Nadu

Tamil Nadu electoral politics was dominated by two main political parties namely the Indian National Congress and the Dravida Munnetra Kazhagam (DMK) till the beginning of 1970 since independence. After the demise of K. Kamaraj and the formation of the All India Anna Dravida Munnetra Kazhagam (AIADMK) by M. G. Ramachandran the political process was dominated by both the (DMK) and the (AIADMK). Ever since the first general election to Tamil Nadu Legislative Assembly the National and regional political parties under the leadership of great stalwarts could not emerge victoriously in the election on their own. They need the support of smaller parties. It continued even after 1970's and both the DMK and the AIADMK sought the help of smaller parties to face the election under the leadership of M. Karunanidhi and M. G. Ramachandran respectively. Both leaders had very rich political experience and mass following. This trend had continued till the last general election to Tamil Nadu Legislative Assembly. But now in the present election a variety of political formations have emerged and it created a new trend in the political process while the political parties face the Assembly elections on 16th May, 2016.

The new trend is that almost all smaller political parties have started accusing both the DMK and the AIADMK and made scathing attack on them. They brought allegations against both the DMK and the AIADMK for their corrupt practices and following a specific practice of paternalism. Both parties brought Tamil Nadu politics to the lowest ebb by indulging in corruption in governance, administration and public life. They have been pursuing populist policies to lure the voters apart from pursuing pro-poor policies and programmes. It is to be noted here that in India both the DMK and the AIADMK are known for their pro poor policies. Even before Amartya Sen talked about social development the DMK under its leadership of M. Karunanidhi introduced slew of social development programme in Tamil Nadu. In the same the AIADMK under the leadership of M.G. Ramachandran introduced an array of direct benefit social security schemes to the ultra poor in Tamil Nadu. Till date major segments of the middle class and lower middle class are with the DMK and major segments of the poor are with the AIADMK. Yet they are being attacked by all smaller parties. It is alleged that voters have been bribed by both political parties by using the money which they amassed while they were in power alternatively. These two political parties have adopted client pattern policy to keep the party cadres intact, and they followed big brother attitude while maintaining relationship with the smaller parties. These two political parties have adopted a paternalistic attitude towards other political parties. They form alliances with smaller parties to face the elections. Once election is over these small parties are treated very badly and shabbily. Further the two political parties have been captured by a set of families. The DMK has been captured by M. Karunanidhi family (now it is alleged that it is being captured by M.K. Stalin family). The AIADMK has been captured by the family of Sasikala who is the close associate of J. Jayalalitha. But this phenomenon is new in both the parties. Till Vaiko came out with sizable number of district secretaries from the DMK, the party was organised scientifically and democratically. In the same way as long as M.G. Ramachandran was in the leadership no family has come nearer to the party. It was his will that prevailed in the party. The two political parties have adopted a corporate approach to run the parties and the activities have been modeled on companies. It is also a new culture. Joining political parties has been made as a business venture to make profit. These two political parties have developed a new style of political mobilization by spending huge amount of money. Huge money is spent for party conferences and meetings and thereby politics has been made costlier. As long as they collected money from the public and cadres, they practiced very simple way of mobilization of people for political activities. These two political parties have been alleged to have made huge money through corrupt means when it is in government and through the strength of money power, they do politics. This kind of politics has made every political party has to make money for politics or they have to give space for the expansion of both the parties. This practice and process made the small parties more vulnerable. The two political parties have been spending unimaginably huge money for election and by which they keep these small parties far away from them in electioneering. When these small parties aligned with the two dominant political parties, they depend on these two political parties for election fund. This trend has been effectively captured by the former Election Commissioner of India Gopalsamy that Tamil Nadu is the only state where voters have been bribed by the political parties. This has been amplified by the present Election Commissioner of India made observation that the biggest challenge before the commission is the practice of 'cash for voters' in Tamil Nadu.

All these small parties are unable to join together to face the two dominant political parties in the election as their social base prevent them to join together to oppose both the DMK and the AIADMK. Yet they form their own formations. In one account all these small parties kept away from these two dominant political parties and made scathing attack on them. Of these smaller parties, there are some who are strong national and regional in character, and from the very beginning of this election they distanced themselves from these two political parties. There are some smaller parties not so strong in vote base waited for alliance with the AIADMK but they have not been accommodated by the AIADMK and hence these small parties joined with smaller alliances.

The AIADMK has shown its victorious face in the election fray as there is no anti incumbent wave and hence some of the smaller parties evinced interest in joining with the AIADMK. Whereas the DMK from the very beginning shown its weakness by unilaterally inviting the Indian National Congress for its front and subsequently begged with Desiya Murpokku Dravida Kazhagam (DMDK) led by actor Vijayakant to come for alliance despite the attack on the DMK by the leader of the DMDK Vijayakant. The Indian National Congress is so weak as the BJP in Tamil Nadu but it has been given 41 seats which is unexpected and it is because of the weakness of the DMK front. The Indian National Congress has used this opportunity to get 41 seats. A few Muslim outfits have got more number of seats from the DMK. Till last minute the DMK waited for the DMDK which has given an impression that DMK is in desperate mood. Even after the announcement of the candidates, never DMK faced such a protest against the selection of candidates by the party cadres as it witnessed now throughout the state. It has indicated the weak position of the party. This has been attributed to a fact that the DMK is undergoing a change and it moves from the fold of the leader M. Karunanidhi to M.K. Stalin. M.K. Stalin emerged as an undisputed leader of the DMK. It has come to a level that a candidate announced by the DMK party has openly refused to contest in the election. First time this party faced such a kind of protest by the cadres against the selection of candidates. This protest held even in front of the house of the leader M. Karunanidhi.

Having seen and anticipated all these political scenario and development Pattali Makkal Katchi (PMK) under the guardianship of Dr. Ramadoss took a stand that it has to form its own alliance to face the election. It declared Dr. Anbumani Ramadoss as Chief Ministerial Candidate and chalked out its own course of political activities to face this election. This party has followed the model of Prime Minister Modi in conducting election campaign. The party proclaimed its development agenda as Modi did in 2014 election. For the one year the party has conducted the election campaign. No political party is willing to move closer to PMK as they believe that party is still in the caste line as it attaches its linkages with the caste organisation "Vanniar Sangam". Here one has to understand that the same PMK has moved out from the caste barrier but it could not succeed. Hence, again it went back to caste. It is only the caste gives life to that party. The party would have been finished if the caste has not extended support to it. Against this background one has to look at this party. There is no doubt that caste base is its strength and its weakness also. The party strongly felt that it can attract the new voters roughly around 10 million with their development agenda. This party considered this new voter is aspirational class and they can be drawn towards development agenda. For one year they spent huge money and energy to organise regional conferences and other political activities. Till date not even a single political party moved closer to the PMK for alliance despite its attractive election campaign by adopting all modern methods and tools. It looks like the exact Modi campaign.

Of the smaller political parties, the Clarian calls for wipeout the two dominant political parties the DMK and the AIADMK came from Marumalarchi Dravida Munnetra Kazhagam (MDMK) leader Vaiko and Viduthalai Chiruthai Katchi (VCK) leader Thol. Thriumavalavan as they have been humiliated by these two political parties. They pitched for a coalition government in Tamil Nadu and they argued that it is the only way to change the course of politics of Tamil Nadu. The two communist parties have joined with them and formed the front "Peoples Welfare Front" (PWF). They prepared a common minimum programme as their base for doing politics unitedly in Tamil Nadu. This was considered by the DMK as a most dangerous step to prevent the party to come to power by these smaller parties. The DMK considered that the AIADMK is so strong and hence it made the DMK to look for forming a formidable alliance. Normally the DMK under the leadership of M. Karunanidhi form a formidable alliance to face the AIADMK in the earlier elections. This time this possibility was thwarted by this new formation of a front by the MDMK and VCK along with two left political parties. Not only forming this front it also invited the DMDK and the Tamil Maanila Congress (Moopanar) TMC to the front. This new initiative will spoil the efforts of the DMK and it is considered as a help to the AIADMK. Hence, the DMK branded the PWF as the team 'B' of the AIADMK. Since the DMK has desperately looking for vibrant and strong alliance against the AIADMK, the PWF prevents the smaller parties joining with the DMK. Of the smaller parties the DMDK under the leadership of Actor Vijayakant has got a mass following with the vote share of 5 to 8% in Tamil Nadu. The DMK desperately tried to woo the DMDK towards its side and failed. It joined with the PWF. The DMK has been alleged that it made attempts to break the MDMK party which was considered responsible for formation of the PWF. Now it has been alleged that the DMK has worked to break the DMDK also. In the meanwhile the Tamil Manila Congress Moopanar TMC under the leadership of G.K. Vasan after the AIADMK shut the door for alliance joined with the PWF. After its joining with the PWF, it is alleged that the DMK started breaking Tamil Maanila Congress (Moopanar) also. It is not really breaking that party, but a few leaders have been made to leave the party. By doing so an image has been created among the public through media that the political parties are handling towards a split. There are other formations in the electoral politics in Tamil Nadu. BJP is left alone with a smaller party to be in the fray. Nam Thamizhar Iyyakkam is yet another party put candidates in all 234 constituencies. A few new political parties formed recently and they also put candidates. The AIADMK with a strong leader without having alliance with smaller parties which are worthy of bringing votes, is contesting in the election without having any anti incumbency wave. The DMK with a few smaller parties in the election fray with formidable challenges. The third front with credible leaders and parties along with good vote share of the DMDK in the election fray. PMK with a slogan of change and development is in the race. What is going to emerge from the election will write a new chapter in the electoral history of Tamil Nadu.

From the electoral process one can predict the following options:

a.   The AIADMK will emerge victoriously; b) A fractured verdict will end in coalition formation. If the first one happens, it indicates the current style of politics is approved by the people. If the second option materializes and it is a remarkable change in the attitude and behavior of the people. It is nothing but seeking an alternative to two Dravidian Political parties.

6. An Unusual Performance in Legislative Politics

M. Karunanidhi popularly called Kalaingar and the former Chief Minister of Tamil Nadu turned 94 and he has been in legislative politics in the past six decades without any gap. In order to remember his contribution towards legislative politics a programme was organised at Chennai with the active participation of national leaders recently. It is a remarkable journey of a man who hailed from obscurity without having any background, be it caste or class, or education and reached the zenith of glory simply because of his multifaceted talents and hard work coupled with commitment for the emancipation of the Non-Brahmins despite many shortfalls in his political career as other politicians. Had he known Hindi joined in national politics, he could have become an acclaimed national leader. From 1957 to the last general election held in for Legislative Assembly, he successfully contested and won the election and served in Tamil Nadu Legislature for sixty years. A man who failed in school final, without any background emerged victoriously in all the political struggles by contextualizing himself from the period of C. Rajagopalachari to J. Jayalalitha sustained in politics for eight decades. It is not a small achievement. It is a history of sorts. In this context, it is necessary to assess his commitment in promoting legislative democracy and deepening of it through evolving legislative debates more matured and meaningful. It is an unequivocal fact that M. Karunanidhi stood for the cause of democracy by waging a struggle against emergency. He faced emergency with a brave face. He paid a heavy price for it.

He took politics to the people for social transformation of the Tamil community through his communicative skill and ability. He effectively used media and film to reach out to the masses. Despite his poor formal educational background, he exemplified and excelled in promoting democracy through achieving social equality and social justice in the last six decades. When he contested in 1957 general election in the rising sun symbol, he was in the fray as an independent candidate. He got the rising sun symbol and later it became a party symbol. His devotion to legislative proceedings is evident from his astute preparation for speeches in Legislative Assembly both as Chief Minister and opposition leader. His arguments, observations and speeches are always scientifically strengthened through appropriate evidences. His respect to legislature is known through his presence in the Legislative Assembly fully from morning to evening and reaching the house before time and on time. His listening to the voices of the opposition and responding to the arguments of the opposition members are evidences to prove that how he was valuing the arguments of the members.

When he was the Chief Minister he allowed the Assembly to function more number of days compared to other periods. His response to the members both through reply and arguments convinced the members which enabled them to function more effectively to prepare for presentations in the Legislative Assembly. His listening capacity and methodology of taking notes from the speeches of the members and more specifically the opposition and giving reply to all the points and questions raised are always unique. He made the house to enjoy while he gave reply to the speeches of the member as the leader of the house. He drew the attention of everyone. He used to allow the opposition party members to speak more time and while giving reply, for all the major points pointed out by the members would be covered. His consultative process in the decision making will prove amply that he was always open to learn and advise. His thoroughness in preparation for legislative debate and deep involvement in listening to the voices of the elected representatives of the people are noteworthy. When the former Legislative Assembly secretary Delhi Durai interacted with me, he observed that M. Karunanidhi's preparedness for Assembly meetings is extraordinary. He elaborated that during the Assembly session, he (Mr. M. Karunanidhi) keenly and closely watched the movements of the opposition leaders and he prepared himself to face any question in the assembly in any form at any time. In such a way, he took meticulous care in collecting authentic information from all sources to give any reply to any issue raised by members in the Assembly.

His political sagacity can be understood through his friendly approach towards his severest critics. He was sensitive to the issues of dalits and women while dealing with those issues in the Legislative Assembly. He never lost his equipoise when he faced criticism from the members of opposition. His memory is very sharp and hence while giving reply or making observation, he used to quote extensively evidences from old records. He made the entire official machinery alert in preparing notes for his legislative work. His devotion to argument is impeccable. He demonstrated his creative genius in keeping the Legislative Assembly transaction with high order and dignity. His 60 years of legislative activities and 80 years of political activities without having sound socio-economic and education background made him the tallest leader of our time. Now everyone feels the vaccum created by him in Tamil Nadu politics at a critical juncture after the demise of J. Jayalalitha.

7. Are they serious on the issues of the country?

A student of mine interrupted emotionally my lecture in the class while I was interacting with them on the subject 'transformational leadership' and asked me "are the opposition leaders whether they belong to regional political parties or national political parties, serious on the issues of the people and the country?" I replied that "it seems that they are serious in forming alliance in winning 2019 general election by defeating the Narendra Modi led BJP". She immediately reacted sharply that "every party leader is aiming the Prime Minister post or some share in the powers of the central government and they are not much worried about the issues of the country which are serious in nature. Every leader is interested in saving his or her own party and through which the interest of certain families which control the parties has to be protected". She continued further that "Prime Minister Narendra Modi has promised us that he will act not as a Prime Minister but as protector of the people. Protection means, protecting the country, public institutions, values and ethics which we have evolved over a period of time. While noticing the events that are happening in the country one can easily judge what he promised and what he delivered in the last four years. I am hailing from a poor family and more specifically from a Dalit family, I always look how my freedom and liberty are protected and how I am treated in the society? How my family economic status is being improved? And how my entitlements are ensured? To get my entitlements I have been asked to open a bank account. I have opened the account but I was asked to maintain a minimum balance. Later I was asked to remit the old notes in the bank. The poorest will believe the banks and the post office for their worthiness. But now all hopes are belied. Our public institutions have been made to lose the trust of the people. A strong man is a Prime Minister and yet the public institutions are not protected. He came with a promise and pledge to root out corruption from India and a development agenda.

Four years have gone yet to see any tangible impact of the new government under the leadership of Narendra Modi. Concretely, we could not see the impact of the initiatives of Narendra Modi in retrieving the black money. Poor tolerated patiently during the period of demonetization by accepting the promise of the Prime Minister with an assumption that something will come out from this exercise and rich are going to be affected. It is shocks that the worst affected were the poor and nothing came out of the exercise. Poor could not gain anything out of it as promised by the Prime Minister. Raids have been conducted in the premises of the politicians, business men, middle men, houses and offices by the different agencies of the government of India. What is the net result? Neither cases have been filed nor they are allowed come clean through the process of inquiry. As a result, the agencies involved in investigation and raids are fastly losing their credibility among the public. Having seen all the weakness of the ruling party under the leadership of Narendra Modi, the main opposition the Indian National Congress and the other political parties which are opposing Narendra Modi have neither chalked out strategy to unify the opposing forces nor evolved alternative programmes to the current programmes of the BJP on development. Opposition parties strongly believe that people are tired of listening to the speeches and promises of Narendra Modi and the negative impact created by the policies and programmes of the BJP government in the life of the poor would make the people to support opposition parties. With this belief only, the opposition parties are not taking serious attempt to unify the opposing forces and to evolve alternative programmes. Narendra Modi not only relied on the weakness of UPA II. He came as a messiah by pushing back his own party leaders in New Delhi through capturing the imagination of the people and for which attractive programmes have been given. On the one hand, he indicated the lapses of the UPA II and on the other hand he gave new programmes which were very attractive. Now nothing materialised but the opposition is not using the weakness and lapses of Narendra Modi government. The opposition leaders are contented with what they have organisationally. Day by day they are giving sense to the public that they are not serious in removing BJP from power and they are serious only in safeguarding the interest of their party. If the politics of opposition is really analysed seriously one can come to a conclusion that a few families interests are more important than the issues of the poor or the country. Today's youth want change otherwise they will change the government. Now the opposition parties have to realise their larger role to save the country and the people. All opposition parties both the regional and national have to join together and chalk out alternative programme to save farming, farmers, forest and tribal, animals and nomads, sea and fisher folk, crafts men and crafts. Above all, the governance institutions have to be saved as they are losing the trust of the people fastly in India. People will take a call but the political parties have to prepare themselves to face the new context created by Narendra Modi". After her observation I told her that to see the impact of Narendra Modi's initiatives, you have to wait for five more years. She immediately replied that "Narendra Modi is going to be in power for another five years as there is no leader to challenge Narendra Modi" She said. Here is a take a way for the opposition parties from the perception of an educated youth about the current trend in Indian politics. I value her observation as she is active in social media and moreover she was in a group which supported Modi during 2014 general election.

8. Congress Manifesto: State Vs People

A birds eye view of the "Election Manifesto 2019" of the Indian National Congress gives a signal that it moves towards its original constituents and tried to remedy the old misconceived deeds.

Indian National Congress has taken a open stand to side with people and more specifically the poor and the marginalized by following the basic principle of Mahatma Gandhi "the people are the sovereign", through the Election Manifesto. This document provides the party's perspective, position and stand on all the aspects of politics, governance and development. Since 1960 it slowly and 1980 fastly drifted away from its original constituents namely the poor marginalized, minorities Dalits, and Tribals. A perception has been developed among the poor that the congress party has moved away as it has started following the neoliberal policies. This perception has been used by the regional political parties and weakened the base of the Indian National Congress by expanding their bases. As a result the Indian National Congress has lost its roots in many of the states. It is a fact to be noted that though it followed neoliberal policies, Indian National Congress continuously evolved and implemented propoor policies and programmes with huge outlays. Indian National Congress was tough enough to deal with the regional parties when they struggled for regional aspirations. The Indian National Congress has always got a concern for the poor. All entitlements of the poor have been given in the form of rights during UPA regime. Despite all, arguments have been projected that there is no difference between the congress and BJP. The Indian National Congress has been for the poor and with poor through its programmes even during the neoliberal era. Hence it cannot be compared with BJP. The Indian National Congress has been a platform rather than a party wherein left, right centre can work together to serve the Indian masses. The BJP cannot accommodate all. Through the comprehensive Manifesto, the Indian National Congress demonstrated that it would stand by the side of the affected because of the repressive policies and activities of the BJP government and BJP as a party in the last five years. Further in unequivocal term through the assurances in the Election Manifesto, the Indian National Congress made it that people are sovereign and the state has to work for the people without depriving their rights. Through its manifesto it gave a message that it would like to keep the people in the North East and Kashmir as citizens not as subjects by giving assurance that it would examine the powers given to Army. It gives a sense that the Indian National Congress has taken a bold step to move away from the earlier tradition by accommodating the regional aspirations. Extensive regional consultations have been conducted to elicit the views of the people for the preparation of the manifesto. While doing so experts have been invited and sought their views and opinions. The same have been scrutinized and wetted by the domain experts to make it more doable as they are to be delivered if it comes to power. The promises given in the manifesto have intensified its intensions to strengthen the institutional mechanism created during the previous UPA regimes meant for poor and the marginalized. The schemes announced in the manifesto are to address and solve the acute problems faced by the forming community, pastoral community, tribal community, fishing community and craft communities which constitute 78% of the population in India. Through the manifesto it gives a signal that it is a contextualized National Political party with a concern for the poor, minority and the marginalized. And at the same times it gives a sense that this party will be realistic in handling the regional issues. It is almost a common minimum programme with an operational framework. Revival of planning commission and enlarging the rights regime have raised hope for the regional political parties to have tie up with the Indian National Congress. Revival of planning commission indicates the fact that the allocation of resources based on an accepted scientific formula and not on the discretion of the central government. Series of measures have been indicated in the manifesto to strengthen the local bodies more specifically by sharing GST pool to local bodies have indicated its commitment in strenthing local bodies. The whole manifesto has brought a new paradigm of empowering the people, making the people as citizens not as subjects and restoring the soveringuity of the people which is fundamental as advocated by M.K.Gandhi. It is not a wish list but a well thought out document implementable. If it reaches the masses, it will be the game changer in this election. It needs systematic and serious effort on the part of the party cadres to take it to the masses if it really wants to be a serious player in capturing power at the centre.

9. Political Struggle vs Events

Tamil Nadu, state was once a progressive state, both in ideas and actions, a model for social reform and innovative development activities. Be it freedom struggle or social reform or protecting states rights or in evolving pro poor schemes, programmes and policies. Tamil Nadu is a pioneering state paved way for other states to emulate and in such way our leaders earn the respect in the country. From freedom struggle to the present Tamil Nadu has produced galaxy of leaders with reputation and respect. They are both national and regional leaders. The national leaders had regional outlook to look at the issues of the people and the regional leaders had the national outlook with patriotism and in such a way Tamil Nadu was known to the world through the outstanding leaders till the demise of M.Karunanidhi and J.Jayalalitha.

Now Tamil Nadu is a state facing slew of crises due economic globalization activities. It is a fast urbanizing state by making the life of the rustic folk more difficult and distress. Half of the population are in the urban areas. Fast urbanization will increase the speed of economic activities and further equally damages the ecology and environment. No doubt Tamil Nadu is the biggest beneficiary of globalization and equally worst affected state in terms of ecology and environment. Fast growing corruption in every walk of public life, governance and development due to growth of economic activities has eaten away the contributions made by the leaders of Tamil Nadu in the past. Both farmers and farm labourers move out from agriculture due to severe strain in farming activities. Public institutions have lost their reputation, charm and credibility. Equally the officials have lost their reputation once built up through their honest and hard work. As a result, politics, society, governance and economy have gone to the lowest ebb which is being echoed by all the political parties. All the political parties are leveling charges against the AIADMK government and yet nothing could be done. In the office of the chief secretary ED raids have been conducted, highest police officials office had been raided, CBI went into the Minster house and premises of his office, five murders happened in the resort of J.Jayalalitha, sexual assault on 200 women in Pollachi involving a gang of youth and a college women teacher lured women students to meet the sexual desire of the higher officials in an University, have brought down the reputation built over the years by our leaders. Two months back the President of the BJP made a scathing attack on Tamil Nadu that it is the most corrupt state in India. Gopalsamy the former Election Commissioner observed that Tamil Nadu is a pioneering state to initiate the cash for votes practice which is a menace to the whole electoral politics and its system to day. The anger of the public in Tamil Nadu was witnessed in Jallikattu agitation, Neduvasal and Kathiramangalam and sterlite agitations. Government employees and teachers were on strike for some time to protect the public institutions. All the political parties expressed their solidarity with the agitating groups but never they participated as an integral part of the agitation. Yet nothing comes out from the government as the Government feels that they are all the peoples agitations and hence they thought that the people's agitations will move nowhere. At times people argue that the present government has lost its moral authority. Yet, the political parties have not organized a single political struggle on the issues and crises of the tamil society. Of course political events namely public meetings, conferences, are being organized by the political parties continuously. Even for those events also people have been mobilized not to participate meaningfully in any of the objective but to show the strength of the mass by paying money to the participants. Completely the political parties have lost the trust of the people. People can act decisively only in the General Election but in between elections the political parties have to constantly mobilize the people to get the best services from the government. The political parties have to act both inside and outside the legislature to enhance the performance of the government. It is a pity that there is no meaningful debate and discourse takes place inside the Legislature Assembly in Tamil Nadu.

In Tamil Nadu, there had been a practice since Independence to mobilize people for political struggle to address the issues of the people. In this process people were educated and informed about the political processes and procedures. After the initiation of economic globalization, political parties moved into corporate mode of activities by abandoning the practice of mobilizing people for political struggles. They have started corporatizing the party activities by investing huge money into party structure and activities. As a result political parties instead of mobilizing the people for political struggle, they conduct only political events and therefore people have to wait upto the next general election to see any change in their life.Life style of the party leaders has been changed and thereby the gap between the people and the parties has been increased and the gap has been filled in by the market forces. In this short span of time one could see large number of people from the business world moved into the parliament and legislature by increasing the cost of electioneering. Yet another important aspect is that there is no political orientation for the youth in the past three decades. The new framework of market oriented politics has brought a new culture that money power will bring stability of the political parties by marketing the parties through media and commodifying the votes through cash for votes. Unless the whole framework of politics is changed from corporatization to struggle based politics, politics in India will lose its foundation.

10. Deepening of Democracy

The theorists and specialists on democracy argued, at the dawn of independence when India declared it is going to adopt parliamentary form of democracy, that it is going to be a short lived phenomenon as Indian society is afflicted with factors which are detrimental to the practice of democracy. It was their observation based on the facts and not their wish. The factors such as hierarchical social divisions, extreme economic inequalities, discriminatory practices, illetary, absence of strong middle class and intense social conflicts in India are antithetical to democracy. Theoretically the arguments are valid based on the experience of the societies in the world. Contrary to the theoretical views democracy is in practice in India which is a puzzle to the scholars of democracy.

In the same way democracy is in vogue in many of the countries in the world despite the presence of the antithetical factors. The quality of democracy varies depending on the intensity of the antidemocratic forces working in the society. It is also evident that democracy is every expanding phenomenon in the world. Twenty first century witnessed the speedy expansion of democracy due to democracy promotion of external agencies and internal struggle of the masses. Thus it is always a process by which democracy is promoted, and deepened. The quality of democracy varies across the countries from tribalistic to participatory political culture. Democracy promotion and deepening are not easy tasks and they are being done through a process of struggle. In India people struggled for freedom but not for democracy. It was granted to the people by our leaders.

After India got independence, institutions and organizations have been created and electoral process had been initiated to bring democratic practice in Indian society. No doubt elections have been conducted ever since independence with a break of two years of emergency in are uninterrupted way and thereby all political activities have been organized centering around election. As a result what we found in India is that Indian democracy is institutional and not behavioural. The activities initiated by Jawaharlal Nehru at the dawn of Independence for promotion and deepening of democracy has been given a go by subsequently. As a result democracy in India survives through election but the core values of democracy are in deep deficit. Why is that India witnesses such a kind of serious deficit of core values of democracy in Indian society and polity despite a vibrant constitution to include everyone in India to enjoy all the benefits of democracy? is a question to be answered. It is effectively argued that the Indian masses have been oriented by the political parties through a process of political mobilization by using the antithetical factors to democracy such as caste and religion for electoral politics to win the election instead of pursuing development politics. Our politicians by perpetuating the politics of caste and religion, they have not integrated the communities rather worked for dividing the communities. Their mastery lies only in using the caste, religion, language, culture and region and not in pursuing development politics which ultimately works against perpetuating the core values of democracy. The core values of democracy such as liberty, equality, justice, fairness, equity, respecting the dessert voice, participation, deliberation, discourse debate, and freedom of expression are only in academic discourses and deliberations and not in the practice at the community level in everyday life.

Research studies show that majority did not understand the meaning of the core values of democracy. Even the political institutions which are to work for democracy promotion and deepening of democracy through their activities, defray from practicing the core values in their own institutional activities. It is the role of the state and the political parties to dismantle the barriers and obstacles in democratization of the societies. But in reality, the state and the political parties in the last seven decades have reinforced the anti democratic structures and values to seek votes. The scholars used to appreciate India for being atleast in electoral democracy despite the presence of anti democratic forces. Further the opportunities which are created for deepening of democracy such as decentralization of powers, and building peoples institutions have not been used effectively by the political parties, civil society organizations and the middle classes.

In the last two decades both bilateral and multilateral agencies have argued based on the evidences that there is a close correlation between democracy and development. Hence all the UN agencies time and again reiterated the need for democratization of communities, organizations and institutions to achieve equitable development and thereby enabling the people to lead a civilized life with dignity. But in India, institutions which ought to promote democracy defray from the core responsibility and allow India to face deficit democracy. In order to tide over the deficit, an array of steps have to be taken from changing the school curricula to introducing political reform to change the course of politics.

11. Electoral Alliance in Context

The political parties in Tamil Nadu are facing an acid test in the ensuing Lok Sabha election as the two dominant political parties have lost their leaders who established emotional funds with their cadres. So this election takes place in the absence of both charismatic leaders M.Karunanidhi and J.Jayalalitha. Till the last election electoral arithmatics played a decisive role in deciding the victory of the party. But now in the absence of the two leaders, electoral chemistry has a role to play. The AIADMK is not the

AIADMK of the past under J.Jayalalitha. at present it has a symbol, party office and power is but not enjoying the whole hearted emotional support of the party cadres as it enjoyed during the period of M.G.Ramachandran and J.Jayalalitha. Their relationship with the cadres is emotional. But it is not case with either Edapadi Palanisamy or O.Panneer Selvam.

After the split and formation of the new party Amma Makkal Munnetra Kazhagam (AMMK) under the stewardship of the T.T.V. Dinakaran, no one knows the cadre strength of the AIADMK. The AIADMK as a party is weak but it is in power and hence it is able to put up a show that it has got strength. The BJP wants some weak political entity which will enable the BJP to establish its hold in Tamil Nadu politics. The AIADMK has been weakned in interfering in the internal matter of the AIADMK by the BJP. Yet it supports the AIADMK to continue in power. This is the popular perception. As a result T.T.V. Dinakaran has emerged as a force to reckon with in Tamil Nadu politics. T.T.V. Dinakaran has taken a clear cut anti BJP stand and through which he gained popularity. In this context a very big youth movement began to show up in the form of Jallikkattu agitation. It was a platform for many of the youth groups to ventilate their grievances against the state establishments and the political parties.

Even after Jallikkattu, they have been active in social media. Following Jallikattu there have been many micro movements sprang up with the active participation of the public to protect natural resources and environment from exploitation by the big companies. All those agitations have been tacitly supported by educated youth oriented in Jallikkattu agitation. The centres reluctance in sharing resources due to Tamil Nadu, conduct of common entrance test to fill up medical seats in Tamil Nadu medical colleges, releasing of small amount of money to carryout relief and rehabilitation works in the areas affected in Gaja cyclone have made the sensible Tamil population to think that Modi government is not favourable to Tamil Nadu. The repeated harassment of the AIADMK government through central vigilance and anti corruption machineries without taking any further action on the evidences and enabling the AIADMK government to be in power have given a message to the people that BJP is no longer a party meant for cleaning India. Further the AIADMK Ministers especially the Deputy Chief Minister and Finance Minister O.Panneerselvam openly criticized the central government for not releasing the funds due to the Tamil Nadu government. Apart from the above the Teachers and government employees were against the present government as it has not considered even the genuine demands as agreed and promised by J.Jayalalitha. Totally both the centre and state governments have earned the wrath of the people and almost all the political parties were against the state government. To counter the anti incumbency of both governments, and to face the impact caused by the split by T.T.V. dinakaran, it is necessary to get the support from various parties to stabilize the position of AIADMK. The image of the two leaders M.G.R and J.Jayalalitha and the value of the symbol have gone. Against this background the current AIADMK has to move in a practical track without following the footsteps of J.Jayalalitha forming alliance with smaller parties.

To counter all the forces which are working against this state and central government much has to be done in forming alliance with more number of smaller parties and strategic electioneering to project itself as a winning alliance. In this election two crore youth voters are playing their crucial rule in deciding the fate of the parties. From the social media one could infer the mood of the youth as they are against the existing process of politics, governance and administration. This election will give answer to the following questions: Whether the vote bank politics will continue in this election in the changing political scenario; will the money power decide the course of politics; will the youth force came out from Jallikkattu are active and influencing the voters to decide a fair choice of the party. The results of this election will indicate whether Tamil Nadu politics will remain in the same binary politics with old practices or move in a new different path and pave way for new course and new processes and practice.

12. Electoral Politics Mars Democracy

First time in India election has been canceled in two assembly constituencies in Tamil Nadu owing to the practice of giving cash for vote adopted by two major political parties in Tamil Nadu. The Election Commission has given explanation to the cancellation of the election in two constituencies that it has got enough evidences to the fact that the political parties have distributed cash for votes. Now it becomes a subject for discourse all over the state. It is a shame on us and it becomes a menace to our democracy. It brings discredit to the whole electoral process. Repeatedly complaints have been given by many political parties to the chief electoral officer at Chennai and the Election Commission office at Delhi that cash is being distributed massively by the two major political parties in Tamil Nadu and they openly went to press and made allegation that the chief electoral officer is helpless as he could not act on his own and he acts as per the order of the commission from New Delhi.

The Election Commission of India has repeatedly answered that steps have been taken to improve the institutional mechanism to conduct fair and free election. It is true that police force has been strengthened and numbers of poll observers have been increased. For finance related issues income tax departments and enforcement directorate have been involved in the electoral process. Institutional machinery has been strengthened and all the institutions have been geared up to work vigorously. All these machineries have been working along with the officials of Government of Tamil Nadu as they were in the electoral process under the control of the Election Commission. No one argue that those machineries have not worked. They have worked but not effectively to check the malpractices as malpractices are huge as a culture. More than sixty cores of rupees have been captured as the individuals and parties violated the election code and cases have been registered against many individuals.

Any honest officer involved in the electoral process will say how the whole electoral process has been vitiated by the dubious and corrupt practices of the dominant political parties in Tamil Nadu. "Cash for Votes" and "Thirumangalam Formula" has become a culture in Tamil Nadu politics. Everyone knows, it came from Karnataka via Andhra Pradesh to Tamil Nadu and it became a culture in Tamil Nadu now. It is a truism that in Tamil Nadu the dominant political parties are running the party originations as corporate companies. Promoting profit values rather than the values of service among the party cadres. People associate themselves with those political parties do political activities and invest money with the thinking that they get everything back with compound interest. Even by doing business one cannot earn such profit as they earn while the parties are in power. In such a way political culture has been promoted in Tamil Nadu. Globalization has contributed substantially for escalating the cost of political activities. Globalization has changed the nature and character of political culture. The concept of service has been replaced by the concept of profit. In this process ordinary poor voters have been oriented to perceive that it is part of the electoral process. A stage has come in Tamil Nadu that if a place is neglected in distribution of cash, people from that place will contact the representatives of political parties and ask them why they have been neglected. In such a way system has been developed. When the election schedule was announced the Chief Election Commission made a statement about Tamil Nadu that it is the biggest challenge of the commission to tackle "Cash for Votes" practice in Tamil Nadu. Against this background systematically steps have been taken by the commission. They are institutional in nature. Expanding the institutional machinery is first step and it has move further. Beyond the first step the commission could not move and use its full power and capacity to arrest this practice of "Cash for Votes". In the context of vitiating political culture developed by the main stream political parties, the Election Commission could not act firmly. As a result political parties, intellectuals, media have brought an argument that the Election Commission could not go beyond giving warning signals to these erring political parties. Now everyone accuses the Election Commission for its inaction. When the Election Commission, found evidence for bribing voters, why actions have not been initiated. Yet another argument has been developed that in the context of corrupt political culture nurtured by the main stream political parties what the Election Commission will do in the absence of reform in the electoral process. The candidates are violating the election codes and norms starting from election expenditure. Everyone in Tamil Nadu knows that candidates who have got capacity to spend minimum of three crore rupees will get tickets in the dominant political parties. Apart from the candidates parties are also giving money. A party has declared that it has collected 100 crores for election expenses. Election Commission has put a ceiling that the candidate cannot exceed 28 lakhs rupees as election expenditure. Election Commission itself knows that all candidates have violated the rule in the election by exceeding Rs. 28 Lakhs. This amount is not enough to carry out even to meet the minimum of expenditure. It is only a paper work they do while submitting accounts to election Commission. To tackle all the crises in the electoral process serious electoral reform has to be thought of. Unless serious reforms are introduced in the conduct of election, we are weakening our democracy. Our democracy is only a minimal and deficit and that to with all kinds of ills. A good governance can emanate from a clean electoral process. If the electoral process is dubious and fraudulent, it will destabilize the base of our democracy. Hence series of steps are necessary to reform the conduct of election especially to tackle " Cash for Votes".

In the begging of 2000 the Department of culture has taken initiative to organize workshop in different places to bring electoral reform. Subash Kashyap has been authorized to coordinate the activities. Finally it culminated in a National conference atKolkata. Finally they submitted a report of electoral reforms. It became a document entitled "National Reassurance through Electoral Reforms" published by Rashtriya Jagriti Sansthan and Shipra, New Delhi.

On that lines,a serious workshop has to be organized in Tamil Nadu with the active involve of representatives political parties, media, academia, intellectuals, judges to create suggestions and recommendations to tackle the menace of "Cash for Votes" and otherwise it will eat away the vitals of our democracy.

13. Governance Deficit in Tamil Nadu

Thomas paine used to argue that Government is a curse for the people as it sits on the head and shoulder of the people. Yet we need it as we need protection. So protecting the people is the core function of the government. Now many of our leaders think that protecting the territories by using army is the only protective function of the government. Protective function encompasses safety and dignity of the people and they are also the core responsibilities of the government. In a country like India, protecting the weak and marginalized from the exploitation and dominance of the other groups is an yet another core responsibility as Indian society is communitarian in nature. In India it is in the hands of the state government. The recent event of sexual assault which exploded in Pollachi is rocking the entire nation and shacking the governance mechanism in Tamil Nadu as it has been handled in an inappropriate way by the police. Tamil Nadu state government was once rated as one of a few well governed states in India, when J.Jayalalitha was the Chief Minister. But now its name has gone down to the lowest ebb as Tamil Nadu has witnessed the event of sexual assault on a group of young girls by a gang of youth in Pollachi. It is not a stray event with the involvement of one or two. It has got a chain of events over the past few years done in an organized way through a protective mechanism. Thanks to the social media the deep malaise has been unearthed and brought to the notice of the public despite the silence of the mainstream media. It is not an ordinary event to be ignored. It is alleged that a very big gang involved in sexual assault with the support of higher level politicians and police officials for the past four or five years. More than hundred girls have been made as victims. Truth will come out only after a proper investigation. One year back a similar event took place in Madurai Kamaraj University. Women students of an affiliated college have been alleged to be lured by a college women teacher to meet the sexual demand of the higher level officials to achieve some benefits for those who involved in it. Till date the inquiry and trial is on to find out the truth. Teachers involved in the racket have been released after one year on bail. Both events have brought down the reputation of our government and administrative machinery along with reputation of our educational system and its processes. Once our police was compared with Scotland Yard in terms its bravery and turpitude. But now all have gone and the politics is being looked at with contempt as police has stoop down to the lowest level of serving the political masters instead of ensuring the safety of the girls and women.

The highest police officer without knowing the procedures laid down by the court, has revealed the names of the victim and her brother. It reveals the brutality and high handedness of the police in dealing with such sensitive serious issues. The way in which the police handled the issue indicates the fact that how police force in Tamil Nadu is being used to protect the political class instead of protecting the people. Had J.Jayalalitha been alive and active in politics, she could have taken everybody involved in it to task and appropriate action would have been taken sternly. As long as she was the Chief Minister, she was firm in maintaining Law and Order in the state. No anti social element would be spared and in such a way J.Jayalalitha had acted in the past in governing the state. Even party men dared to go to police station to rescue party men who have committed crime. There was no compromise on safety of women during J.Jayalaitha's regime. As a result Tamil Nadu has been hailed as a peaceful state compared to its neighboring states. She was always pro poor and pro women and she was very sensitive on gender issues. Her innovative pro-poor pro-women activities in governance and service drew the attention of Mother Therasa and Hillary Clinton. Both of them visited J.Jayalalitha and appreciated the leadership of J.Jayalalitha.

Here it is to be noted that arguments have been projected that the severity, cruelty and vulgarity of the young boys in handling the young girls for sexual and monetary benefits despite resistance indicate the linkage with higher ups who are in political and administrative system. It is natural to have such suspicion. Having seen the anger of the public and wrath of the students, the Government has handed over the investigation to the CBI as a face saving strategy. The event held in Kongu belt which is dominated by the Vellala Gounders supposed to be the supportive area for the present AIADMK regime. The dream of consolidating the vote bank of these regions in favour of the AIADMK has been dismantled through this event. The whole media started accusing the police for not handling the issue firmly. Rule of law, Justice and fairness have gone. Governance and administration become weak day by day.

While going through the process and procedures adopted by the Government of Tamil Nadu one will easily indicate the deficiency in Governance and administration. Unless the whole process and procedures of governance and public administration in Tamil Nadu is revamped, the credibility built by the leaders over a period of time will be lost. Hence attention is needed to remove the governance deficiency and to improve efficiency in governance and administration. The culture of "Rule of Law" has to be restored instead of "Ruling party law".

14. Implications of the By Elections in Tamil Nadu

Nanguneri and Vikravandi, the two Assembly constituencies held by the Indian National Congress and the DMK respectively, have been snatched away by the AIADMK with a huge margin, in the recent by election in Tamil Nadu, gave a shock to the DMK and the Jubiliation to the AIADMK as it is considered as a precursor for 2021 general election to the Tamil Nadu Legislative Assembly. After the demise of the leader J.Jayalalitha and the split in the party, the AIADMK has witnessed continuous defeat in the by elections and a rout in the Lok Sabha election. The continuous success and the triumph in Lok Sabha election by the DMK has been considered that the leadership question has been put to rest as M.K.Stalin has emerged as leader in Tamil Nadu Politics. Though Edapadi Palanisamy is in power, with all the support of the central government, and the machinery he could not emerge as a leader. He will be considered as powerful as long as he is in power and hence he cannot be a leader in real sense. There is yet another argument among the opinion makers that if Edapadi Palanisamy is weak, and M.K.Stalin is so strong as leader, why the weak government by Edapadi Palanisamy is not destabilized and dislodged. It continues because of the weak leadership of M.K.Stalin.

No one predicted that Edapadi Palanisamy will continue in power for such a long period after the demise of J.Jayalalitha by managing series of crises. He has managed the central government, opposition party the DMK, and the internal split by O.Panneerselvam and subsequently by T.T.V.Dinakaran. Above all he managed the people without much resistance from the people. It does not mean Tamil Nadu has no serious issue. People have been facing plethora of problems in all fronts. Yet the present regime has not given any opportunity to the opposition to mobilize the people against the government. For the past two years he slowly consolidated his position in the government as well in the party and yet it is not known whether the party workers are with Edapadi Palanisamy. He is neither away nor nearer to the BJP and the central government. He gives a sense to the people that he is not willing to align with BJP but the context warrant him to have truck with the BJP. Though the DMK has taken a clear stand that it is opposing the BJP, people have not bought the argument as it has not taken up the peoples issues for a political struggle. Even on a sensitive issue like Hindi, the DMK has not taken the political struggle forward despite media has given leap and the DMK withdrew all of a sudden from its commitment to wage a struggle. Though the present government is weak it cannot be taken on by the DMK through a process of mobilizing people for a political struggle which gives a signal that the DMK is also politically weak. Further there are a few smaller political parties have determined to work for the defeat of the DMK as it prevented almost all the smaller parties to emerge as a force to reckon with. For these parties, the AIADMK is not a threat. But the DMK is a real threat. Hence the smaller parties role and the withdrawl of T.T.V.Dinakaran and Kamala Hasan from the electoral context enabled the AIADMK to wretched the seats from the Indian National Congress and the DMK in the by election.

The AIADMK votes have been slowly consolidated as T.T.V.Dinakaran is not in the fray. Further the entire alliance partners have been totally involved in the electioneering to give an image that the AIADMK is in the race to win the election confidently. Moreover the Chief Minister and his team made it a point to show their strength in the election through their continuous mobilization. Apart from the above there is no anti incumbency wave in the state as the present government is responding to the immediate needs of the people. The AIADMK has indicated to the electorate that if the DMK comes to power, it is not the official government run the administration but only the party men will run the whole machinery and in such a way party tyranny will be imposed on the people. This was being used by J.Jayalalitha for a long. Further it is to be noted that the last by election to Vellore parliamentary constituency, the DMK won in a slender margin which was interpreted in the media that it indicates Hindu votes are slowly consolidated against the DMK.

Basically this by election indicates a few messages to the political parties by the people. One, it is not a cakewalk for the DMK to win the Assembly election by projecting themselves as Anti Modi. There was anti congress sentiments created in Tamil Nadu and that sentiment was initially changed by M.G.R. by alligning with Indian National Congress later totally that sentiment has been changed by the DMK through its alliance with the Indian National Congress. In the same way the Anti Modi wave has been slowly disappearing because of the AIADMK led by Edapadi Palanisamy, the Chief Minister of Tamil Nadu and its allies more particularly the PMK. Hence this by election gives a clue that if the AIADMK forms a viable alliance, with all those parties which were with AIADMK, the future of the DMK in the coming Assembly election in Tamil Nadu will be bleak. The Lok Sabha election was not between the AIADMK and the DMK. If Sasikala comes out and takes the lead in the AIADMK and asks T.T.V.Dinakaran to fall in line, the AIADMK votes will be consolidated. Further till date Edapadi Palanisamy has maintained the image that he is able to manage the government and the party intact. There is yet another question whether Edapadi Palanisamy will have that charisma to maintain that party after he comes out from power, is to be seen. If Sasikala takes the lead, Dinakaran fall in line with the AIADMK, Edapadi leads the government, the party will be in tact to face the DMK with alliance partners and that will give an image that it is a winning alliance. Unless the DMK reposition itself and reorganize the party to suit the new context, it is not a cake walk for the DMK to come to power.

15. Is there any new narrative in Tamil Nadu politics?

Tamil Nadu was once considered as a model state to other provinces for laying foundation for strong economic development through agriculture and industry. It was achieved by K. Kamaraj through his visionary leadership. Subsequently under the DMK regime with M. Karunanidhi as leader established a strong governance framework to achieve social development even before the concept was contextually conceptualized by the academics and more particularly Amartya Sen. Revolutionary social development schemes had been launched by M. Karunanidhi and thereby his governance and administration as model for other states to implement social development schemes and programmes. Subsequently, M.G. Ramachandran created a path breaking framework to work for the poor by directly delivering benefits to the poor. When it was announced it was criticized by many but after seeing the implications of the schemes in the life and livelihood of the poor, everyone showered encomium on him. M.G. Ramachandran with determination carried out all the pro-poor schemes unmindful of the criticisms against those schemes as freebies by his adversaries and conventional economists and development exponents. Later, Jayalalitha deepened the pro-poor policies and schemes and established it as a model state for pro-poor governance. It does not mean that Tamil Nadu has no serious issue. It has plethora of problems. They are also to be attended to seriously and urgently by our political and policy communities. Both C. Rajagopalachari and C.N. Annadurai were in helm of affairs for a short period and they wanted to take the politics of Tamil Nadu into a different path. But they could not succeed. C. Rajagopalachari and C.N. Annadurai were in power only for a short period. Thus, K. Kamaraj, M. Karunanidhi, M.G.Ramachandran and J. Jayalalitha have made indelible mark in Tamil Nadu politics, governance and administration through their policies and programmes. All the four leaders are visionary and strong committed leaders. Barring J. Jayalalitha, all the three leaders hailed from a humble background rose to the altitude through their hardwork. They had remarkable leadership qualities and perspectives. Now the era is over. J. Jayalalitha is no more and M. Karunanidhi is confined to his house and thereby both have given space for others to take over. At present, no one in Tamil Nadu is able to match K. Kamaraj, M. Karunanidhi, M.G. Ramachandran and J. Jayalalitha in terms of the visionary leadership. But everyone has nurtured hope to become Chief Minister of Tamil Nadu. Of the political parties, the DMK and the AIADMK have organizational strength and cadres. But there is no scope for other political parties in the next four years to nurture such a scope. The DMK has narrowly missed this opportunity to form the government in the last Assembly election and now it wants to capitalize the fluid situation created in Tamil Nadu politics after the demise of J. Jayalalitha. But the AIADMK is in tact. The party functionaries MLAs and MPs are solidly behind the general secretary V.K. Sasikala.

AIADMK has developed a culture that the party has to work under one leader. The party is proud to call itself a party with army discipline. It means no debate but to obey the order of the leader. The leader is above groups. Everyone will get a chance to be part of governance and its spoils if party comes to power. No other party has given such a hope to the party workers. Party workers can get any berth at any level at any time if the leader wishes. This proposition has made the party workers loyal to the leadership althrough. The party functionaries know that they have four years to enjoy power. Hence, they need a leader. They know who can manage the party without divisions. Hence, the party functionaries, MLAs and MPs have unanimously chosen V.K.Sasikala. This is the strength and character of the party. The problems are not in the party AIADMK and among its workers. It is only in other political parties which have nurtured hope to get some benefits out of this situation. They have been nurturing such a kind of aspiration but they are waitlisted. But V.K.Sasikala has got a chance to become the Chief Minister which is unacceptable to them. In Tamil Nadu nobody visualized such a kind of turning point in the life of V.K.Sasikala. She herself never dreamt of this new turn. If anybody nurtures aspiration to become Chief Minister within the AIADMK, It can be understandable. It was expected but it did not happen. Hence, the leaders who developed such a kind of aspiration in other political parties made noise which has no meaning. The social media engineered by middle men now to create opinion about this issue. Without knowing the legalities and established procedures, they make opinion and observation that they do not want Sasikala as Chief Minister as people in the US mobilizing against the newly elected president. It is a pity that now social media works as a business venture creating an opinion which is being used by the leaders of some of the political parties that it is the popular opinion. If anyone invests money, opinion can be created and spread throughout and that practice we have seen in the recent elections. Political party leaders have made observations based on the observations made in the social media. They consider the opinion emerged in social media is public opinion. But millions of people who work from dawn to dusk for their livelihood have their own opinions but they have not expressed their opinion. They express their opinion only during election. Because, they have no leisure to do such kind of activity and they do not have such a kind of technology available with them. But, these political leaders have not taken into account the opinion of the poor who have no access to such technology. The political party leaders could not take the politics to the next higher level and for which they have to enhance their leadership qualities. Enormous opportunities are in Tamil Nadu politics for nurturing of new leadership. But it is not taking place. The problem we find today in Tamil Nadu politics is the paucity of leadership. The crisis is in leadership.

16. Leadership Question in Tamil Nadu

Recently Rajnikanth again made a statement that "leadership vacuum persist still in Tamil Nadu" triggered yet another controversy and both the DMK and the AIADMK leaders reacted and responded by arguing that there is no such leadership vacuum as Edapadi Palanisamy and M.K.Stalin have emerged as leaders and people have recognized them as leaders since both are discharging the respective responsibilities as Chief Minister and opposition leader. They are giving messages to the public through media that the binary politics will continue. Why Rajnikanth made such a comment at this juncture is a question to be pondered over. After the Lok Sabha election, this question has not been raised as DMK won the Lok Sabha election sweepingly in Tamil Nadu. The DMK media wing and the leaders have proclaimed that the electoral victory has demonstrated that people have recognized M.K.Stalin as leader and this trend will continue in the next Legislative Assembly Election also. People of Tamil Nadu have learnt the art of changing the regimes through ballot even the iconic leaders were in Tamil Nadu Politics. DMK and the AIADMK have come to power alternatively. In the last 2016 Election J.Jayalalitha broke the trend and created a record that the AIADMK got victory consecutively. It was unexpected and yet the DMK also won more than 80 seats under the leadership of M.K.Stalin. Getting votes from the people in Tamil Nadu is not an easy affair. Both the DMK and the AIADMK have crossed the stage of using the caste card to corner votes for electoral victory. By liberally announcing populist schemes competitively they have faced the election in Tamil Nadu. After certain period, beyond populism huge money has been invested to purchase votes by both the parties. Thus competitive populism coupled with cash for votes made the smaller parties far away from this type of competition. But they were put under the mercy of the two political giant parties. For their survival, they have to align either with the DMK or with the AIADMK. All these parties have done it with reluctance.

Every one knows in Tamil Nadu, the present set of leaders do not have the leadership qualities of Rajaji, K.Kamaraj, C.N.Annadurai, M.Karunanidhi, M.G.Ramachandran and J.Jayalalitha. They were on their own. They caronated themselves. To days leaders are not of that type. They have been brought to this level by circumstances. They cannot be compared with those leaders of the past. Though all the leaders were from this region with strong regional bond, they had national perspective and national recognition also. Their influence in national politics was also high. Their contribution to national politics was unfathomable. They were not only political leaders, they were mass leaders. They had distinct leadership qualities which drew the attention of the national leaders and the masses. Tamil population is expecting such a kind of leadership at present. Rajnikanth has expressed that mood of the people not about the positions the leaders occupied now. Why he made such a kind of statement now. There is a reason behind it. The present AIADMK party despite in power with the same old symbol of the leaves have faced defeat after defeat in the election till the Lok Sabha election. Media and the opinion makers have come to the conclusion that AIADMK is in the last phase of the political life as DMK under M.K.Stalin emerged victoriously in the Lok Sabha Election. Hence many started writing and projecting that M.K.Stalin has emerged as leader. Two important events which have made Rajnikanth to make such statement. One the Vellore Lok Sabha by election. Though the DMK won the election, the margin of victory has raised a question where has gone the vote share of the DMK and its ally? Because the victory margin is very thin even though the consolidated Muslim vote bank went in favour of the DMK. This has raised a doubt whether the mood of the people has changed. Secondly in the recent by election the AIADMK has snatched away both the seats Nanguneri and Vikravandi from the Indian National Congress and the DMK respectively. Both the DMK and the AIADMK faced the by election with the same alliance partners. If the Lok Sabha election trend continued, both the constituencies, the Indian National Congress and the DMK would have retained the seats comfortably. Thirdly the electoral victory margin is very thin. Huge difference in the margin of the electoral victory of the AIADMK candidates in both the constituencies. This change has created questions in the minds of the opinion makers. Really is the DMK taking steps to introspect as it is a well organized scientific party with a cadre pack up? But the reality is some changes are taking place in the minds of the voters in Tamil Nadu. The question is whether the leaders of the present context in Tamil Nadu have the ability, skill, knowledge, perspective, commitment, passion, capacity, capability, to create new narratives in Tamil Nadu politics, as Rajaji, K.Kamaraj, C.N.Annadurai, M.Karunanidhi, M.G.Ramachandran and J.Jayalalitha created in the past. There is a general feeling that the present day leaders do not have such a kind of ability. This has been reflected by Rajnikanth.

Further one has to understand that Ranjikanth is not making senseless statements. He is not a person to make senseless emotional statements without some base analysis. He was closer to power circle and tested his influence many times in Tamil Nadu politics and saw the ups and downs. In this context he made that observation that Tamil Nadu has got leadership vacuum not from the perspective of facing election by the leaders of the parties. Hence his statement has got some valid grounds.

17. Narendra Modi's New Narrative

A few IT specialist and now activists in environment education recently visited me. They are known to me from the days of Jallikattu agitation in Tamil Nadu. I have been following a few groups which have emerged from that struggle and they are active in working with farmers, women and youth in the rural areas of Tamil Nadu. They have determined to work with the people in rural areas by giving up their jobs in IT sector as they feel that the rural areas of Tamil Nadu are in deep trouble which made the poor to migrate from rural areas to urban cities and towns to seek employment opportunities. Tamil Nadu is the fast urbanizing state. Rural urban population ratio is almost 50:50. Rural distress and vulnerability of the poor drew their attention towards finding technological and organizational solution. They pinned their hope on the leaders of the people at the grassroots institutions and they believe with their active cooperation, vulnerability could be reduced. Since I am working with grassroots institutions by building the capacity of the elected representatives more specifically the women and Dalits and doing action research on many of the rural issues, the youth groups constantly in touch with me and interact with me to get some input for their rural transformation activities.

This time when they came, they started interacting with me about national politics with the belief that I have more information since I have contact with political leaders. In fact, I was keen to get to know their understanding and observations about the current politics as they are in social media and they are in development politics. I feel that it is important to know their views as they are youth not affiliated to any political party but critical of the entire functioning of the party system in India and mere specifically in Tamil Nadu. Mere more than one crore youth voters are in such a state of mind in Tamil Nadu. Hence, I asked them to respond. When I asked them, they informed that "National politics gains momentum and Narendra Modi and his team took stock of the reality and worked out appropriate strategies to pluck all the weakness on their side to kick start the election campaign. But the main opposition party the Indian National Congress has not learnt any lesion from the past experience as ruling party and even in recent years as a main opposition. The leaders of the Congress have never involved in introspection. They have been giving wrong signals to the public. Knowing fully well that the party is organizationally weak everywhere they have not taken any step to strengthen the organisation. To counter the BJP and Narendra Modi, the party has to work in a mission mode with a fire of "do or die". Rahul Gandhi plays his solo. Neither he gives confidence and image that he is consolidating the party organizationally nor he takes efforts to consolidate opposition parties both regional and national to put up a brave face jointly. Whereas, Narendra Modi quickly introspected and did a course correction in his communication".

They further lamented that "Narendra Modi has a new narrative now. He started lamenting that he has taken all the steps to end corruption and to bring fair governance with rule of law. He never looked at decision from the perspective of votes and victory of his party. He kept the interest of the country and its future in the backdrop and not party in the background. To get best results from his measures one has to wait for some time and with some pain. For the interest of the country, people have to bear the pain and people are cooperating". Yet economy has experienced slow down, he has accepted and he further says that he is taking institutional reforms to end corruption and put premium for honesty in public life. Narendra Modi said "It is my duty to protect honest people in this country. It is a war between honest and dishonest". "In such a way, new narrative is brought to public political sphere by Narendra Modi. Whereas, Rahul Gandhi and the congress party have not understood the fact that the party needs new faces to counter Narendra Modi and equally new narrative to oppose Narendra Modi or to arrest his influence. Rahul Gandhi may be good in heart, politics needs strategy and communication to reach out to the masses. The BJP and Narendra Modi are on the offensive and Rahul Gandhi and the congress are in the defensive. In this context, to save the country, first the congress party has to be saved. If the congress has to be saved it needs a leader with image to counter Narendra Modi. Narendra Modi and the BJP are aware of the public mood but at the same time they are also aware of the weakness of the congress party. If the congress is able to project a leader like Goplakrishna Gandhi and hundred other reputed opinion makers, scientists, media persons and intellectuals with good image, it will be very difficult to deal with them by the BJP and Mr. Narendra Modi".

"In the best interest of the Nation, the congress party has to take an aggressive position to face the challenges posited by Narendra Modi. The issues that India confronts are very deeper and serious. Farming community, tribal community, craft community, trading community, and fishing community are the worst affected in the present era of globalization of economy. The opposition parties have failed to change the existing narrative into poor versus rich. Realistically speaking, the congress party is not interested in defeating Narendra Modi but a group of people with vested interest captured the party for their own survival which made many stalwarts to flee from this party. Once Indian National Congress was a platform and it provided enormous space for many for their political activities. But now it has been lodged with a group of families. This is the fate of the congress party and the country" observed by them in a few minutes before we start our work.

18. Old Calculations New Strategies

The political parties in Tamil Nadu are facing an unprecedented challenges in the current Lok Sabha election as the two dominant political parties have lost their leaders who established emotional bonds with their cadres. So this election takes place in the absence of both charismatic leaders M.Karunanidhi and J.Jayalalitha. Hence every party feels that it is a new context and it needs new strategies. Old formulas of the icon leaders will not work this time. Till the last election electoral arithmatics played a decisive role in deciding the victory of the parties. But now in the absence of the two leaders, electoral chemistry has a role to play. The AIADMK is not the AIADMK of the past under J.Jayalalitha. At present it has a symbol, a party office and power but it is not enjoying the whole hearted emotional support of the party cadres as it enjoyed during the period of M.G.Ramachandran and J.Jayalalitha. Thus the present leadership is forming alliance with smaller parties and liberally giving tickets to them with an aim of getting those votes to win the election. This act itself indicates that the party is so weak now.

Secondly the DMK has been perceived that it is a winning party as the ruling AIADMK is facing a real threat from T.T.V.Dinakaran who has snatched away a major junk of the AIADMK cadres. Since AMMK is contesting in the election under T.T.V. Dinakaran's leadership, a major portion of the AIADMK votes will go with T.T.V. Dinakaran. In this case the DMK can easily win the election. The reality is different. The youths involved in Jallikkattu movement have been critical of both the Dravidian parties and the BJP also. There are about two crore youth in the social media vehemently criticizing the BJP, AIADMK and to some extent the DMK. This opportunity has been consistently utilized by T.T.V. Dinakaran.

Even after Jallikkattu agitation the youths have been active in social media by highlighting the critical issues which are affecting the development of Tamil Nadu. Following Jallikattu there have been many micro movements sprang up with the active participation of the public to protect natural resources and environment from exploitation by the big companies. All those agitations have been tacitly supported by educated youth oriented in Jallikkattu agitation. The centres reluctance in sharing resources due to Tamil Nadu, conduct of common entrance test to fill up medical seats in Tamil Nadu medical colleges, releasing of small amount of money to carry-out relief and rehabilitation works in the areas affected in Gaja cyclone have made the sensible Tamil population to think that Modi government is not favourable to Tamil Nadu. The repeated harassment of the AIADMK government through central vigilance and anti corruption machineries without taking any further action on the evidences and enabling the AIADMK government to be in power have given a message to the people that BJP is no longer a party meant for cleaning India.

Further the AIADMK Ministers especially the Deputy Chief Minister and Finance Minister O.Panneerselvam openly criticized the central government for not releasing the funds due to the Tamil Nadu government. Apart from the above the Teachers and government employees were against the present government as it has not considered even the genuine demands as agreed and promised by J.Jayalalitha. Totally both the centre and state governments have earned the wrath of the people and almost all the political parties were against the state government. To counter the anti incumbency of both governments, and to face the impact caused by the split by T.T.V. dinakaran, it is necessary to get the support from various parties to stabilize the position of AIADMK. Against this background the current AIADMK has to move in a practical track without following the footsteps of J.Jayalalitha forming alliance with smaller parties. It is a kind of old calculation. The reality is different. At present huge youth population around twenty million are in social media rejecting the present day politics, governance and administration.

In this election they are going to play their crucial rule in deciding the fate of the parties. From the social media one could infer the mood of the youth. This election will give answer to the following questions: Whether the vote bank politics will continue in this election in the changing political scenario; will the money power decide the course of politics; will the youth force came out from Jallikkattu are active and influencing the voters to decide a fair choice of the party. The results of this election will indicate whether Tamil Nadu politics will remain in the same binary politics with old practices or move in a new different path and pave way for new course and new processes and practice.

19. People's Movement for New Course of Politics

After the demise of J. Jayalalitha, politics in Tamil Nadu undergoes a sea change. It indicates that it moves from party politics to people politics. People have developed an antipathy towards the party politics as political parties are evincing keen interest only in forming electoral alliance rather than forming alliance among the political parties to find solutions to the problems of the people by exerting pressure on the government jointly. Political parties are leveling charges against each other and spending time only in blame game. By listening to the arguments of the political leaders one will form a totally a negative feeling that our political parties have lost their relevance in the present context. On many of the critical issues of development political parties individually express their concern and solidarity but not joining together to fight against the government to find solutions to the problems. They accuse each other and indicate the degree of misdeed each one did in the past. The political parties in the recent years have not evinced any interest to launch a prolonged struggle on the serious issues faced by the people and more particularly the poor. Politics has been turned towards money spinning exercise. There is no ideological discourse in politics in the recent years. Corruption was the only subject in the political discourse in the past two decades. Politics without values and ethnics keeps the youth away from politics. Aginst this backdrop, people especially in the rural areas mobilize themselves to fight against the state to solve many of the critical issues of development as their life and livelihood are at risk. Political parties normally do such mobilization in the past but now they are not taking any step to mobilize people for a struggle. Instead they organize agitations party wise on the same issues for a few hours in a day apart from issuing press statements. When people mobilize themselves the political parties come and show their solidarity with the people who are in the struggle. Tamil Nadu has witnessed series of people struggle. People organised themselves in Kudankulam against the establishment of the nuclear plant. It was a well organised people struggle for a long period. Second such a mass mobilization took place in Marina Beach for Jallikkattu. It was a mammoth congregation of people mostly youth organised made the state to respond. Many groups have been formed voluntarily and they are active in social media. They are keeping the online participation consciousness alive on many of the social issues which are critical to the development of Tamil Nadu. Youth are active in this process but without the ideological perspective. They are not identified with any political party. They raise series of issues in their day to day interactions in social media. Recently Neduvasal agitation to protect agriculture and environment from the scheme launched by the government to take methane from the agriculture lands and now Kathiramangalam people agitation against ONCG on oil exploration, held in Tamil Nadu draw the attention of the public and the activists in the social media. The struggle is on for more than hundred days. Large number of youth groups are visiting and expressing their solidarity with the agitating villagers. Yet another people mobilization takes place to oppose the opening of the state owned liquor shops. This mobilization has been done by the women locally and they participated in the protest forcefully and sometime violently with anger against the state. Now the death of Anitha a student due to the implementation of NEET triggered the agitation and for which students are being mobilized. Normally, these kinds of mobilizations usually will be done by the political parties. But now they are being done by people themselves. The political parties are visiting all those places and expressed their solidarity with them. Most of the people who are in struggle expressed that they want to keep away from the political parties as they feel their cause will be diluted by giving political colour.

In these agitations, the political parties are criticizing each other for the sorry state of affairs in Tamil Nadu. People want solutions to those problems and not moral and oral support. Most of the agitations are for protecting nature, natural resources and livelihood opportunities. It indicates the huge environmental and ecological loss Tamil Nadu has incurred. As a result, livelihood of the poor and farmers are at stake. Many of the agitations are taking place only in the rural areas. The above people struggle brought to light the heavy damage done to ecology and environment by exploiting the natural resources in the name of development. In the seventy years development activities, villages have been damaged and villagers have been marginalised. They are disempowered. Rural Tamil Nadu faces serious ecological and environmental crises. Unfortunately, the mainstream political parties could not understand the critical issues of development properly and perspectively. The present political parties do not have intellectual background to understand the implications of these agitations and the issues confronted by the state. But in the social media conversations take place among the youth on various issues affecting the state Tamil Nadu. People want an alternative approach to the present development model. In the same way, the political process has to be changed from party politics to people politics. The people politics has to revolve around green politics. Nobody has got a clue to take it forward. The political parties are waiting for election. People are expecting a totally a new way of political process and an alternative approach of development. It is the need of the hour today in Tamil Nadu.

20. Rajini in Tamil Nadu Politics

Rajnikanth repeatedly reiterate a statement that "there is a leadership vacuum persist still in Tamil Nadu" which triggered arguments in both the DMK and the AIADMK. The leaders of both the parties responded by arguing that there is no such leadership vacuum as Edapadi Palanisamy and M.K.Stalin have emerged as leaders and people have recognized them as leaders since both are discharging the respective responsibilities as Chief Minister and opposition leader. They are giving messages to the public through media that the binary politics will continue. Why Rajnikanth made such a comment at this juncture is a question to be pondered over. After the Lok Sabha election, this question has not been raised as DMK won the Lok Sabha election sweepingly in Tamil Nadu. The DMK media wing and the leaders have proclaimed that the electoral victory has demonstrated that people have recognized M.K.Stalin as leader and this trend will continue in the next Legislative Assembly Election also. People of Tamil Nadu have learnt the art of changing the regimes through ballot even the iconic leaders were in Tamil Nadu Politics. DMK and the AIADMK have come to power alternatively. In the last 2016 Election J.Jayalalitha broke the trend and created a record that the AIADMK got victory consecutively. It was unexpected and yet the DMK also won more than 80 seats under the leadership of M.K.Stalin. Getting votes from the people in Tamil Nadu is not an easy affair. Both the DMK and the AIADMK have crossed the stage of using the caste card to corner votes for electoral victory. By liberally announcing populist schemes competitively they have faced the election in Tamil Nadu. After certain period, beyond populism huge money has been invested to purchase votes by both the parties. Thus competitive populism coupled with cash for votes made the smaller parties far away from this type of competition. But they were put under the mercy of the two political giant parties. For their survival, they have to align either with the DMK or with the AIADMK. All these parties have done it with reluctance.

Every one knows in Tamil Nadu, the present set of leaders do not have the leadership qualities of Rajaji, K.Kamaraj, C.N.Annadurai, M.Karunanidhi, M.G.Ramachandran and J.Jayalalitha. They were on their own. They caronated themselves. Leaders of to-day are not of that type as we have seen in the past. They have been brought to these positions by circumstances. They cannot be compared with those leaders of the past. Though all the leaders were from this region with strong regional bond, they had national perspective and national recognition also. Their influence in national politics was also high. Their contribution to national politics was unfathomable. They were not only political leaders, they were mass leaders. They had distinct leadership qualities which drew the attention of the national leaders and the masses. Tamil population is expecting such a kind of leadership at present. Rajnikanth has made such a statement as people perceived the leadership qualities not attached with posts and positions. Why he made such a kind of statement now. There is a reason behind it. The present AIADMK party despite in power with the same old symbol of the two leaves have faced defeat after defeat in the elections including Lok Sabha election. Media and the opinion makers have come to the conclusion that AIADMK is in the last phase of the political life as DMK under M.K.Stalin emerged victoriously in the Lok Sabha Election. Hence many started writing and projecting that M.K.Stalin has emerged as leader. Two important events which have made Rajnikanth to make such a statement. One the Vellore Lok Sabha by election. The DMK has won and yet the margin of victory has raised a question where has gone the vote share of the DMK and its allies? Because the victory margin is very thin even though the consolidated Muslim vote bank went in favour of the DMK. This has raised a doubt whether the mood of the people has changed. Secondly in the recent by election the AIADMK has snatched away both the seats Nanguneri and Vikravandi from the Indian National Congress and the DMK respectively. Both the DMK and the AIADMK faced the by election with the same alliance partners. If the Lok Sabha election trend continued, both the constituencies, the Indian National Congress and the DMK would have retained the seats comfortably. Thirdly the electoral victory margin is not very thin. Huge difference in the margin of the electoral victory of the AIADMK candidates in both the constituencies created a doubt about the winnability of the DMK in the next Assembly election. This change has created questions in the minds of the opinion makers. Really is the DMK taking steps to introspect as it is a well organized scientific party with a cadre pack up? But the reality is some changes are taking place in the minds of the voters in Tamil Nadu. The question is whether the leaders of the present context in Tamil Nadu have the ability, skill, knowledge, perspective, commitment, passion, capacity, capability, to create new narratives in Tamil Nadu politics, as Rajaji, K.Kamaraj, C.N.Annadurai, M.Karunanidhi, M.G.Ramachandran and J.Jayalalitha created in the past. There is a general feeling that the present day leaders do not have such a kind of ability. This has been reflected by Rajnikanth.

Further one has to understand that Ranjikanth is not making senseless statements. He is not a person to make senseless emotional statements without some base analysis. He was closer to power circle and tested his influence many times in Tamil Nadu politics and saw the ups and downs. In this context he made that observation that Tamil Nadu has got leadership vacuum not from the perspective of facing election by the leaders of the parties. Hence he decided to come to politics to contest in the next general election to legislative Assembly.

21. Sarkar Controversy in Tamil Nadu

Sarkar (Government) is a Tamil movie acted by Vijay a popular, young and leading actor in Tamil Nadu and directed by Murugadoss. It was released on the day of Deepavali. Within a few days of its release one the Ministers of the AIADMK government have criticized that the film has shown the AIADMK and it leaders in bad light and hence those scenes have to be removed. Cadres of the AIADMK have organized protest meetings in front of the cinema houses allover Tamil Nadu. Within a few days the objectionable scenes as indicated by the AIADMK government have been removed. It is to be noted here that the film was produced by the Sun Group owned by Maaran brothers. The controversy and agitations have created curiosity among the ordinary viewers and as result the film gained much popularity. If a sensible individual views it he or she will come to a conclusion that it is an effective film to be screened in every village and in every street of towns and municipalities to create awareness among the voters about the significance of the ballot paper. This film can be recommended by the Election Commission of India to be screened all over the country in different languages. Apart from the importance of the ballot paper it brings to the notice of the people that the centralized system of party control has to be dispensed with an alternative system of decentralized people centric evolutionary politics to bring accountability on the part of the elected representatives.

Further, how valuable citizens have been reduced as voters by the political parties, as beneficiaries by the government as petitioners by the bureaucracy and customers and consumers by the market. People are the primary agents to bring transformation in society and politics but in reality they are the most dishonored and disrespected individuals in the society. The film has brought to light the decentralized model of politics to cleanse the corrupt government, administration and politics. This has been suggested in Gorwal Committee at the dawn of independence that the Indian National Congress to search for talented committed social workers for the party to contest in the general election on behalf of the party. The same decentralized model was suggested by Rahul Gandhi for the youth congress. Unfortunately, it was not allowed to emerge as successful venture in the party by the old body guards of the party as the new crop of leaders will outwit the old generation politicians from the field in terms of performance.

There is yet another message has been conveyed convincingly and powerfully to the people that raising question is the hallmark of democracy. In our democracy, questioning is totally prohibited in the name of discipline in all the democratic institutions. In this film, it has been highlighted that without raising question equality cannot be achieved and democracy will not mature. All these message have communicated through the actor Vijay by writing a powerful dialogue in this film.

In the electoral process of a democracy, if a party gets huge majority by weakening the opposition party in terms of its strength, it is not a victory for democracy. This aspect has been convincingly scripted and communicated through the powerful dialogue delivered by the hero. It is out and out a political movie with hard ideas communicated in a simple way. It is a highly educate movie.

The dialogues scripted for the film criticized both the Dravidian parties not only the AIADMK. Why then the AIADMK ministers alone unnecessarily raised objections and asked them to cut a few scenes in the movie. They assumed that it is a movie completely criticized the AIADMK. Really, it is not so. The film out rightly condemned both the parties as they involved in practicing cash for votes and delivering freebies. The film argues for an alternative arrangement to the existing political party framework of politics.

Deeper democratic values are highlighted in a simple way to the public. Since Sun pictures involved in production, the DMK kept quiet. Of all the fan clubs, Vijay fan clubs has got more number of youths. He has a huge following also. He takes a different line unlike Kamal and Rajinikanth. He took an open stand against the central government and the state government. When GST was welcomed by all cine actors, he was the only person opposed it. Kamal and Rajini both are old but he is young. Yet, he indicates that he will enter into politics. This creates fear among political parties. Whenever, Vijay produces films of this sort, it is being opposed by political parties and through which curiosity has been raised among the people and thereby huge advertisement is being given free of cost. This film also had the same fate but it succeeded by earning more than their expectation. This movie has to be recommended by the Election Commission to be screened all over the country in the respective regional languages for the benefit of the public. The Election Commission has repeatedly made it clear that it faces the problem of cash for votes in South India more particularly in Tamil Nadu. In this context, this film is a welcome one to create awareness among the people about the value of votes. The entire team has to be appreciated. It is an excellent movie to create voters awareness among the people. It out rightly attacks all unethical electoral political practices to cleanse body politics. It is one of the best political movie taken in the recent past in Tamil.

22. Shaping Electoral Alliance

In Tamil Nadu forming electoral alliance to face the ensuring Lok Sabha election becomes difficult for every leader and party as the leaders look at each other equal in the absence of two mass leaders J.Jayalalitha and M.Karunanidhi. However popular they were both M.G.Ramachandra and M.Karunanidhi both faced the elections only with alliance. But J.Jayalalitha broke that practice by facing the last Lok Sabha election without forming alliance with any party and won 37 seats and thereby she made a history of sorts. After her demise the party is divided. The leaders and functionaries are with the ruling AIADMK and the major Junk of the cadres are with AMMK under the leadership of T.T.V. Dinakaran. Apart from the cadres of AIADMK T.T.V Dinakaran snatched away a huge youth force from many political parties.

A sizeable number of youth without having any political background moved towards him by seeing his leadership qualities by facing all round challenges from the Central Government, State Government, Court, CBI, enforcement Directorate and other political rivals within the family and the political parties. Hence media has come to a conclusion that he is going to emerge as a factor to reckon with in Tamil Nadu politics. Many vibrant, capacitated and passionate youth who could not see any facture for some of the parties and leaders have moved over and joined with T.T.V.Dinakaran. The youth who have fed up with the conventional politics of the DMK, the AIADMK, and other small parties have joined with AMMK. As a result one could see large number of youth with T.T.V. Dinakaran. Even before the major parties starting the election campaign, T.T.V. Dinakaran has began the campaign and pulling the crowd. As of now in Tamil Nadu politics, there is no crowd pulling leader but one could see huge crowd mostly youth in his meetings.

If it is women or middle aged men or old age men in any political party meetings, one could come to a conclusion that they are hired by the party for the event. Whereas in Dinakaran's meet one could see the youth groups large in number. Moreover his source of funds has been monitored by the Government agencies and as a result T.T.V. Dinakaran could not in comfort zone in financing for mobilization of people for his meetings. Hence

T.T.V.Dinakaran factor made every major party in Jittery and hence they are in search of parties to form formidable alliance. In this process all the parties are having an eye on the PMK as it has got a consolidated vote share of 5 to 6% which is transferable. No other party among the smaller both national and regional parties has got such vote share in a consolidated form. All parties are sending emissaries to the PMK which is necessary to give a sense that party which goes to election with PMK is a winnable front.

But it is not so easy to manage the PMK as it is guided by Dr.Ramadoss a seasoned politician worked with both J.Jayalalitha and M.Karunanidhi with rich political experience. Though he headed a small party he moved with both J.Jayalalitha and M.Karunanidhi as a strong leader equal to them through his tough bargaining power. This time the PMK is a glittering star going to decide the fate of the parties in Tamil Nadu Lok Sabha election. Hence facing the PMK and its founder Dr.Ramadoss will be a touch task for both the DMK and the AIADMK. For him both the DMK and the AIADMK are under his mercy this time. Vijayakant an actor once emerged as an alternative with 8% vote share disappeared from the scene. At one point of time Rajini gave a voice against the PMK in an election, but PMK emerged victoriously. Thus both the PMK and its leader over a period emerged as a deciding factor.

To move further to capture the central stage, PMK wants to use this opportunity to form an alliance with a party which can liberally give seats to the PMK. Thus the PMK keeps every one guessing to whom it is going to form alliance. As of now huge opportunities are for the AMMK and the PMK. It is not so easy to undermine both the AMMK under T.T.V. Dinakaran and PMK under Dr.Ramadoss and Dr.Anbumani Ramadoss. Both parties role is crucial for deciding the course of politics in Tamil Nadu.

23. Skilling the Representatives of the People

Bursting crackers is joyful act everyone does in our social setting during festivals. But in Germany it requires certification from an institute. When I was in Germany as a visiting professor I came to know this fact while witnessing a cracker festival in cologne city. It was amazing to see burying and burning of dead bodies in the cemetery and crematorium respectively by a set of professionals in a professional way in the heart of the city itself. For the above acts, these professionals should get needed certificates from the certification institute. For them any act is a professional one. It was curious to see that more than 380 such professional skills approved by the Government of Germany. But in India, not even fifty skills have been approved by our government. Policy making is a highly a professional and skillful act and it is being done in the legislative and decision making bodies with the participation of the elected representatives of the people without having any professional training to the elected representatives. This has been indicated in many times by the scholars who have done research extensively in the area of Indian Legislative behavior and performance. I have also done an empirical study to analyse the role perception of the legislators. It was continued to Tamil Nadu. In this regard, I interviewed 174 Members of Legislative Assembly when M.G. Ramachandran was the Chief Minister. It was published by Konark Publishers. In this work, it was concluded that the poor performance of the elected representatives was attributed to poor perception of the legislators on the role to be performed by the elected representatives both inside and outside the legislature. Performances of the elected representatives have gone down not only in quantity but also in quality. Substance, content, style and methods are also qualitatively weak and poor. It is because our legislators have not been consciously trained for higher level legislative debate in the house and political discourse outside the house. In this regard, it has been indicated that there is no policy to skill our elected representatives. There is no policy to train our members of National Parliament, Members of State Legislatures and Members of Local Bodies both urban and rural. At least for local body leaders there are training institutions all over the country despite absence of a training policy. But for the Members of Parliament and Members of State Legislatures barring the Bureau of Parliamentary studies and training located in parliament annex building there is no specialized training institute. Even the Bureau of Parliamentary studies has neither requisite capacity nor the Members of Parliament are interested in attending training in this institute. There is yet another interesting aspect one can notice among our Members of Parliament and Legislatures that they generally do not like to be trained. The moment they become Members of any house, they feel that they are leaders and attending training is beneath the dignity. They feel that they have to speak and others have to listen. Any leader shown any interest in training is news.

When Chandrababu Naidu in his previous regime organised such a kind of training for the legislators and it was very big news in the media. When Rajiv Gandhi asked the members of parliament to attend the programmes organised by the academic institutions, they were news for the media. These are imperatives and essentials for the elected representatives to perform the roles and responsibilities in the legislative bodies.

Legislative business is the most professional business as it decides the fate of millions of people which requires skill not only for communication but to do the work within the framework of rules of the houses. Even valuable ideas pertinent to policy or decision may not reach the policy maker if that idea is not put within the framework of rules of the house. Every member of the house either in parliament or state legislature has to perform two major functions theoretically. In the best interest of the country and best interest of the people they have to do interest aggregation and interest articulation. They have to collect the problems and issues of the people for onward transmission to the decision making bodies. But while doing this job, the members have to put them into the framework of rules of the houses. It is not an ordinary work. It needs research acumen. The works involved are of research in nature. Further, in my opinion there is no manual for Members of Parliament or State Legislature supplied to each and every member that can be easily understandable to them. Simplifying the practice manual to the level of an ordinary member is yet another need. How to organise their office for legislative work and constituency work is yet another professional job. Many of our representatives of the people do not have professional offices to enable to discharge the responsibilities both in the house and outside the house. Professionally equipped office will alone enable them to connect with people, connect with information, connect with institutions and connect with needed data. Technically qualified people can alone help the representation of the people. To manage the technical office the elected representatives should have capacity. It is to be enhanced. Edmund Burk was representing Bristol constituency in the England parliament. But his speeches in the parliament became a subject of learning in the universities. For a meaningful work in the parliament and in state legislature lot of framework is needed. Hence, training is the imperative need. It is not a onetime affair and it is a continuous one. It requires a policy and an institution. Senior Members of Parliament Legislative Assembly based on their experience can be made as resource persons for this training. Equally senior bureaucrats and academics who have done creditable research work on Legislative behavior can be drawn as resource persons. A permanent academy has to be set up at Delhi and state capitals for offering such a kind of training. It can be in collaboration with world reputed leadership schools like Kennedy School of Government, Leadership school in Singapore National University or Leadership school in Upasala, University of Sweden. Customized courses could be evolved for involving world level scholars who are on the job for several years.

24. Tackling Deficit Democracy through Democracy Promotion

Aspiration to be in democratic governance is increasing exponentially in geometric proportion among the people in the world. It is evident from the report published by the Freedom House that one fourth of the world politics were democratic in 1950 and most of them were from the west. But in the year 2005, out of 192 countries, 123 countries had come to the fold of democracy in their polity and governance. For the first time democracy has acquired majority status on a world scale after the year 2000. Just it became a wave in the world. It started from Portugal and moving fastly in the world. The speed of expansion of democracy in the world is unprecedented which causes the problem of quality. Democracy expansion in the west was slow, steady and phenomenal through a process of hard struggle. Further, it is to be understood that democracy promotion and democratization activities of the western societies were evolved though a process struggle. But the present day democracy promotion activities are engineered by external forces. The moot question is whether people who are involved in democracy promotion and democratization are aware of the meaning of democracy as it varies across the world.

The expansion of democracy took place in the world through democracy promotion policy adopted by many of the western governments. Human collectivities who are in the authoritarian regimes are struggling to establish democratic political regimes. They do it with a broader understanding and notion that democracy is nothing but changing political regimes with the electoral participation of ordinary citizens. Changing political regimes is being perceived by the people as the most excited transformation they cherish in the nature of democracy. While seeing the countries' practices, procedures and processes of the institutions of governance which are in democracy in the recent years because of democracy promotion and democratization, one would come to a conclusion that democracies are in different forms and at different levels. The nature of democracy and its typology are basically the outcome of the nature of interaction between government and the people over the process of governance and development. At present the changes are fast in the society because of globalization. Hence, all democracies are in transition and they move from one level to another. The basic question here is that whether democracy gets strengthened in the process and its quality gets improvement in the fast changing world.

How to comprehend democracy is yet another question as it is defined broadly that it is a set of institutions and organisations with a set of processes and procedures to involve the people in electing a regime to govern the society. The whole functioning of the institutions and organisations are based on attitude and behavior of the people who are involved in politics. Democracy is not a mechanical process of mere electing a regime. People's participation in all the activities will reflect the belief, attitude, values, norms and behaviour of the people. Though it ultimately reflects in political regime and its governance activities, the essence of democracy lies in values, norms, attitudes, beliefs, behavior of the people in relation to formation of political regimes and the conduct of the same. Thus democracy is an inclusive concept covering the socio economic aspects of the human society. That is the reason why we see varieties of democracies in the world based on the socio economic and cultural moorings of the human societies.

The essence of democracy lies in practicing equality, fairness, justice, equity in socio economic political life of the society. Empirically the behavioural social scientists conceptualize democracy from the core values and norms of democracy and their practices both in the society, economy and polity through their institutional mechanisms. They evaluate the democracies in the world and classify the societies and countries in the ranges from minimal democracy to progressive democracy interms of democratic processes, procedures and practices. Societies are in progressive and regressive forms interms of democratic practices in the world. Societies come to democracy out of excitement but while practicing the core values, they found extreme difficulties and as a result they may retreat also. But regression and progression are well within the democratic framework. Most of the occasions the socio cultural and economic conditions of the societies have strongly contributed for the regressive trend in democratic governance. Democracy by its core strength, it has to bring change in the socio economic cultural moorings of the society. Many of the occasions and in many of the societies, it does not have such a strength and hence world has witnessed that more number of countries are in minimal democracy. Wherever democracy promotion and democratization is strong, democracy moves progressively and moves to different levels by overcoming the obstacles. One set of nations in the world are working for reforming democracy. Yet another group of nations are in democratization process countries which are advocating reform in democracy have reached certain state in democracy and hence they want to move further. There are countries which are struggling to establish minimum practices, and processes in democracy and hence they are in democratization processes.

All basically depends on democracy promotion activities. People tend to move towards democracy not for the sake of democracy alone. Societies move towards democratic regimes with the hope that they can improve their socio economic conditions of their life. Their life would be transformed through the democratic process. If such a transformation is not taking place, people tend to look for alternative regimes. But in the world, it has been seen that democracy takes different shapes, forms and modes. Even in India, still our democracy is in minimal level and basic in form and it has not used its full potential to transform the poor. As a result, many argue that we have to redefine and rethink our democracy. In this context alone decentralization was thought of as a powerful tool to deepen our democracy and to transform the life of the poor, excluded and marginalised by involving them in the process of development and governance. We have seen the onset of stagnation in decentralization also. Hence, India has to work for democracy promotion and decentralization of powers to make our democracy vibrant and decentralization active in transforming the life of the poor. When the political class is reluctant to do the above who will do this work is a major question. It is the responsibility of higher learning institutions, middle class and intellectuals to do democracy promotion work and decentralization work through our educational institutions and media.

25. The Search is for a New Narrative in Tamil Polity

In Tamil Nadu, what we are witnessing after the demise of J. Jayalalitha and the disappearance of M. Karunanidhi from the public space is a leadership crisis. It is being increasingly felt day by day in the political space as politics is being done on and around the death of J. Jayalalitha and the imprisonment of V.K. Sasikala based on the judgment of the Supreme Court. How long they lament on J. Jayalalitha's death? Even the main opposition party which is also involved in the discourse. It is a pity that Tamil Nadu politics has not moved an inch beyond the old narratives. Since there is no new narrative in Tamil Nadu politics based on the real issues of Tamil Nadu, the Tamil society faces plethora of problems due to huge rainfall deficit (64%) inadequate water supply, illegal mining, illegal sand quarrying, unregulated real estate, poor quality of education from primary to higher learning, stagnated industrialization, continuing formers suicide, absence of provisions in PDS shops, continuing law and order problems, regularized corruption in every walk of life, continuing the disappearance of commons, and depleting natural resources, loss of ecology, rising unemployment, disturbed fisher folk by the Sri Lankan army including killing of fishermen in the sea. All these issues are deeply rooted and it is not so easy to find readymade solution. Despite the seriousness, the issues have not drawn the attention of the politicians to create new narratives in Tamil Nadu politics. No doubt, Tamil Nadu is one of the fast developing and urbanizing states in India. rural urban divide in terms of population is 50:50 in Tamil Nadu.

Tamil Nadu politics has been always a trend setter for the other states. K. Kamaraj had laid foundation for the strong economic development through building the basics for agriculture development and industrialization. In the same way M. Karunanidhi had laid foundation for administering social development even before the concept gained currency in other Indian states. M.G. Ramachandran set a new trend in helping the poor through direct transfer of benefits. By following the tradition of M.G.R., J. Jayalalitha has implemented pro-poor pro-women and pro-children schemes which became model to other states. It is one of the progressive states in India despite certain negative trends like continuing and soaring corrupt practices in public sphere and authoritarianism in politics. Practice of democracy has not been strengthened yet development has been achieved. Till date Tamil Nadu is known for its performance in taking care of the poor. There is no distress migration in Tamil Nadu. For this, whole credit goes to our leaders who relentlessly pursued pro-poor policies.

K. Kamaraj and M. Karunanidhi, M.G. Ramachandran and J. Jayalalitha had distinct leadership qualities and styles and they made indelible marks in governance, administration and process of development in Tamil Nadu. E.V. Ramasamy Periyar and C.N. Annadurai made a significant contribution in changing the discourses of politics through their ideas in Tamil Nadu politics. Having seen the leadership qualities of all those giants, the present day leadership could not lent anything substantial to create a new narrative after the demise of J. Jayalalitha. Had M. Karunanidhi is active today he would have taken politics to a different level. Even at the age of 92, he was up to date and he has the perspective to look at issues. It is unfortunate now we do not have such leadership qualities among the leaders of the parties. A few political parties talk about the real issues but they are in feeble voice which has not drawn the attention of the media. As a result, the Tamil media both electronic and print narrating and spinning stories on an around the death of J. Jayalalitha. It seems that some forces are working constantly that the real issues should not come to public space for discourse through media. Hence, in media every day one could see the non-issues in the debates. Public, youth, students, opinion makers are in search of alternative politics and in search of new leaders with a different style. Jallikattu and Neduvasal agitations have demonstrated the loss of credibility on the part of the political parties and their leaders among the public. People have started feeling that there is no credible leader to lead Tamil society. People have lost hope in the political parties as they perpetuate the corporate style of functioning. Political parties barring a few smaller parties have no real concern on the issues but even their activities always around formations of alliance to win a few seats in the election and to form government if it is a major political front. It is a total vacuum in Tamil Nadu politics and what is going on in Tamil Nadu at present is only a political show and people are witnessing it as a cinema rather than a political discourse. The search is "where is my leader?"

26. Underestimating the Change

Change is the eternal phenomenon and the speed of change is the recent phenomenon as technology drives fast the change. To achieve anything in the world, one has to understand the speed and direction of change and act according to the changing speed. While working fastly by understanding the speed of change one should not forget the role of professionalism to get the best results. So one has to orient himself or herself to work fastly and professionally in whatever field one works to get intended outcome. For a long, people lamented that we could not find change in politics as we find it other fields especially in the market. Market is so dynamic and people who are not dynamic in the market will be kept out of it. Politicians are also in the market as consumers but they could not imbibe anything from the market to change the narrative of politics excepting treating or making voter as a tradable commodity. They have been using the old retrograde parochial political tools and strategies to manage the electoral politics. Over a period of time people have acquired awareness and knowledge through socialization and political mobilization. As a result, people have come to a conclusion that political establishments are backward looking and selfish to the core and they make money for themselves and for party and for politics. Since cost of politics has been escalated, the political parties have to mobilize huge resources unethically. They transform the political parties into their properties. This perception has been created and strengthened in the era of globalization as corruption in public life in geometric proportion, damaged the whole body politics, public life and public service. As a result, people were fed up with this trend and look for alternative. There was total stagnation in national politics at one point of time.

Narendra Modi from a state carefully carved out a design and a framework of political action to change the course of politics. By adopting a high risk mode he ventured into political action in his party to transform his party and his image. He did and brought 360 degree change through a difficult process. In this process he has enhanced his skill, capacity and capability to reach out to the masses and opinion makers. His careful design and activities regenerated the party to get a victory in the election to the surprise of many political pandits. Both the BJP and Narendra Modi have come to the stage with new outlook and approach. Despite resistance from all quarters he managed to change both his party and his image. In every act of Narendra Modi one could see determination, fire, direction and hard work which are totally absent in the congress and the regional parties aligned with the congress. Narendra Modi exhibited his conviction and determination in every political act he pursued. For the people who were in despire and desperation, he became a messiah. He came at a political juncture at the national level where there were full of managers, brokers, chief executive officers in the helm of affairs in most of the political parties both in the region and at the centre. Whereas, Narendra Modi exhibited his leadership qualities to turn every challenge into opportunity. His track record of governance and achievement in economic growth achieved in Gujarat made the right wing intellectuals to support him through their writings. His contrast is Rahul Gandhi. He was given ten years both in government and party to reform governance and his party. Neither he could cleanse his party nor support Manmohan Singh to achieve the best to change the course of politics in India. Power was with him to transform the party yet he could not do so as the old guards guarded the wested interest thereby the party cadres have been disillusioned in this process. The best performers and the best workers who have got the field grip have been made to soar over the degeneration of the party election after election. Despite all setback they are not prepared themselves to reposition the party. Even now the party has not taken any preparatory work visibly to face the next election. The party looks like the last days of Mohal Empire. Contrary the Narendra Modi team has moved far ahead by pushing the Indian National Congress back further. He demonstrates through his decisions and determinations to act without wavering. He has given a sign that he has started a new era. Whether we like or not, he has given a sense by putting an end to institutions and practices which are historic in nature and far reaching consequences. This is not an ordinary step.

All his decisions have not started yielding results. All he has done is building only hope through his communicative ability. He sensed that people have lost hope in many of the institutions and practices. Beyond that he has convictions that these institutions have lost their soul and spirit and the practices became rituals. Hence, he has captured the imagination of the people with his communicative ability. He convinced the people that what is going on in India is chaos in the name of politics, governance and administration and which is being used by self seekers and corrupt politicians and administrators. This has to be stopped and a new direction has to be given. He also informed the people that he will take decisions which are hard in nature and they are to be tolerated for the sake of this country. Thus, he started dismantling great institutions like the planning commission and taking difficult decisions like demonetization and GST. His live contact with masses and his continuous mobilization mode bewildering everyone in the opposition camp. Anna Hazare's anti corruption movement and Abdul Kalam's speeches on development consciousness among the educated youth in this country helped Modi's campaign for new consciousness for new India and development. When a new class of people aspiring to engage themselves for development looking for new messages and framework of engagements and Narendra Modi emerged as a new messiah to cater to the needs of the aspirational class. He keeps on engaging the masses. In this context, the opposition parties have indulged in attacking only Modi without evolving an alternative approach and new naaratives. This trend provides enough scope to BJP to continue to sweep the next election also. The worry that India faces is the absence of opposition. The opposition parties have not even shaped themselves as the real opposition. This is the pity of the Indian politics today.

27. What ails Indian National Congress?

Our political pandits started arguing that the Indian National Congress is in a fix and moving in the beaten track to find solution to the organizational problems, which will not help the party to come back to the centre stage as an alternative to the ruling dispensation. They lamented that the party is facing unprecedented problems in different fronts which need a major surgery and not cosmetic solutions to cure the ills. Because the Indian National Congress faces problem in organizational restructuring, ideological repositioning, finding right leadership at right place in the organisation to lead the party and above all the trust deficit. These problems are not unique to the Indian National Congress alone. Many of the regional political parties once they were in the centre stage to decide the future of the central government, have being facing the same problems. Many second level leaders in Indian National Congress, and other regional parties have noticed this syndrome and started moving towards the BJP to enjoy the green pastures. The BJP has strategically used them to advance their political march towards the power centre. The BJP knows pretty well that organizational strength, contextualized ideological position of the party, adoption of the most advance technology to reach out to the masses, projecting powerful leadership to communicate and convince the masses, creation of a new consciousness among the people and weakening the stand of the opposition parties by touching the weaknesses of the opposition parties are the factors to achieve what it wanted to achieve. The BJP has demonstrated in the recent years that it never contended with the electoral victory. Its aim is to penetrate into the masses by using the success. When the BJP achieved electoral victory in a state it will consolidate its positions first and then only it will move towards the next phase or area. Conquest and consolidation is its strategy. Whereas the Indian National Congress has not learnt the art and as a result despite it remained in power for ten years, it could not consolidate and strengthen the party organizationally. They have been continuously searching for strategies and strategist PRs for electoral victory and not for penetrating into the masses. Infact the Indian National Congress is the Mother of political parties in India as British parliament. It was born out of a movement drawing the support of the masses more particularly the rustic folk in the rural areas namely the farming community, pastoral community, craft community, fishing community and tribal community. They were drawn towards the party emotionally as the leaders built the trust through their moral turpitude and engage with the people. Over a period of time the Indian National Congress concentrated much on electoral process and government formation and management of government rather than engagement with people. In the last thirty years, the party has absolutely moved away from its original constituents and concentrating much on electoral strategies and process and thereby the party has started facing trust deficit. In the era of globalization of economy the party has lost its trust as the benefits of the economy reached the rich and the middlemen and managers of the party despite its propoor policies and programmes. The Indian National Congress never bother to see whether the chalked out schemes and programmes have reached the needy by involving the party cadres. At this juncture the BJP moved into the space which was left by the Indian National Congress. It is not only the space left by the congress has been used but also the values such as patriotism, nationalism, sacrifice, service, yoga, naturopathy and so on so forth.

Indian National Congress has to start its introspection by searching its soul. A proper introspection will tell where the congress failed. It should be a soul searching introspection. This exercise has to be done not with managers and middlemen of the party but with congress minded intallectuals and the opinion makers. They are critical of the Indian National Congress as it moved away from its original constituents. They have concern for the poor and they feel that the Indian National Congress has lost its support base from its core constituents. Hence the Indian National Congress need not bother about the immediate electoral outcome and it has to work for rejuvenating the party and build its organizational strength by contextualizing the ideology. M.K.Gandhi will substantially guide the party, if the party leadership analyses the fall of the party in the backdrop of the Gandhian ideology and framework of building mass movement. It has full five years and hence it can reposition itself by taking up the cause of the poor and by which a new consciousness can be created that it is a new congress and it is a Neo congress.

28. What is New in Indian Politics?

A student of mine came to my room to take leave after completing her master programme on 'Development Management'. When she enters I along with my colleagues we were in a discourse on state and national politics of today. A friend of mine who was sitting by my side asked the student to tell us about her perception about the current political scenario as she belongs to the youth of today. Without any hesitation she told us by showing her mobile phone that the technologies of today has transformed the thought process of the people through the continuous innovations and changed the life of the ordinary people in this country. She further said that she could not see any meaningful transformation or change in the field of politics. She told us that it is sad to note that the political parties with old people captured the political parties and kept them under the control of their families as business houses moving in the beaten track without much change in the political discourses and processes. Youth are so tired of the regressive politics and they hate the hegemonic political culture developed by these political parties and leaders. This enabled Mr. Narendra Modi to be firm in taking politics to a new ground and chalking out his agenda of activities unmindful of the opposition parties as they are weak and outdated. She further argued with us that it is only Narendra Modi started adopting the business and big pank approach to reach out to the masses as brand reach out to the consumers. She has not stopped with the above observation and she went on to argue that at present no one is able to counter his influence in Indian society at least now as the political parties both national and regional however strong they are with vote banks, they cannot match Mr. Narendra Modi as he is the man of the time and need and others are of the past. They are not only irrelevant but also outdated. Having listened patiently to her arguments, I asked her to list out the achievements of our Prime Minister Narendra Modi. She said that without having any background he reached several positions only through his performance and connected himself with the masses. He carefully created an image that he is going to deliver. He appropriately evolved strategies to keep his image above the images of all the leaders among the masses. When the development aspirations of youth were on the peak in the era of globalization he captured the opportunities through evolving appropriate strategies to project his image as savior of the country and a performer. Despite all negative projections against him, he emerged victoriously by managing the oppositions. It is interesting to note that she argued with me the poor competency and capability of other leaders who oppose our Prime Minister. She asked me a question, "why Rahul Gandhi, though he is young, could not connect himself with the masses more specifically with young despite his hard work and sincerity?". I informed that he was caught in a circumstance and context which worked against him. But she told that Rahul Gandhi has not exhibited his fire and not demonstrated his capacity as a leader to perform either in the party or in governance during ten years of UPA regime. He neither demonstrated his leadership nor proved his ability to deliver through the government by taking over certain responsibilities. Further, she said that youth needs new leadership, new styles and approaches for politics. Youth looked at the emergence of Narendra Modi from the humble background with curiosity and admiration. Narendra Modi is a new type of leader hails from humble background and performs differently she added. She moved further in her argument that countering Narendra Modi is not so easy as the conventional political leaders of both national and regional political parties have moved away from the youth. I intervened and asked her, how to counter Narendra Modi. She said that all the political parties have to field new leaders to run the parties. She said that there is no dearth of leaders in India. It is only the families in all the political parties barring a few blocking the emergence of new brand of leaders.

She informed me that the political parties are trying to field a common candidate to contest in the presidential election. Even name has been suggested. This is not the way to approach the problem. The political parties have to identify a common candidate for the Prime Minister post in the next election in the year 2019. The political parties should not waste their time in the presidential election. First the Indian National Congress has to ask Gopala Krishna Gandhi to lead the party at present. Let him be the president of the Indian National Congress. The face of Indian National Congress will be changed. He will give totally a new direction to the party. His image will help the party to rejuvenate itself from the present deep slumber. Let him initiate identifying one hundred leaders from every walk of life to lead the party and thereby he can coordinate the political parties to form a front to face the 2019 election. When young leaders with unblemish background join hands with Gopala Krishna Gandhi, the political scenario will be changed. As long as the Indian National Congress and other political parties keep continuing the present style of functioning with the present set of leaders, with the same vote bank approach, the prospect of Narendra Modi to continue in power for another decade is bright. The political parties have to adopt a different strategy to draw the attention of the youth who bring changes in governance. After hearing from her argument, I interacting with a young faculty in our university, on the same theme. The young faculty whom I interacted with made it very clear that the observation of the student on the present conditions of politics is absolutely a realistic. The faculty member added a few points pertinent to this discourse. All the political leaders from the ruling parties both national and regional in the past have earned a bad name among the masses because of non performance, poor performance and wrong performance in governance. But Narendra Modi though he was also in power more than a decade, fortunately he maintained his record strait that he performed well in governance and he had not faced corruption charges. This enabled him to control over the party and government. From all the above observations and arguments, what I feel is that it is high time to reorient our political parties by restructuring the parties and their strategies.

29. Where is the Leader?

Whenever there is a political crisis in the country, there will be some leaders who have got the recognition and acceptability of the major political parties to work together despite ideological differences to save the country. In this context Jayaprakash Narayan, popularly called with reverence as JP, Harkishan Singh Surjeet the general secretary of the communist party of India (Marcist) have played crucial roles in the past to bring unity among the opposition parties to play a constructive role in reshaping politics for a better course of action. Though Jayaprakash Narayan a Gandhian leader and Harkishan Singh, the leader of a party, both had a good image reputation among the public and the trust of the political parties, they had managed to move with the political parties with different ideologies. They succeeded in their attempts as they had clean image. Both of them had reputation and integrity in public life. It is the past history. Why it is remembered here is that in an intellectual circle, there was a discourse as to who will play the role of Jaya Prakash Narayan or Harkishan Singh Surjeet at present to bring unity among the opposition parties. A group of opinion makers argued that the collapse of the opposition unity is due to the absence of such tall and acceptable leaders in National Politics. Yet another group of people argued that this time Ms Sonia Gandhi can play that role as he retired from active politics and she has the will power to do it. In 2004, it was only Sonia Gandhi knocked at the door of Ram vilas Paswan and Mayawati to bring a cohesive front to oppose the BJP when Vajpayee was in the helm of affairs. She has done it successfully and brought a change in the central government in the year 2004.

She was reluctant to take the political role despite the invitation of many senior leaders in Indian National Congress after the death of Rajiv Gandhi. It was only during the period of Sitharam Kesari she took over the responsibility by declaring that the Nehru family has given life for the unity, integrity and secularism of India and that purpose cannot be shattered in to pieces. Hence as a member of that family she felt that it is her responsibility to revive the party and rejuvenate it for the central stage. Nobody expected that she would bring the party to the level of success it achieved in 2004 general election. Though mandate was given to her leadership, she has not taken the Prime Minister post but continuously guided the government through National Advisory Council. Through the National Advisory Council, all propoor policies and programmes have been suggested to the government and saw to it that all have been evolved and implemented with huge outlays. Not only that, when the government was vigorously implementing the neoliberal policies, she exerted pressure on the Government to enact laws to ensure the entitlements of the poor. As a result Rights Revolution happened in India during that period. Many in the Indian National Congress belittled those revolutionary steps as they are neoliberals they had no faith in all those acts and schemes. For those who stood for the poor considered all those acts and schemes are revolutionary in nature. Hence even the top leaders have not spoken much about the much debated revolutionary propoor schemes and acts. Propoor global scheme like MGNRGA was implemented in India only during that period. It is one of the most globally appreciated scheme for the poor. One of the members of the National Advisory Committee, in the sidelines of a National Conference said privately that she could see in the arguments of Sonia Gandhi on many of the propoor schemes, the Catholic Christian values – concern for the poor. In such a way she assiduously taken up the cause of the poor during the entire regime. At present a leader who has immense faith in dialogue, democracy, plurality and concern for the poor is the need of the hour. Among the political leaders she has all qualities to bring every one in the comity of the parties to form a front to function as credible and constructive opposition by bringing all opposition parties. Vibrant opposition lies not in the status and recognition but in action. Having taken the pledge join in active politics with a aim of continuing the Indian National Congress as a propoor, and pro people party, she could act as a mediator to bring together all opposition parties under one umbrella to work unitedly to serve the people as an effective and vibrant opposition front. It is the need of the hour to India.

30. Why intellectuals criticize the opposition?

People, more specifically the intellectual class other than identifying themselves with political parties who oppose the present government at the centre, severely criticize the Indian National Congress and other opposition parties, not with a target and aim of supporting the ruling regime though it inadvertently helps BJP and its leadership but with the hope of sensitizing the opposition parties to understand the ground reality of the political mood of the people and opinion makers of the society. In reality, the opposition leaders and parties exhibit continuously their inability, inertness, and refusal to learn and act fastly and professionally to control the damage done to them by the ruling class. It is equivalent to that of the damage done to the DMK during emergency which helped the MGR to maintain his image as savior of the poor. The DMK took nearly thirteen years to recuperate from the bad image it had earned during emergency. The opposition parties both national and regional are clueless to redeem their parties from the damages and yet they are comfortable as they are protected through their positions. It gives a message to their party cadres that they are in party position, parliament and state legislature to protect themselves, their assets and their business not the interest of the people and more specifically the poor. Left parties are not in this category but their contextualization is a problematic one and hence they are also shrinking. All political parties need new faces and new brand of leadership with different approaches and strategies to lead the parties. It does not mean that these political parties do not have enough new crops of leaders. They have modicum of leaders with potentials and skills to change the narratives and paradigms of Indian polity. But they are not allowed to emerge as leaders on their own. This syndrome paved the way for the continuous success of the present ruling regime at the centre. Their success lies not in satisfying the needs of the poor through their performance but their connections with the masses through their promises. The credibility loss of the opposition parties enables the ruling party in comfort zone. In this process the Prime Minister has got rich ability to communicate with the masses and convincingly keeping the masses with him. It is an irony that the UPA has got a track record of performance which is historic in nature from the perspective of the poor. But they are fully swallowed by the unchecked corrupt practices of some of the leaders in the government during the time. It is also a known fact that UPA has got efficient performers in governance but the country witnessed total inefficiency in the leadership to control the mischief mongers. This continues even today since these parties do not have leadership, people at different levels in the parties behave as they like and give a perception that these political parties do not have cohesiveness, sense of purpose and absence of agenda, everyone wants to safeguard their skin through the positions they acquire in the party and parliamentary institutions. To oppose Narendra Modi the leader, the opposition groups need leader, they need agenda, programme of action and strategy. People who oppose Narendra Modi from the political parties have no image among the public. Already they have been tainted and lost their credibility. Caste, class and religion or region or culture or language will not work at present. Gone are the days are over. Even the branded political families cannot pull the crowd and get votes by showing their faces. Narrative has been totally changed by Narendra Modi. Narendra Modi has given a perception to the people that he is a leader, in the office with a sense of purpose with direction and strategy. He is in conversation with the masses and nobody from the opposition parties has got such linkages with masses in India as Narendra Modi. To oppose Narendra Modi a leader has to emerge and that leader should have moral turpitude with clean image among the people along with a record of performance. It is rare to find match in the opposition parties. There is one such person available but now he has been made to move closer to Narendra Modi. It is none other than Nitish Kumar. He has got all credentials but the opposition groups have failed to make use of him. Nitish Kumar was the first person took initiative to field a common candidate from the opposition parties to contest in the election for the post of President of India. Had the Indian National Congress followed him fastly, the candidate from the opposition groups might have been announced first much earlier to the announcement of the candidate of the NDA. The Indian National Congress and the opposition parties delayed the process deliberately to fail the mission. Finally they followed a ceremony of fielding a candidate. Gopal Krishna Gandhi was contacted in this regard and he was left abruptly. Had the opposition announced the candidature of Gopala Krishna Gandhi, before announcement of the NDA course of action would have been different? In the same way now itself the opposition parties should have prepared a common candidate for the post of Prime Minister in the 2019 election. It is unfortunate they have missed the opportunity. BJP leaders are openly commenting that who is there to oppose Narendra Bhai Modi. As long as Rahul is in the fray for the post of Prime Minster, we are rest assured that we will be in power. The other opposition party leaders at different levels are commenting on the non-seriousness of the congress leadership on the issues faced by the nation. This kind of directionless and purposeless political activity of the Indian National Congress made every supporter of the congress party to move away from it and criticize the style of politics perpetuated by the Indian National Congress. The above conditions led the intellectuals to write series of articles about the debacle and directionless politics of the Indian National Congress. Thus in the 2019 what will happen in the election has been already predicted by everyone that BJP has no opposition. In such a way narrative goes. Thus opposition has to wait for yet another Nitish Kumar to emerge to oppose Narendra Modi.

31. Will the parties learn lessons?

In a democracy election plays a significant role in deciding the fate of the leaders and the parties and ultimately people decide their fate also. The political parties and leaders will have a perception that they can manage the people through their strategies money and organizational power. It is being done competitively by the political parties. In the same way people also manage the parties and leaders through their strategies, perceptions, and decisive political actions through ballot. People are supreme and they are sovereign in any democracy. In India democracy gets maturity only through election however defects the electoral system has got. Through every election series of messages are given to the parties and leaders. Parties carefully study the election results and learn from the results to change their course of action. People never spare parties and leaders when the parties and leaders are indifferent towards the feelings and demands.

No doubt, parties and leaders try to create a consciousness among the people through their communicative ability and through which elections are fought. The victory of the parties and the leaders depend on how well people are influenced by the parties and their leaders. People cannot be deceived or fooled by the parties and leaders continuously. People have their own evaluative standard through which the parties and leaders are assessed. It varies from time to time. It varies from state to state. Yet at time the whole nation will have only one standard framework of evaluation. Based on the evaluation of the parties and leaders by the people, electoral victories are decided.

Against that background, the current electoral verdict in Haryana and Maharastra has to be looked at. The opposition parties have not learnt the lessons in 2019 parliamentary election and yet with all weaknesses and disabilities, contested in the election without much hope. They are not united, they have not repositioned themselves and organizationally they are not revamped. With all the disabilities they have approached the election. They have not created a general mood that the BJP is going to be defeated. Equally the BJP has approached the election with a belief that whatever the BJP and its big dua Narendra Modi and Amitshah say, people will accept and in such a level the BJP leadership has gone up. Absolutely they were in euphoric mood that people will believe the word of the current Prime Minister and in such a way trust has been built up by the Prime Minister. No leader can match Narendra Modi and no one will take on Narendra Modi. So the distance between the BJP and the opposition parties is vast in terms of reaching out the masses. The BJP as party and its leadership have not realized the fact that people will also have a sense to assess the reality from their own life situation rather than on the speeches of the leaders. Many of the occasions people take decision based on the economic rationality from their own life situation. Mere rhetoric will not help when there is a vast gap between their promises and activities.

The two Assembly elections Maharastra and Haryana gave shock to the BJP and the surprise to the Indian National Congress. Why it is a shock to BJP? It is because everyone in the party felt that the charisma and communication ability of the leadership will pay a rich dividend as the opposition parties are in disarray and more specifically the opposition parties were not in a position to give an image that they are the credible alternative. The mainstream media barring a few exception, felt that the opposition cannot go nearer to the ruling as the leadership deficit is visible in the Indian National Congress coupled with organizational weakness. Hence the BJP second line leaders felt that people could be carried away on the leadership score by covering their mismanagement of governance and failures. All their calculations went wrong in this legislative Assembly election in both states.

In the opposition front, especially on the Indian National Congress the state level leadership has taken responsibility and managed the show. Yet they could not give an image that the party is facing the election in full vigour with the strong central and state leadership with credibility. Lukewarm attitude of the leaders is visible although. Hence they relied on the state leadership. But the election results are a very big surprise to the Indian National Congress.

The inference is that people are conveying a few messages to the political parties. They are: one, "People cannot be taken for granted by the BJP that they will be sawayed by the speeches of the leaders alone. We will assess the performance of the party in power and act accordingly". Unless BJP mends itself, it is very difficult to face the next election. It has to perform in governance and thereby they have to touch the life of the people. In the same way it conveys to the Indian National Congress that "people are willing to act in support of Indian National Congress provided the Indian National Congress reorganize, and reposition itself to face the people with alternative development programme". It is sad that a party with a history over a century known for its concern for the tribal, forming, fishing pastoral and craft communities, is facing a leadership crisis. It has to take series of critical decisions to revamp the party to the confidence and trust of the original constituents of the Indian National Congress. The party has to nurture regional leadership and they are to be given independence to build the party from the scratch.

It is only during the time of crises, the leaders have to act fastly, firmly and professionally to face the challenges to give an image that it would emerge victoriously. By this time the Indian National Congress would have reorganized the party, evolved strategies and alternative programmes to win the trust and confidence of the masses. In the same way it would have brought several thousand new faces with credibility to give a sense that it emerges as an alternative to the BJP with new faces and programmes. In India political parties gaining victory not because of their positive strength but due to the failure of the opposition. In Indian politics people are really strengthening democracy despite the poor performance of the political parties. It is right time for political parties to think as to how parties can come out from conventional mode of politics and move in alternative direction of doing development politics rather than continuing in divisive politics perpetuating caste and religion.

32. Corporate Social Responsibility to Total Social Responsibility

After visiting the Kizhakkampalam Grama Panchayat, Alwa in Kerala, I fixed an appointment with the managing director of KITEX (a Kids Wear Manufacturing Company) Mr. Sabu Jacob with an objective of getting the details behind the creation of 20-20 trust and its work in the entire panchayat through the elected representative sponsored by the trust. Why an Industrialist spends time and money for the panchayats instead of focusing his attention on the expansion of his industrial actives to make more profit. It is the question made me to meet him. When I met him in his office, on 8th February, 2018 I started the conversation with him by asking "why you have created 20-20 trust? Is it for spending the CSR money as other industries?" The response came in unequivocal term that it is not CSR activities but it is a TSR activity. Further, I asked him to explain the concept TSR. He said that "it is a Total Social Responsibility (TSR) of the company to transform the communities and not the Corporate Social Responsibility (CSR) of ear-marking some amount of money for social development activities". While hearing that explanation I provoked him by raising yet another question. "Are you responsible for the development of the village?" He said "yes". I argued that there are government departments and political parties to take care of the people. Immediately he retarded and replied that "it is a shame on the part of the politicians to keep the villagers especially the poor to lead a life in sub human living conditions. I have seen the houses provided to the poor by the government. They are in dilapidated condition and toilets have no doors. Living conditions of the poor are in deplorable conditions in the villages. Yet the political parties alternatively capture power in the state and panchayats. Peoples conditions remain the same. For the outsiders Kerala is a socially developed state by quoting the human development indicators. When we visited the areas where poor live, I felt very bad about the political parties. They know how to get votes but they do not know how to enable the poor to lead a decent human life. Absolutely the political parties do not have imagination, creativity, passion and commitment. They want to develop their parties but not the poor people. This condition has enabled me to take up responsibility". In this village, 89 families are leading their life under the shades of trabalin, 220 families have no electricity connection in the village, and 230 families have no toilets. They are the neglected or excluded. What the political parties have done for them? They also belong to either UDF or LDF. Despite their political affiliation their life has not been improved. It means what? Our politics is bereft of development ideas. Our politicians are much worried about the election not about the life of the people. Working with kizhakkampalam Grama Panchayat is not the corporate social responsibility. It is a total responsibility of our company to transform the life of the people". He further lamented that "I am not doing any charity. My family both father and mother had generosity and love towards the community and hence I too have a passion to work with people to transform them. It is the village where from I hailed and I feel that it is my duty to work with them for their upliftment. Hence, I am working. It is my desire to work with the people and make the village as a model village for the whole of the country in the year 2020. Today in the village 550 families have been destroyed and economically ruined due to the practice of taking alcohol by the men of those families. People that too the poor could not enjoy life. They are in suffering. Who will bring happiness to their life? Political parties want strong men to nurture and expand the party. I want only leaders and facilitators to help people to come up in life. In every aspect of human life one will find discrimination even in Kerala society. This has to be removed by empowering the poor. If it is a public school, the quality of education is poor and hence it caters to the needs of the poor. If it is a primary health centre, it will have only minimum facility not state of the art facility. If it is a balwadi, one cannot expect quality in maintenance. At present public institutions are being run with multiple deficiencies and as a result the quality of service is poor. Poor has no choice and hence they have to rely on public institutions. This has to be changed by equipping the public institutions on par with private institutions". He further added. "Why this dual standard of life? Poor has to lead a life with inadequate basic facilities. Rich has a high standard of life in the same village. Why the political parties are not sensitive towards the dual standard of life. Everyone talks about consumption parity not about the standard of life. My basic objective is to transform the village life by enabling everyone to lead a decent dignified human life. What minimum standard has to be followed for a decent human life should be provided for everyone. What the government have not achieved in the 70 years, have to be achieved through this new initiative of 20-20. It should be with the participation of people. The 20-20 will be a facilitator and supporter to the people of that village. People should realize their value of life. Reviving the life of 550 families which have lost their life in alcoholism is the challenging task. Poor have to understand the value of their life. They should know the value of their kids. They should know the value of nature. Basic work in the village is to create basic awareness about decent human life. The whole transformative process could be achieved with the active involvement of the community. The whole transformative process is centering on consciousness and valuing people. Even the poorest in the village should realize their worthiness and they should also lead a decent life as the rich and they will be respected as the rich in the same village. Most of the activities can be done in the consciousness of the people" he observed. Finally, he said that "it is not mere infrastructure development project from the external agency. It is a new consciousness creation among the people in the village and it is development consciousness. Thus, it is a total company responsibility not corporate social responsibility. The company is part of the community" will the companies take such responsibility?

33. Emerging Theses in Tamil Nadu Politics

The void created by the death of J. Jayalalitha and the absence of M. Karunanidhi in Tamil politics has enabled the political forces to produce many new theses as the course of Tamil politics in the past was dominated by the strong leadership from the days of K. Kamaraj. The six and half decade's political history of Tamil Nadu was the portrayal of the activities of four indomitable leaders namely K. Kamaraj, M. Karunanidhi, M. G. Ramachandran and J. Jayalalitha in governance. All the four were decisive, determinant, forceful and concern for the poor and performers. All the four had established distinct record of performance in their regimes. Each one has demonstrated the distinctive perspective. But now there is no such tall charismatic personality in Tamil Nadu politics. Yet someone has to emerge. Who will emerge as a strong leader in Tamil Nadu politics? How the political parties are going to decide the course of action? are the key questions. When the activities of the political parties at present are analysed, one will find the emergence of new theses. There are many theses emerging from the political process in Tamil Nadu politics at present.

Thesis - I

The DMK, the main opposition party with its full strength expecting the fall of the AIADMK government on its own and is ready to face the election as the party has got a successor to M. Karunanidhi Mr. M.K. Stalin. M.K. Stalin exhibited his sobriety by conducting himself diligently in the activities of the Legislative Assembly and outside the Assembly. He exhibited his hard work in keeping the party cadres intact and dynamic. Through his consensus politics, he is able to draw a few political parties towards the DMK. The parties which are moving closer to the DMK for common issues are going to stay with the DMK to face the election as partners. M.K. Stalin has not involved in any scam and he made it very clear that he will not allow corruption to take place if he is voted to power. Since he promised that he will not allow any such corruption as in the past, many looked at Stalin with hope. Many of the opinion makers have come to support M.K.Stalin. The numerical strength of the party and the strength of other parties which are going to be with the DMK are enough to get electoral victory. With this assumption, the DMK is performing its political task at this juncture. It does not want to form the government through dubious means but ready to face the election with the hope of winning it. Many opinion makers formed this proposition that the DMK has got an yet another opportunity.

Thesis- II

Indian National Congress has lost its hope to regain or recapture power from the Dravidian parties as it struggles for its existence. In this context, the BJP has created a framework to dismantle the politics of the ethnic nationalism based on the language and culture. The BJP has been expecting an opportunity and now it has come through the demise of J. Jayalalitha and disappearance of Dr. M. Karunanidhi from active politics. There is no dominant leader in Tamil Nadu politics at present. It wanted to use the new opportunity to expand its base and get into the Legislative Assembly to form the government. The leaders of the BJP believe that the image of the Prime Minister Modi and the new outlook of aspirational class will help in this regard. Knowing fully it is an uphill task, it has decided to take the risk. At the same time, it perceives that is possible only through forming a mega alliance with a few other political parties. It also needs crowd puller to fetch votes. In this regard, the party is hoping on the actor Rajnikanth as he has hinted his entry into politics. To perform the task, they want to see the AIADMK without a strong leader. Hence, they want to keep Mrs. Sasikala and her family out of the AIADMK. At the same time, all the leaders of the AIADMK should be in tact to take the direction from the high command of the BJP and Modi and act upon. In this process, the BJP has underestimated the power of Sasikala family and overestimated the popularity of

OPS. As a result, unexpected turn of events like NEET examinations are happening which are not in favour of the BJP.

Thesis – III

A few smaller political parties in the recent past wanted to keep the DMK and the AIADMK away from Tamil Nadu politics, and for which they formed a front to face the election. They faced the last general election to Legislative Assembly. They failed miserably in the election. After the election also they continued their strategy. Now a new opportunity comes in the form of an actor Rajnikanth. Rajnikanth can mobilize the masses and organise a party at present to take Tamil Nadu politics into a difficult direction. His popularity can be used at this juncture to mobilize votes. He is being motivated by various groups including the BJP to enter into politics. They believe that he will be the fittest person to dislodge the two Dravidian parties. With this belief the smaller parties are exerting pressure on Rajnikanth to enter into politics.

There is yet another political party the Pattali Makkal Katchi (PMK) has followed the footsteps of Narendra Modi to create a new narrative in Tamil Nadu politics through its new development agenda. Of all the political parties, the PMK is trying to organise development politics in the past one decade. It performs Green politics in Tamil Nadu. By practicing development politics, the PMK is trying to change the outlook of the party. It tries to come out from the caste fold through a struggle in the political process in Tamil Nadu. It has got clear-cut agenda, strategy and commitment. Yet, a section of the media and a few political parties tried their level best to prevent them becoming a mainstream political party. Yet, the PMK is working tirelessly with their own agenda. The party is trying to capture the imagination of the youth. They relying on the youth and the women based on their development agenda. It also tries to keep itself away from both the Dravidian parties. It has been accusing both parties that they have spoiled the state through their policies and corrupt practices.

What is really happening in Tamil Nadu and what will be the future course of action? Globalization of economy has brought unexpected change in Tamil Nadu. For the past three decades there is no ideological debate in the political discourses. Yet pro-poor schemes of the ruling parties have drawn the attention of the poor towards the two Dravidian parties. They survive on the competitive populist policies pursued by both parties. During the same period it is alleged that corruption has been regularized to the level of eating away the vitals of politics. Against this background, the political parties mainly the two Dravidian political parties have made politics costlier as they do politics as business. As a result, the smaller parties cannot do politics without money. In such a way, the cost of political activities has been increased. In the last general election held in 2015, a third force had been created but failed miserably. Against this background, one has to visualize the future. Unequivocally the trend indicates that the DMK emerges as winning party as it has got sufficient voters backing. Everywhere confusion prevails. The AIADMK vote bank is being disturbed and confused instead consolidated. Even if Rajnikanth organizes a party aligned with BJP and the AIADMK, the front cannot convince the voters what for this coalition. At present the DMK with its working president have given a perception that it will deliver goods. M.K.Stalin has got a reasonably a good political background with a sober leadership style attracts the major sections of the Tamil society. Next emerging force is the PMK. It may be forced to align with the BJP front and it will get sizeable number of seats, if they get seats in the regions where it is strong. All other predictions are fluid. If any other thesis emerges it may be due to a new leadership and a new strategy which are not visible at present.

34. How to make the State Pro-Poor?
Jaya has shown the way

Miss J. Jayalalitha, the former Chief Minister of Tamil Nadu, has left an in-delible mark in the politics, governance and administration of Tamil Nadu. One can bring any amount of criticism against her on the style of politics but no one can argue or criticize Jayalalitha on one count. Her pro-poor governance and pro-poor policies and schemes are the real models for other states in the context of globalization and increasing the gap between the rich and the poor. It was believed that M. Karunanidhi cannot be matched with any other leader, but can be tackled only by M. G. Ramachandran. But that has been changed and a new observation has been made that Jayalalitha cannot be matched with any other leader and she can be tackled only by Karunanidhi. In the initial stages, Jayalalitha kept the mass created by M.G. R by projecting Karunanidhi as corrupt and anti-poor.

Anti-Karunanidhi sentiments have been created by M. G. R among a segment of Tamil society and that group had been continuously nurtured and developed by Jayalalitha successfully. Along with anti-Karunanidhi sentiments, she had followed the footsteps of M. G. R by evolving innovative pro-poor policies, programmes and schemes and implemented effectively by her which has made the poor to identify with Jayalalitha. M.G. R was the first Chief Minister in India who thought of introducing direct benefit schemes to the poor by negating the trickledown theory of economists. Jayalalitha has developed this practice more effectively and by doing so, she made Tamil Nadu as a model state for poor-friendly policies, programmes and schemes.

Without any hesitation, she declared that she is with the poor and the poor are with her. Despite leading a bourgeois life, she worked for proletariats and subalterns. Till to-day, there are 369 development schemes operated through the departments of the State government and local governments. In Tamil Nadu, we have schemes for the welfare of poor people from cradle to grave. Tamil Nadu is far better than many other developed states like Gujarat, in terms of human development indicators, because of the pro-poor schemes and programmes implemented by the Government of Tamil Nadu.

It is a paradox that the AIADMK came into being as an offshoot of a non-Brahmin movement, which was being headed by an orthodox Brahmin, by giving an image to the public that she was more than a non-Brahmin in taking the welfare of non-Brahmin Tamils. Her identity is always with non-Brahmins, but never with Brahmins. She had given a new orientation to the party that AIADMK will believe in the Hindu tradition, not in Aadhi Sankarar's path but in Ramanujar's path. In the same way, she gave clarity to the concept of patriotism and protecting the rights of the state. On all the occasions, she was unequivocal in keeping the national interests paramount, but at the same time, protecting the interest of the state. History will recognize the stand taken by her in opposing the GST, despite the efforts of the central government in persuading her to support the bill. It was a lone opposition but powerful in argument. Her arguments for opposing

GST cannot be repudiated by anyone who values the importance of cooperative federalism. Even the DMK which claimed that it worked for state autonomy has not opposed GST in parliament. While DMK supported the GST, AIADMK walked out during the voting in Parliament. She kept her image very high among the people of Tamil Nadu during 2014 election by resisting the Modi wave.

Thirteen cases were filed after the General Elections in 1996 in order to decimate her political career. She faced all the cases and got acquitted in eleven cases which is not an ordinary issue. Keeping the party's morale and facing the cases were real challenges which she did it with a sense of courage and conviction. She proved unequivocally that cases were foisted by the DMK with an objective of eliminating her from politics.

On gendered governance, she made history of sorts. All her programmes are path breaking whether it is "cradle baby scheme" meant for abandoned children, or establishing private rooms in bus stand and other public places meant for lactating mothers, or giving reservation of seats for women and dalits consecutively for two terms in local bodies, or reserving 50% of seats for women in local bodies, or maternity leave for women for one year or financial assistance for the poor pregnant women or assistance to single girl child or providing bi-cycle to school going girls, she is unique and all are models to be emulated by other states. In the same way, she is unique in implementing pro-poor schemes. All are in the name of "Amma". Amma canteen, Amma medicals, Amma water, Amma cement, Amma Green houses for the poor, and a few others tremendously helped the poor. Even though all these schemes have been criticized by the opposition groups and parties as freebies for vote catching, she relentlessly pursued all those policies without paying any heed to the arguments of the economists that these are anti-growth activities. In protecting the interest of Tamil Nadu, she followed the legalistic approach. She got historic judgments in the Supreme Court on Mullai Periyar Dam and Cauvery water issues which brought a name among the farmers.

It is unfortunate that she is no more. Had she been alive and active in national politics, she would turn the whole hindutva politics into poor vs. rich politics. She is the first Chief Minister in India who demonstrated that regional leaders are in no way inferior to national leaders. She negated the master-servant relationship fostered by the central government towards the state governments. She never considered the central government as a master. She considered herself the Prime Minister of Tamil Nadu.

Her courage has been demonstrated by arresting the Chief of Kanchi Mutt Sankarachariayar. Though she was an orthodox Brahmin, she arrested him which cannot be dreamt of by Karunanidhi. At the same time, her approach, policies, and schemes were meant for promoting all religious activities in the state, by liberally allocating money, not only to Muslims but also to the Hindus and Christians.

In the era of globalization, one can learn from Tamil Nadu under the leadership of Jayalalitha as to how to protect the poor, how to use globalization for the benefit of economic growth of the state, and how to save the poor from the onslaught of globalization. Tamil Nadu government, under the leadership of Jayalalitha, is the role model. There is no distress migration in this state. Tamil Nadu is again the role model regarding the use of MGNREGA for the benefit of the poor, more specifically the women.

Here is a model for how to reach the unreached. "THAI" scheme is meant for reaching out to the unreached areas where the marginalised communities are living by providing all basic amenities through a hamlet level planning. She allocated huge money for that scheme. All the residential areas where SC and ST are living now got all facilities. This is unique in Tamil Nadu. An assessment has been made by the magazine Economist, about development, governance and performance of a few developed states, based on which an article was published in a leading journal Economic and Political Weekly (Economic and Political Weekly, 3rd September, 2016). In this evaluation, Tamil Nadu has come above even Gujarat.

Party men and women had reposed unflinching faith in her as she recognized the work of a grassroot level worker. Though she was incommunicado, she has mechanism to reach out to the party workers and the poor. Till date, masses visiting her burial ground is unabatingly surging. So far, 420 party cadres died because of bereavement. People, cutting a cross party lines, openly made statements about the single handed achievements made by her in politics and governance. She followed the footsteps of M.G. R in leaving everything to the people and not to her family. Like her mentor, she also left the party to the cadres to decide. She is a brave woman, developed on her own, and stood on her own strength. She is open to take stand, with all qualities of a national leader, but located in the regional politics. She silently empowers the poor and women through her governance and programmes. Poor have been empowered to evaluate the performance of the party in power.

35. Is loan waiver a solution to the farmer's crises?

Our policy and political communities are known for their quick and simplistic way of finding solutions to complicated problems and thereby we witness perennially the same problem recurring seriously regime after regime. Whenever the political parties facing election, in order to get the support of all sections the political class use to promise freebies and of them loan waiver to farmers is one and significant. The farmers' problems are not so simple as industrialization and globalization have complicated the problems of farming and forming communities. Intensified farm practices tuned by Green Revolution escalated the problems of the farmers. Since both globalization and industrialization have drawn the attention of the policy community, intellectuals and scientists, farming activities have been reduced into an insignificant economic activity. The needed infrastructure facilities, credit facilities, scientific and technological support, market facilities, input requirements, value addition to agri products needed to farm sector have been neglected over a period of time. All institutional and organizational mechanism available for the farming communities have been systematically dismantled for the benefit of the industrialization. As a result, the farming communities have faced serious ecological and environmental crisis. The lopsided policies pursued by both central and state governments made farming more difficult and profitably unviable. In order to cover up the wrong policies pursued in favour of industrialization to boost up the economic growth farmers have been given loan waiver and free electricity which also ultimately affect the existing eco-system of the farming. All these activities systematically made farming difficult and farmers in deep crises. Thus, farmer's suicides took place in massive scale to the tune of 300000. It is a shame on the policy and scientific communities. Thanks to the rural editor of The Hindu, Mr. Sainath who has brought to light the plight of the farmers and made the policy community to open their eyes towards farmers. As a result, 'Farmers Commission' instead of 'Agriculture Commission' was constituted with world renounced agriculture scientist Prof. M. S. Swaminathan as its chairperson. With great difficulty Prof. M. S. Swaminathan has extensively travelled and met the farmers and worked with experts and activists and finally submitted his report. I was also involved in the field work with lot of expectation worked with Prof. M. S. Swaminathan. A golden opportunity we had as Mr. Sharad Pawar as Agriculture Minister in UPA government to implement the major recommendations. Since it was a comprehensive report with lot of recommendations to enable farmers to come out from debt trap and to provide and create needed eco-system to make Agriculture more productive and profitable, everyone expected quick and everlasting solutions from the central Agriculture Ministry. It is unfortunate the cricket industry has taken much of his time and as a result he could not find time to fight with the neo-liberal economic politicians within the UPA regime to find everlasting solutions to the crises of the farming community. By seeing the crises, the BJP has included this issue as a major one and promised a slew of solutions. This promise has made the farmers to expect more relief and meaningful solutions as the Governemnt is headed by a person who has done meaningful work for farming practices in Gujarat when he was the Chief Minister. The BJP manifesto openly stated that it will implement the recommendation of Prof. M. S. Swaminathan's committee report. It is not loan waiver, but to create a needed eco-system conducive to increase productivity, increase profit and thereby the farmer's status will be enhanced. As per the promise, the present government could have taken decision fastly. It should have taken decision to keep agriculture in the concurrent list and it should have advised the state governments to constitute state farmers commission. Further, the state governments should be enabled to follow the model APMC act to facilitate the farmers to sell their products through a new market mechanism. All agricultural universities should have been enabled to work with farmers by evolving suitable technologies to add values to agricultural products before they go to market. Basic infrastructural facilities should have been created. But nothing came out from the new government also. Even though the Prime Minister has rich experience in Gujarat in addressing farmer's issue, he has not devoted much attention on agricultural side as he was drawn towards the economic growth. It is to be remembered that still 58% of our rural populace depends on agriculture for their livelihood. Now everyone indulged in blame game by politicizing the issue. The need of the hour is relief to farmers. But it does not stop with this simple solution of loan waiver. State governments have to constitute immediately a farmers commission with a time frame. Basic infrastructure has to be created for farming in the rural areas. In this infrastructure creation water management, credit management, agri input management are the core elements. Further, needed appropriate technology extension has to be provided through agriculture universities and Krishi Vigyan Kendras. To enable the farmers to get remunerative price for their products, the model APMC act has to be in place in every state. To add values to the product, newer technologies needed to farmers have to be in place as we find in West European countries. First, the state governments have to constitute a farmers commission. Second, the model APMC act has to be implemented. Third, cooperatives have to be freed from the clutches of the politicians and they should be handed over to farmers for their credit facilities. Thirdly, all the needed infrastructure namely the water storage facilities have to be created by regenerating the water bodies. Fourthly, storage facilities have to be created for farm products storage. Fifthly, the small and appropriate technologies have to be created to help small formers to add values to agricultural products. Sixthly, agriculture universities' extension wings have to be strengthened. Seventhly, rural entrepreneurship courses have to be introduced in agriculture universities to educate the farming communities. Eight, social education has to be imparted to the people through Gram Sabha with the active involvements of higher learning institutions. Nine, every Gram Panchayat has to take steps to evolve a micro perspective development plan in which agriculture plan should be a component. In every state there should be a separate agriculture budget to be presented annually in the state legislative assemblies. Thus, a massive alternative initiative has to be taken to solve the problems of the formers and not a loan waiver alone.

36. R. K Nagar By-election Blister

In electoral politics in every election, electorates use to give messages to the political parties both to the victor and vanquished. Wise leaders and the parties will learn lesson and rework and reorient themselves and their parties. Some of the parties and some of the leaders are always successful as they are contextualizing themselves to suit the requirements of the context. Primarily electioneering is a process whereby the leaders and parties are involving themselves in creating a public opinion in favour of them through a set of strategies and approaches. R.K. Nagar by-election has given a shock wave to many. R. K. Nagar by-election was cancelled in April and reelection was conducted on 21st December, 2017 as per the direction of the court. In the by election the voters of the R. K. Nagar gave many surprises to the political parties and opinion makers. First, in the recent past an independent candidate with a huge margin won the election and defeated the ruling party AIADMK's candidate and made the DMK supposed to be the winner to lose the deposit money. The margin has shaken up the belief, aspiration and calculations of the parties, leaders and the opinion makers. Money power played a big role in deciding the electoral victory for the past three decades and more intensely in the last two decades. It is to be remembered that it is a south Indian phenomenon barring Kerala. It is to be noted here that in Tamil Nadu many factors played their role in deciding the electoral victory and of which money is one. It played its role in this election also. But money alone has not decided the electoral victory of the candidate. There are some other factors played crucially in this electoral process. The electorates are matured and conscious when they go to pooling booths. They cannot be easily cheated by the political parties and the candidates. Election by election voters are becoming tough and made the political parties to become submissive before them. Over a period of time through media that too electronic media views, news, opinions are reaching the ordinary citizens as every household has got television set with cable connections at a cheaper rate. People especially poor have been oriented by M.G. Ramachandran and J. Jayalalitha by identifying themselves with the poor and the poor have been empowered through the pro-poor policies and programmes. J. Jayalalitha has protected the poor, women and fisher folk as her mentor M.G.R. In any reform, imposed by the centre which affects the pro-poor measures, she strongly opposed it and protected the poor by continuing the scheme unmindful of the pressure of the central government. For both M.G. Ramachandran and J. Jeyalalitha, reform meant pro-poor not economy. In such a way, the poor have been empowered in Tamil Nadu. Tamil Nadu is one of the best state in maintaining the public distribution system by serving the needs of the poor. It was well structured by M.G. Ramachandran and nurtured by J. Jayalalitha. Further, when states rights are being affected, it is J. Jayalalitha who became furious and opposed it tooth and nail. Through all means she fought for state's rights. She maintained that she is an iron lady meant for poor and she proclaimed that she is with the poor and poor are with them. Now the present AIADMK has given a sense to the public that the leaders are in the hands of the BJP. Further, the pro-poor schemes well maintained by J. Jayalalitha have been dismantled through the reform packages of the central government. PDS is the best example and it is not in good condition. In the same way, fisher folk and farmers are in distress and they are not protected by this regime. People especially poor have come to a conclusion that the AIADMK government is weak and it is under tremendous pressure from the central government. The BJP failed miserably in Tamil Nadu due to legacy of EVR tried its level best to sneak through the weak AIADMK government which is unacceptable to the public of Tamil Nadu. This is being indicated by T.T.V. Dinakaran very effectively in the discourses during electioneering and opposed the AIADMK government and the BJP.

Generally, people that too poor in Tamil Nadu will not allow the state machinery to harass the leaders too much. If anyone is being harassed by the state machinery much, they tend to get the public support. When J. Jayalalitha was harassed by fostering series of cases after 1996 election on the charges of corruption, people felt that it was too much and hence in the next election DMK was defeated despite its best performance in governance. In the same way, T.T.V. Dinakaran was excessively harassed by the state machinery. But T.T.V. Dinakaran bravely faced all the troubles given by the state. People compare the stand of T.T.V. Dinakaran and M.K. Stalin in opposing the BJP government and its policies. From their perspective, T.T.V. Dinakaran is considered as a smart leader to tackle the BJP government. The AIADMK cadres always need strong leader and it was provided by J. Jayalalitha. After her demise the cadres feel that T.T.V. Dinakaran will give such a kind of leadership and hence they wanted to be with T.T.V. Dinakaran.

Corruption and money distribution are the regularized activities in Tamil Nadu electoral politics in the last three decades. There is no difference between the AIADMK and the DMK. Both have perfected it as an art and science. To retrieve the politics from this syndrome both PMK and Peoples Welfare Front tried in the last general election. But both failed. In this election, the DMK under the leadership of M.K. Stalin has taken a decision not to give money for votes and it is a welcome sign. He wants to change the course of politics now onwards. But the result has raised many questions on his leadership. People in Tamil Nadu do not like dictate politics of the BJP government at the centre in the party affairs of the AIADMK. Further, people do not like the way the present AIADMK leaders respond to the dictates of the centre without any resistance. As a result, they found T.T.V. Dinakaran. He will emerge as a leader of the AIADMK. Up to the next general election, the leadership of OPS and EPS will be respected as they got power. It will be over when election is declared. R.K. Nagar has given a message that Tamil Nadu needs a strong leader to tackle the centre and to protect the pro-poor policies. Money is not the sole factor decided the R.K. Nagar by poll. Narrowing down the larger discourse to money for votes is a kind of escapism on the part of all the political parties and leaders. There is a distinct political culture nurtured in Tamil Nadu which is unique and at the same time there are some aberrations in the Tamil Nadu political system. To remove the aberrations, a massive change has to be initiated to change the course of politics which needs a new leader who has some distinct qualities. Otherwise the present trend will continue in the next election also. One should not think that through money votes can be purchased. Money is one of the factors.

37. Rajini Factor in Tamil Nadu Politics

After the demise of J. Jayalalitha and withdrawal of M. Karunanidhi from active politics due to aging prompted many to enter into politics of Tamil Nadu with a basic assumption that there is leadership vacuum. While using this opportunity, those who are trying to test water project an argument that the system of politics, governance and administration is weak and not in tune with fundamentals of democratic values. This attack is directly on the DMK and the AIADMK as they are responsible for the present state of affairs in politics, governance and administration. This argument is being projected by all the smaller political parties in Tamil Nadu which have aligned with both the AIADMK and the DMK in facing general elections in the past and formed electoral alternative fronts to Dravidian parties and faced the general election in 2014. The alternative fronts one under Pattali Makkal Katchi (PMK) and Peoples Welfare Front (PWF) got defeated and totally rejected by the people. Both the Dravidian parties emerged as ruling party and the opposition party in Tamil Nadu Legislative Assembly.

Now Rajinikanth is trying or is being forced to try at this juncture to test his ability to emerge as factor to reckon with in Tamil Nadu politics. He was also very close to the DMK president M. Karunanidhi. He also gave support to the DMK openly at one point of time. In the same way, he opposed the PMK openly gave a call to defeat the PMK candidates in the general election. But all the PMK candidates emerged victoriously despite his powerful opposition. In Tamil Nadu, both the Dravidian political parties are very strong organizationally. Their connections with grassroots are very strong. The DMK is scientifically organised party which cannot be disturbed very easily. In the same way, the AIADMK is strengthened through its cadres with the emotional attachment. Both parties have been headed by two strong leaders namely J. Jayalalitha and M. Karunanidhi. The AIADMK is being disturbed by the central government by removing Sasikala family and as a result the cadres of the AIADMK could be lured towards a new political formation. With this proposition Rajinikanth is being pressurized to come to the political space organizationally as a political party. Everyone knows that the DMK is organizationally strong and yet it has not done an aggressive politics strategically to topple the weak AIADMK government. From this point of view everyone feels that the DMK has got a weak leadership. On the other hand, the AIADMK even after the merger of two factions O. Panneerselvam (OPS) E. Palanisamy (EPS), it is not strengthened instead it has been weakened as T.T.V. Dinakaran emerged as a leader. Thus, the design of BJP did not materialize with the AIADMK, it tries now through Rajinikanth. In Tamil Nadu politics to drive out the two Dravidian parties, a formidable force is necessary and Rajinikanth alone cannot remove these forces. Both parties' connections with the poor and the middle class is strong and vibrant. Both are strong in delivering pro-poor schemes and policies. The prime argument of 'system failure' and 'massive corruption in Tamil Nadu' cannot draw the attention of the majority and more particularly the poor. Without organizational strength no one political party can dream of winning election in Tamil Nadu is only a pipe dream. Because these two political parties have reached out to the remotest villages organizationally and the cadres are kept active by lubrication through the corrupt money the parties have earned. Everyone knows in Tamil Nadu that the political parties earn money through corrupt means is in circulation. To cleanse the existing practices of politics, governance and administration, a strong political leader with extraordinary vision for evolving alternative politics, governance and development is needed. At present that leadership is not visible. Rajinikanth does not have such DNA as he is not 24x7 politician. He is 24x7 professional actor and cinema businessman. He cannot be compared with MGR as he has not been active in politics as MGR. Further, when MGR registered his party, he relied on his image alone- but today for politics, party needs huge money apart from image.

To do politics in Tamil Nadu at present, organizational structure, media and mass support are very essential and for which monetary backing is the lifeline. Against this background, his entry is looked at with suspecision whether he will come as a full time politician or looking for option and strategy to operate in the backdrop safely. From the political activities which are going on in Tamil Nadu no one could draw the following theses:

a,   However, weak the DMK is in terms of leadership, it is scientifically organised party and it has got the base support of the masses and hence it can emerge victoriously in the coming election, if it forges alliance with like minded parties.

b,   The AIADMK will realign with the T.T.V.Dinakaran by burying their differences for the beneifits of all and face the election with the orgaisational structure and support of its vote bank from the poor and thereby emerge as opposition or the ruling party and it depends on the realignment of the AIADMK factions.

C,   initiating an alternative either by the PMK or by Rajinikanth and forgoing alliance with all the smaller parties by highlighting the alternative development and governance agenda prepared by the PMK. In this formation, BJP cannot find a place as it could not gain strength instead it will weaken the alliance. One has to wait and see the developments in the years to come.

38. Reforming the Political System

President of India has emphatically argued for the need of electoral reform in India in order to strengthen Indian democracy in the context of deteriorating the values of democracy in the political and electoral process of our political system. This kind of lamentations are not new. It has been reiterated by many luminaries in the past. Yet, there is no concrete action at the ground. As a result, our democracy has been classified as minimal democracy by the scholars who specialize in representative democracy. Our founding fathers and mothers with their sacrifice and sense of commitment laid the foundation for parliamentary democracy in India. Now seventy years are over and we had seven decades of experience in parliamentary democracy. Our literary rate has increased dramatically. Science and technology have been developed to the surprise of many of the developed countries. Yet, we are in minimal democracy. Even in the minimal democracy we have several weaknesses. Conducting election to the parliamentary institutions is regular but with many aberrations like bribing the voters as it happened in R. K. Nagar constituency by-election at Chennai city. Hence, it is time to act and not to repeat the ceremonial speeches. Frustrated citizens need action from responsible officials and leaders who are in the helm of affairs. Day by day people are losing interest and faith in the leaders and institutions as the political activities of the political institutions have been influenced by money power and muscle power and thereby the vox populi supremelex becomes only an empty rhetoric not a reality. Hence, every sane and responsible citizen would argue for electoral reform.

In this context, I put forth a suggestion for a comprehensive reform not only in the electoral process but also the whole process of the political system. Overhauling is needed for the politics of India as it has been afflicted with contagious diseases which are easting away the vitals of Indian democracy. To illustrate the danger in which we live in our democracy a few narratives are given below: I am giving below the news items appeared in the newspapers which have got relevance to the above propositions and demands. A party functionary observed that the Samaswadi Party has to be handed over to Mulayam Singh Yadav and then only it can be rejuvenated. Continuously DMK leader M. Karunanidhi has been asked to elevate M. K. Stalin to be the president of the party. Senior leaders of the congress party used to give press statement that without buying time Rahul Gandhi has to take up the president post. Wall posters carrying statements that the permanent general secretary of the AIADMK party J. Jayalalitha. V. K. Sasikala, O. Panneerselvam and Deepa have staked claim to be the real heir apparent of J. Jayalalitha. All the above statements have reiterated the fact that political parties have been considered as properties. As descendants of family, sons and daughters bequeath the properties of father and mother, political parties have to be owned by the family members.

Once the numerical strength of the members of political parties was considered as assets of the party. Now coffer and physical properties are considered as wealth of the party. A newly appointed president of the state committee of a national party gave a press interview that he has no money to develop the party. He felt that without money one cannot develop a party. This is the perception of a state party president. Many political parties in India have properties more than companies and industrial houses. In such a way, political parties accumulated wealth. All dominant political parties barring a few are having the perception that without money party cannot be developed and cannot face the election. Money is the source through party can be nurtured and developed and gain political power. This perception is shared not only by the party functionaries and members but also the general public. The political parties realized the potentials of the power of the state, and hence by hook or crook they want to capture power. When they capture power, they try to take away huge money for the party and the families of the party functionaries by rent seeking using power. By using the money power they want to come to power and even if they are defeated, they run the party till the next election. To run the party they need huge money as political parties have to spend money for political activities. Nobody does any free work for political party and for all the party activities, parties are paying money to cadres and public.

At the dawn of independence the political parties collected money from the members of the party and general public. But now they have opened a channel towards market. Huge money comes from business houses and through rent seeking. Globalization has increased the volume of economy and as a result huge money comes from the industrial houses and business houses. As a result, one could witness policy corruption in governance. The corruption at the top induced the corrupt practices at every level upto grass-roots. That is why a recently conducted research in 17 states brought to light the fact that per capita bribe is more than percapita tax in India. In such a way, rent seeking habit has entrenched into politics, governance and administration. The money mobilised through rent seeking and other means have been used for political mobilization, election expenditures and bribing voters. South Indian states are competing with each other and of them Tamil

Nadu is open and visible. The quantum spent is very high. There is a new economy called party economics and election economy as knowledge economy. These economies affected the real economy. This trend has obstructed the National Election Commission to conduct a by-election in R. K. Nagar constituency. By cancelling the by-election in R.K. Nagar constituency, the National Election Commission had made a statement that it is not possible to conduct the election fairly. It means the whole electoral process is vitiated and all the political parties are responsible for it. In this context, everyone makes his or her own observation about the electoral process and pointedly make one strong recommendation that the whole electoral process has to be reformed. But I want to make a submission that it is not confined to election alone, it starts from somewhere and it ends in election. So unless the whole political process is cleansed, any minor attempt will be only cosmetic, and it will not provide lasting solution to the problem. In this context, I make the following recommendations:

1. One cannot keep any public office not more than two terms. A political party leader can hold the office only for two terms not more than that. It is applicable to the President of India, Prime Minister of India, Governor or the Chief Minister of a state or Ministers, MPs, MLAs, and Local body leaders. In the life time one cannot hold any public office not more than two terms. No, political party can keep its leaders not more than two terms. Tenure of the office bearers of the political parties can be made uniformly two years. By rotating the position, individuals hold over institutions will be weakened. As a result, organisations and institutions will be strengthened and not the individuals. Now our democracy revolves around individuals not around institutions.

2. Trusts have to be delinked from the political parties. Trust cannot be controlled by the political parties. All the trusts of the political parties separated from the political parties influence. The party leader's family members are in the trust and thereby they control over the coffer. Party can nominate public figures to the trust but they should not be from the parties.

3. It should be made mandatory that political parties have to conduct the election for the party periodically. It has to be monitored by the Election Commission. When the major political parties conduct

party election, the Election Commission has to nominate observers. Political parties which have not conducted the party election periodically should be debarred from electoral contest.

4. Political parties have to submit accounts of income and expenditure and audited statements to Election Commission annually. Audit should be done by only one reputed company nominated by the Election Commission. Parties which have not submitted the audited statements should not be allowed to contest in the general election.

5. Political parties which are not active in Electoral politics have to be removed from the registration. They should not be provided the status as political parties in any governance engagement.

6. Political party's resource mobilization has to be done transparently and the details of the receipts and expenditures should be on the open domain.

7. Lokpal has to be in place. Who gives money, how much they give, to which political party they have given are to be made public. Refusal to lokpal and allowing the corporate to give money without disclosing identity should not be encouraged.

All the above reforms have to be done expeditiously and professionally. In the past, there were committees and commissions to make recommendation to reform the electoral process. As a result, reports were submitted to the National Election Commission. There were seminars and symposia and recommendations had been given from these seminars and symposia. To do the above reforms recommended by commissions and committees the leader should have the will. Unless one has extraordinary will power this challenge cannot be responded. Do we find such leader in India at present is the question.

39. Status of Dalits in Periyar Land

The status of Dalits in Tamil Nadu could be seen in a comparative perspective with the neighboring state Kerala. Kerala is a model for social transformation and social development. It is not a model on all developmental issues. Swami Vivekananda visited south India and made an observation about Kerala that it is a lunatic society as it practiced unseability which is a worst form among the discriminatory practices. In such a way, social relationship was maintained in Kerala. Tamil Nadu is known for its social justice movement and its leader's initiatives in social reforms in Tamil Nadu. We Tamils always called that Tamil Nadu is Periyar land. E.V. Ramasamy Periyar from Tamil Nadu went to Kerala to participate in Vaikom Satyagraha. Now where is Kerala in social justice and where is Tamil Nadu? is the question to be pondered over. Through series of social transformative movements initiated by the left and the spiritual organisations attitude and behaviour of the people have been changed. Within a short span of time roughly three decades, the issue of untouchability has gone from Kerala coupled with the above movement, a movement for science has helped the Kerala society to adopt more of science than the community practices. With the result, Kerala has achieved remarkable progress in social development and social justice. The only crucial issue which Kerala has been facing is the conditions of the Tribals. It is a slur on Kerala now. But in Tamil Nadu, despite the fact that the political parties decented from Dravidian Movement have been in power continuously in five decades and speaking volumes about the social reform movement initiated by the Dravidian Movement, the conditions of the rural poor dalits are in deprable conditions.

In Tamil Nadu nearly 20% of the population is Dalits (19.18% SC and 1.03% ST). Of them 63.2% are literate. 11% of the Dalits own lands. 25,613 Dalits are in the Gram Panchayat as ward members, 3299 Dalits are Gram Panchayat Presidents, and 1598 Dalits are Block Panchayat Councilors. Nearly 20% of the positions have been captured by the Dalits in rural local bodies. Despite the presence of the elected representatives in the rural areas, discriminatory practices widely prevalent in Tamil Nadu. When a study was conducted in 2013 Gram panchayats in 12 districts in Tamil Nadu, it is found out that 33 types of discriminatory practices are in operation in the rural areas. Periodically caste clashes erupted in Tamil Nadu. But in the clashes worst affected are the Dalit women and children. What are the discriminatory practices that are in the society with what intensity have been given below in the form of a table.

Table No: 1 Discriminatory Practices

Sl. No.	Types of Discriminatory Practices	Prevailing Gram panchayats	Percentage (%)
1	Two tumbler system practiced	104	49
2	Denial of permission to enter into common temples	213	100
3	Discrimination in PDS Shops	70	33
4	Discrimination in Graveyard	208	98
5	Discrimination in "Commons" Utilization (Halls)	111	52
6	Discrimination in "Saloon"	142	57
7	Discrimination in water tanks and ponds	145	67
8	Discrimination in Health institutions	33	68
9	Discrimination in Educational Institutions	29	15.9
10	Discrimination in using the public toilets	58	13.4
11	Compelled to carry the dead animals	185	87
12	Denial of permission to use costly dress and jewels	54	25.3
13	Compelled to burn and bury dead bodies and carry death messages to relatives	183	86

Sl. No.	Types of Discriminatory Practices	Prevailing Gram panchayats	Percentage (%)
14	Bonded Agri labourers	114	54
15	Inter-caste marriage was strictly prohibited	213	100
16	Community Panchayats deliver judgment to the Dalits when they involve in petty crimes	105	49
17	Ill-treating the Dalit elders by the caste Hindu youth by using slang	196	92
18	Atrocities against Dalit Women	94	44.1
19	Compelling them to remove sewage of the village	158	74.1
20	Dumping the waste of the villages in the Dalit settlements	104	48.8
21	Property cannot be purchased without the permission of the caste panchayats	63	29.5
22	Dalit children are discriminated in schools	133	62.4
23	Dalit students are involved in cleaning activities in the school	38	17.8
24	Dalit children are ill-treated by using slang	126	59
25	Dalit students are not permitted in public functions in schools	103	48.3

Sl. No.	Types of Discriminatory Practices	Prevailing Gram panchayats	Percentage (%)
26	Panchayats leaders are ill-treated	45	21.1
27	Dalit students are not permitted to play with caste Hindu students	13.3	62.4
28	Animals of the Dalit family should not mingle with the animals of the caste Hindus	33	15.9
29	Caste Hindu students are not permitted to take food when it is prepared by Dalit Cook	63	29.5
30	Postman will not deliver letters to Individual houses of Dalits	33	15.9
31	Discriminatory practices in village administrative office	62	29.5
32	Walls have been constructed to prevent the Dalits to enter into caste Hindu areas	47	22
33	Dalits have to stand and should not sit in the public transport in front of caste Hinwdu	73	34.2

*Source: Computed from G. Palanithurai, **Dalits and Dalit Representatives in Rural Local Governance**, New Delhi: Concept Publishing Company, 2013.*

It is state a known for reformist politics. It is modernized, industrialized and most urbanized state. Despite all, the discriminatory practices are in operation. Of the 33 types of discriminatory practices 13 are very intensive. It is strange to note that there are community panchayats functioning in the villages along with constitutional panchayats. Community panchayats are more powerful than constitutional panchayats in many of the villages in Tamil Nadu. the continuous political mobilization on caste line for politics caste identity becomes strong in the rural areas. The conditions of the Dalits have also not been improved. The potentials of local bodies are not known to many Dalit leaders and organisations. Through local bodies, many of the critical issues of development can be addressed. Local bodies have to address social justice issues. But in reality it is not so. The Dalit rural local body leaders have taken up the issues of social justice at a limited level but faced volley of problems. But they are not properly addressed by the officials. The Dalit political party leaders have not helped the Dalit panchayat leaders when they face problems. Dalit panchayat leaders have faced volley of problems at community level and there is no mechanism to help them. To overcome this issue, the Dalit Panchayat leaders have to be trained. It should be an exclusive training for them. They are to be unionized. They have to be facilitated to form their own association to address their problems on their own. They should be taught how to deal with social justice issue through non-violent means. Support system has to be created by the government to enable the Dalit panchayat leaders to work on social justice issues. Panchayats have tremendous potentials to transform the society at the grassroots. They are to be strengthened and empowered.

40. Where is the leader from 'Jallikattu'?

The agitation launched by the youth and students for Jallikattu has brought to light several new propositions and theses in Tamil Nadu politics. It is unprecedented, unexpected and unique in terms of the nuances used to communicate the messages, mobilization done, conduct of the mobilized youth in the agitation and the messages given to the political class. The millions who participated in the agitation has appealed to the political class that they should not come and participate in this agitation by projecting their party colour. Further, they reiterated that they do not require any material support from the political parties. Refusal of youth in entertaining the political parties in their struggle has given a message that the political parties have lost their credibility from the eyes of the youth and the students as the political parties have not united themselves for the cause of the people of Tamil Nadu. They did not speak in one voice on the issues of Tamil Nadu. Plethora of issues affecting the life, livelihood and development of Tamils and Tamil Nadu. On all the issues people could hear only divisive voices among the political parties. But the political parties are using issues to gain political mileage but not to solve the problems. Blame game is the only activity one could find in the political space and not finding solution and this culture has frustrated everyone and mere specifically the educated youth. Take the case of Cauvery river dispute, Srilankan Tamils issue, fisherman issue, Kudankulam nuclear plant issue, mining of sand and minerals, Paalar river issue, Mullai Periyar issue, Krishna water issue, alcoholism, corruption in public life, governance and administration, the political parties have not united themselves to solve them. It is a known fact that the political parties are the instruments to carry forward the demands of the people to the government and exert pressure on the government to get things done.

But in this agitation the youth and students who involved in protest made a declaration that they do not want any help either materials or moral support from the political parties. They demanded help only from the public. As they expected, public have extended all kinds of support to sustain agitation as it has been facilitated not obstructed by the police and the government machinery. Absolutely there is no resistance from any quarter. As a result, public has also joined and by which it becomes a festival or sometime it appears as a fun. The whole exercise was not in the mode of a struggle but in the form of a congregation.

While going through the opinion expressed, discourse developed, observations made in the venues of agitation and the views exchanged through social media, one could gauge that they have given a new message that Jallikattu is only an opportunity to express their anger over the nature of politics, governance and decisions making on the vital issues of Tamil Nadu both by the central and state governments. The anger is against the political culture that prevails in India and Tamil Nadu. Youth had developed a feeling that the central government has not responded positively to the genuine demands of the Tamils. Youth had accumulated the feelings of anger, depression and despondency and they are being released through this agitation. The pent up feelings and emotions of the youth have been released through this agitation. Since there is no leadership and organization, there is no mechanism to moderate the views, expressions, observations, opinions of the participants inside and outside on various issues through this agitation. Participants have touched whole range of issues of Tamil Nadu. Further, the Government is also bewildered to identify the leader and organisation to initiate talks with them.

There is not even a single organisation which took initiative for this agitation but it is only the message spread through social media brought millions to street and Chennai Merina beach. There is a huge mass but they are regulated by themselves collectively which attracted the public, more of women and children. No violence, no anger, no slang against anyone but focused on the cause of Jallikattu in the initial stage.

Having seen the new trend of expression of the feelings and emotions of the youth, the political leaders, and the media have been perplexed to ponder over the steps to be taken at their level in the light of the sudden unusual expression of the emotions of the youth. The whole media, filmdom, political class have to take a relook on their activities and they have been psychologically made to make statements infavour of the agitating mass and unless otherwise they tend to lose their credibility in the eyes of the agitating youth and students. The whole activities of the youth and students have made us to call it as "Tamil Spring". In such a way, it has progressed.

There is no leadership in the movement and it is being directed by soul force but the expressions are always emotional. Those who gave messages have whipped up the emotions. This movement started with a demand of a permanent solution to organise Jallikattu but in due course many demands have been included. Since there is no leadership how to end this movement is a big problem. How to end and where to end is a problem for the agitators.

It is to be seen in the backdrop of a political culture perpetuated in the last fifty years. In the context of marginalization of the civil society space, there had been no orientation for the youth to look at issues in perspectives and the political parties failed to engage youth through ideological orientation in the past three decades. After the introduction of globalization students have been made as commodities and a product to job market instead of making them as change makers or transformational leaders. In this context, the youth with varied aspirations, dreams looked for opportunities through governance by the political class but they could not get the responses as they wanted. Yet, they were clueless by and endlessly waiting for opportunities. In the eyes of the youth, and the public the political class is the biggest beneficiary of globalization and this made them to develop a perception that the political class is exploitative and corrupt. No political organisation has given opportunity to the youth to channelize their energies and emotions through political activities. Now it has exploded. This event was over. But strong messages are coming out from this agitation to the political class, ruling regimes and the administrative class. Proper understanding, and reorientation is an imperative need of the hour. People who participated in the agitations are not with full understanding and awareness of the basis of Jallikattu. Jallikattu is only the way through which the youth and students have expressed what they wanted to express. It is up to political class, ruling class and administrative segment to reorient themselves to do the job meaningfully and be sensitive to the issues of the people.

In the last thirty to forty years there had been no mass agitation in the colleges and universities. Absolutely the youth in the educational institutions more specifically in higher learning institutions had no political orientation. There is no space for them for any political activities or at least for political discourses. The major segment of the youth who participated in the agitations is the product of the new generation higher learning institutions. There is an absolute disconnect between the educated youth and the political class. This technology driven mobilization has provided opportunity for them to ventilate their emotions, despair and despondency through this Jallikattu agitation. Will the political class mend itself?

Second part of the question is what are the unintended consequences of this agitation? Everyone expected that the movement will produce good leaders and new set of agenda for future activities. Unfortunately, there is no sign of forming an organisation to pursue new course of politics which is alternative to the existing framework of politics. In the seven days period, enough opportunities were there to evolve an organisation. Though they spoke in the course of agitation about whole range of issues in Tamil Nadu, they did not have any vision, goal and strategy to move further. In the absence of a leader and an organisation, how to end the agitation becomes a problematic. The whole movement ended in a sad note of violence and excess police action against a segment of the agitating mass. Since, the participating youth in the agitation had no political orientation and experience without knowing the power of the political class and the state, have moved into the agitation track unintentionally. But the present government have sensed the mood and emotions of the people acted quickly and convincingly to exert pressure on the central government and got the work done. When the deal was clinched, people who were responsible for agitation have not celebrated the victory instead they moved out of the court of agitation insignificantly. It is purely because of the lack of leadership.

41. Where we are in combating the impact of climate change?

People have been increasingly realizing the impact of climate change throughout the world whether they are rich or poor. Both are facing plethora of problems in day to day life and the poor will face severe problems in their livelihood choices. Faster growth depletes natural resources very fastly. Global companies with their giant machines move from one place to another place to exploit the resources and more particularly the minerals. Rules and regulations are being violated with the help of the politicians and the bureaucrats. Sensitive citizens and civil societies vigilantly have taken the violating companies to the task through legal means. But exploitation of natural resources are continuing in the third world countries unabatingly. In this process a few segments of the society got advantages and many face problems. Equally policy communities at the global level are seriously concerned about combating the climate change development and hence series of resolutions have been passed in global institutions and followed by resolutions in national and regional legislative bodies. Many serious legislative decisions have been taken at the national and regional levels. They are being implemented. These are not enough to arrest further damage of the ecology and environment and a strong option was advocated in Paris summit to pursue "Green Growth" which argues that the humanity has to pursue economic activities in a different path. It is an alternative path. This resolve came after a strong realization that the present way of economic activities will not sustain the achievements what humanity has made and more particularly the present day economic activities brought severe issues in developmentalism itself. Now it becomes a development crisis. Green growth, and sustainable developments are not new subjects but they had been brought to light for discourse on development eighty years back. When they were advocated by the ecologists and environmentalist, the mainstream thinkers have branded them as anti development thinkers and non system belivers or anarchists. Until now they are treated as anti state advocates. But now only after seeing the severity of the impact of the climate change they start recognizing the environmentalists and ecologists as scientist. In the development discourse they are being included to share or contribute their input to evolve a development framework which is new and it is considered as 'development beyond'.

Countries like India 68% of the people still in the rural areas and 58% of the total populace are relying on agriculture for their livelihood and hence, actions have to be initiated at the ground. Green growth economic activities have to be initiated at the village level. Ecology and environment have to be nurtured and protected in the rural areas. Environment friendly economic activities have to be initiated. Activities which damage environment have to be totally prohibited. Solar energy augmentation has to be done at the village level. Organic and natural farming have to be encouraged. Biomass burning has to be stopped. Biogas plant has to be set up and the gas has to be used for cooking purposes. Green building norms have to be followed in construction of building in the rural areas. Alternative building technology has to be introduced. Instead of burnt brick, compressed mud block can be used for construction. By doing so, an enormous amount of wood can be saved and emission of huge carbon can be reduced. In such a way smart solutions have to be found out for achieving sustainable development. All the common lands are being used to create green cover. Biodiversity act has to be implemented in the rural areas to protect the rare species which are grown in the locality. All kinds of plastics and polythene usages have to be stopped. Maintaining a perfect sanitation in the villages is the prime activity of the institutions at the grassroots. The whole life style has to be changed at the village level and in this context a behavioural change among the people is the need of the hour. People have been lured to spend and they are encouraged to consume. But now new behavioural traits have to be brought in. In this process people have to be consciented on conservation and nurturing of nature. All the activities of the community have to be oriented to conserve resources and not to spend more. A new paradigm of rural transformation has to be evolved to maintain equilibrium in the relationship between human society and nature. This paradigm is not new, it was advocated hundred years ago by M. K. Gandhi. At that juncture, he was ahead of time. He is more relevant today. To bring such massive transformation in the rural areas among the people in their attitude, behavior and activities, transformational leaders are needed for the rural communities. Appropriately time has come as the Fourteenth Finance Commission made it mandatory that every Gram Panchayat has to develop a perspective plan for the development of the village panchayat areas. Guidelines for preparation of Gram Panchayat Development Plan have been issued. While preparing the Gram panchayat development plan, the panchayat has to keep the climate change, disaster preparedness, green growth, sustainable development in the backdrop. To perform the above the panchayats have to be prepared through capacity building, training and sensitization. People have to be mobilized and sensitized on all those subjects and new transformational leaders have to be prepared. In a conventional training institute one cannot expect that these inputs will be given to the Panchayati Raj elected representatives through training process. In order to integrate the aspects which have been mentioned above, training modules have to be prepared and they are to be integrated with the general training modules meant for training the panchayat leaders.

A new leadership training programme has to be conceptualized to shape transformational leaders. To perform the above task a new leadership school has to be created in all the states or to convert the existing State Institute of Rural Development as new leadership schools. It is the need of the hour.

42. Who should be the President of India?

Whenever there is a discourse on any social or political issue, it is my habit to take it to the youth who are in higher learning institutions with a purpose of sensitizing the youth on those issues and to know their ideas, views and concerns on those issues. When I seek opinion or view, I rely only on youth who have evinced their concern on social issues without taking any party position. Hence, I took the issue namely the President of India election as observed by Nitish Kumar the Chief Minister of Bihar. He opinioned that the present incumbent may be considered for next term as he is the most suitable person for the context. When this was published in the newspapers and debated in the television channels, I took it to the youth to ponder over the issue meaningfully. To my surprise the students who expressed opinion have come with arguments for why the candidate should be preferred. They first informed that they will take a day and think over it and they will communicate to me their opinion, choice and the reason for come to such conclusion. As per their promise next day they came to my room. I asked them what is their opinion and the reason for making the decision. The students have informed me that the best choice for the country and the Prime Minister is the incumbent President Pranab Mukerjee. I asked only about the choice. They brought a fact that the present incumbent is the best choice for not only the country and for the Prime Minister. There is a reason behind it. Many time the Prime Minister told openly that he is guru and guide. He lavishly praised him for his sagacious advice and direction. From the public perception his equation with the present president Pranab Mukerjee is fine. The country is undergoing a topsy-turvy change in economics and politics. Hard decisions have been taken to cleanse up the economy and polity. For many of the hard decisions, the present incumbent has extended whole hearted support knowing fully well the Prime Minister is not telling openly the truth to the public as it would affect the implementation process of many of the decisions. The students gave one example that everybody knows demonetization is not for weed out block money. But Prime Minister told us that it is to curb black money. The basic objective of the demonetization plan to bring the informal economy to formal economy. To make everyone follow rule of law. Prime Minister wants to bring some basic discipline in governance and administration. All decisions whatever he has taken are hard. The present President Pranab Mukerjee without any bias he extended whole hearted support based on the merit of the decision. Knowing fully well that demonetization will help the country without taking political side the president openly supported it. To push GST the Prime Minister has gone up to 25% to state government which is unacceptable to the economists with the reason that the states have to be made fall in line with the centre. It is not an ordinary decision. In such a way that the country is poising for change through hard decisions. In our country any decision can be easily linked with politics. In the past years the president proved himself as a man with stature known for his forthright views. The views are not political. Pranab Mukerjee has rich experience in politics, governance and administration and he would be of much useful to the country. For all the hard decisions to be taken in economy needs support from the President of India as an economist president and not a politician. It is good for the government and the country. His erudition, maturity, equipoise, scholarship, and statesmanship he is second to none. By keeping him in the position, he is not gaining but the country gets rich benefits. Now to his stature finding a candidate is tough task. Apart from the above the context needs him. Against this background, the incumbent president Pranab Mukerjee is the best choice. All the above arguments have been projected by the students. When they have completed the arguments, I asked them whether the points given by them are really yours or the views others also. Because some of the points I never expected from them. After a few seconds, they informed me that it is the considered opinion of their group. Again I asked a question, Group means what? They told me that they are in social media groups. They first floated the idea and subsequently supplied argument also. After a careful deliberations and analysis, they arrive at this conclusion. It is to be noted that today's youth are at a different level in deliberation and decision making. Social media has connected the entire world. Technology enabled them to share opinion, build perspectives and act fastly. Further, the level of knowledge sharing is really going up. Level and intensity of the discussion is being determined by the groups and their calibre. Within a day the idea has been circulated and opinion has been generated based on the facts. In this regard, one could gauge the level of operation of the youth at present. They are influenced by ideas with facts.

43. Will the BJP gain through this process in Tamil Nadu?

After the death of J. Jayalalitha, the AIADMK party continued to be intact for some time and demand came from everyone that Sasikala (Chinamma) has to lead the party as General Secretary. This idea was mooted by some and everyone joined including O. Panneerselvam and others who opposed Sasikala now. Later it moved further that demand came from many that party and the government should be under the leadership of one individual. As a result, O. Panneerselvam has tendered his resignation and Sasikala has been elected as leader of the party to form the Government. O. Panneerselvam was part of the process. Everyone believed that he was reached the position of the Chief Minister from the tea shop only through Sasikala family and that too through T.T.V. Dinakaran. From the day of death of J. Jayalalitha, prominent public figures visited Sasikala that she is going to be the deciding factor in Tamil Nadu Government and the AIADMK party.

Within two days after proposing her name for the Chief Minister scenario has been changed as O. Panneerselvam (O.P.S) went to J. Jeyalalitha Samadhi (memorial) and observed silence and opened up his mind. Trouble started from there for the party, Sasikala and the government. Even before O.P.S came public to criticize Sasikala many sensed that design has been evolved somewhere to give shock wave to all frontline leaders as raids have been conducted in the office room of the Chief Secretary by the enforcement. Officials when O.P.S was in office in the same secretariat.

It was a shock to everyone who were in helm of affairs. O.P.S is known for his loyalty and he has no individuality and always a loyal servant to his master. But all of a sudden he got the courage to oppose Sasikala. Having seen O.P.S prostrated before Sasikala no one believe that O.P.S on his own cannot do anything of this sort. From that day onwards people started lamenting that the BJP has played its card to weaken the leadership of the party and transfer the cadres of the AIADMK to the fold of the BJP. Why BJP evinced keen interest in the internal affairs of the AIADMK party? Is it to save the party or to convert the party cadres into the fold of BJP or any other big game the BJP aimed at in Tamil Nadu? These are the questions likening in the minds of the opinion makers. Political parties in Tamil Nadu are accusing the BJP for its dubious role in the internal affairs of the AIADMK. Apart from the above questions, there are a few questions related to the above argument. They are: who are the individuals involved in framing the design to disturb the AIADMK for the advantage of the BJP? What is the framework developed to perform the task? It is a fact to be recognized that politics will be played out around every opportunity.

One is obvious that the BJP wants desperately to establish a hold in Tamil Nadu and it wants to change the old Dravidian narrative by using this new opportunity. It is not new in Indian politics. This strategy was adopted by the Indian National Congress to create a division in the DMK by using M.G.R. It succeeded in creating the AIADMK but not weakening the DMK as it wanted. Instead of weakening the DMK, the whole strategy has weakened the Indian National Congress itself. Thus, Indian National Congress failed miserably in its attempt and it struggles for its existence till date. Now it needs the support of the DMK for its existence. The BJP perceived that there cannot be a better opportunity than this one as the field is now a level playing one and this cannot be missed. Hence, the BJP has determined to close all the opportunities for the emergence of a strong leadership in the AIADMK as the cadres have been oriented to be under a strong leadership. Hence a demand has been created through a section of the AIADMK leaders to remove Mrs. Sasikala and her family from the party. This proposition was mooted with the perception that Sasikala would provide such a leadership as provided by J. Jayalalitha to that party and thereby J. Jayalalitha legacy will be established again. Nobody has dreamt of this scenario of opposing Mrs. Sasikala from among the cadres. It has come from a distant source. Everyone is asking, why sasikala and her family have to be removed from the AIADMK? Till date there is no answer from anyone for this question. People who demanded the removal of Sasikala has not stated the reason for the demand. Hence, everyone has sensed that this is not the demand of the party cadres and they have been conditioned to pose this question by someone from elsewhere.

BJP knows that either OPS or EPS have no following on their own. Neither they have charisma or acumen to be leaders to manage the party in the long run. It knows that they are not upright politicians as they were part of the AIADMK. Yet, they will be used to convert the cadres to the fold of the BJP. Knowing fully well the power of Sasikala and her family the BJP has taken a bold step of distancing Sasikala and her family from the party and thereby the party can be weakened and the cadres can be absorbed in the BJP as it also opposed vehemently the DMK and its leader. In this process, the arch enemies of the DMK can also be co-opted to build a grand alliance to oppose the DMK. For this task, formation of a new party under the leadership of actor Rajnikanth was enabled and facilitated by the BJP. If everything goes as per the design in the coming election, the DMK can be prevented from capturing power. If one more term the DMK is prevented from capturing power, the DMK party can be weakened further. That is why the BJP wanted the both factions together to work on the design of the BJP. It is a design perceived by the opinion makers from the activities of the BJP and the AIADMK.

But the developments in the recent days after the merger of the two factions of AIADMK indicate that the outcome of the merger has not yielded results in the expected lines of the BJP. In this process, the image of the BJP and the Prime Minister are at stake. Both the BJP and the Prime Minister have taken high risk to turn the events in favour of the BJP in Tamil

Nadu politics. First step what has been taken through OPS has not yielded any results as yet another faction with sizeable number of MLAs under the leadership of T.T.V. Dinakaran to topple the government. Neither he could mobilize popular support nor MLAs despite the support of the Prime Minister. It was a total failure. Second step, by bringing the merger of the two factions, people who were involved in schism in the AIADMK expected that the party would be made in tact to sail smoothly. It has not yielded any result. Now the problem is complicated. So the step two is also a flap. All the above strategies have been mooted by one segment of the BJP. There is another strategy suggested by a few in the same party that the BJP need not interfere in the internal affairs of the AIADMK and if Sasikala emerges on her own, she can be allowed to take over the party. But through a political bargain as adopted by the Indian National Congress with Dravidian parties alternatively, the BJP can adopt and get sizeable number of seats in Lok Sabha and State Assembly and thereby BJP can easily without much risk and investment gain political mileage. In fact it is being spread that New Delhi preferred the first route and handled the factional leaders by using their conditions to wreak the boat. Unfortunately the merger was not smooth and the images of both factional leaders have gone to the lowest ebb. Day by day the way the issues are handled by the Government has created an opinion that the AIADMK ministers and MLAs are not interested on the issues confronted by the people and they are interested in safeguarding their personal interest. They enable the other group Mrs. Sasikala's family to gain advantage out of the current impasse that she is the only leader to handle the party and cadres effectively. But the whole exercise in AIADMK under the direction of the BJP has created a opinion that the AIADMK has no leader and it enable the DMK to come to power as it has a leader with a scientifically orgainsed a party with cadres committed to the leadership of the party and the organisation. The sizeable number of new voters first time comes to electoral politics as voters are with the people movement all over Tamil Nadu. They are going to decide the fate of the Tamil politics in the next election.

Section II
Development

44. A New Social Business for Service

If anyone says that s/he is joining politics with an aim of serving the society and people, no one will appreciate and believe the statement of the person is true because politics has been made in such a way that well-meaning and honest people cannot go nearer to political system in the past thirty years. It is true that politics has been made not to attract honest and sincere person to serve the society. Yet people's aspiration to serve the society has not been diminished. Many are looking for ways and means to serve the poor and society. Many are doing such services silently without the notice of the media. Recently I have seen a new model which we call social entrepreneurship or social business to serve the poor. It is perfectly fitted into the market mode but serve the humanity in an exemplary manner. The best example for this model is Aravind Eye care system - a leading community eye care system in the world. It was started at Madurai and spread across Tamil Nadu and now moving towards other states and other countries. Within a short span of four decades it treated 45 million people. It has undertaken 4.5 million surgeries. Even after four decades service the hospital says it has covered only 10% of the people. It made history of sorts. What is the specialty and what is the uniqueness and how it is being organized and run are amazing and innovative. Hence, it draws the attention of the medical world. It is possible in a most corrupt ridden politics, governance, administration and society. But it is being carried out in a most honest way. Fred Hallows foundation estimates that 32.4 million people in the world are blind. Of them 50% are due to cataract. Of the affected 90% are in the developing countries. It requires much attention from the state and the market. But to solve such a kind of problems of the poor neither the market nor the state have solutions. Currently barring a few countries, both the state and the market failed the poor in attending to their basic needs. Where is the solution for this kind of problem? State has to do the service without cost and the market has to do the same with profit. The context requires a new model of service to help the poor. The Aravind Eye Care system has demonstrated a model whereby delivering service professionally and earn profit and help the poor by delivering the same service free of cost. Get money from the affordable by treating them professionally and from that money do free service to the poor with the same quality of service as it has been done to the affordable.

It is not so simple. It needs a system, strategy, culture and values to sustain this model. Aravind Eye care system has developed all the above in its journey in the last four decades since its inception. It is a business model but it is a social business where service gets primacy and not profit. Profit comes not for any individual but to the hospital for service. It works on deeper spiritual values of the founder and the staff. The trusteeship and generosity of the rich and affordable who contribute for the service played greater role. The affordable need not pay huge sum for eye treatment in Aravind Eye care as they use to pay in private hospitals. They have to pay only less compared to other hospitals. Hence it is profitable for the rich also. People who are paying for the treatment they get from Aravind Eye care system without knowing, are also part of the service to the poor. They are both beneficiaries and contributors. For the success of the model volume plays its role. The volume fetch huge money and the same is responsible for fixing affordable cost.

Recently I had been to Aravind Eye care for a minor surgery in my eye. When I thanked the doctor for his service, he responded to me that Aravind Eye care hospital has to thank you for paying the amount for the treatment. "Because from the amount the hospital collect from the patients, the expenditure for the poor is met. Hence every patient who paid for his or her treatment is also contributing for the service of the poor" observed by the Doctor. There was a man behind the success of the model and its sustainability. Late Dr.G.Venkatasamy, a visionary leader in social business created this model and laid the strong foundation for its sustainability. The vision evolved for this model by the founder Dr.G.Venkatasamy has firmly rooted on the spiritual values of Vivekananda, Sri Aurobindo and M.K.Gandhi. He was deeply influenced by all these spiritual Gurus. The family members who are responsible for running the system have been thoroughly internalized the value system evolved by the founder. In the same way the staff have also been oriented. The uniqueness lies in drawing the support staff from the rural areas that too from the poor socio economic background and oriented them in the culture and values of the Aravind Eye care system to suit the requirement of the new framework of service and more specifically to maintain a culture of service while serving two kinds of patients namely the paid and cost free. It is just like a McDonald model of business with a character of social business. When needless blindness has been eradicated through this model why not other issues like sanitation, diabetics, dental care can be tackled by perfecting the save model. This model has been studied by various business schools and a case study has been conducted by Harvard school of Business. It needs a public discourse. In India every state can organize three on four such hospitals by following the Aravind model.

45. Visioning for a New Global Order through Democracy

A few days ago a letter has been sent to a college in Tamil Nadu by the Higher Education Department asking for explanation about the programme conducted in the premises of the college where the Actor Vijay criticized the functioning of the government of Tamil Nadu. The substance of the letter is how educational institution allows individuals to talk about politics in the premises of the college. The same question was raised by the Government of Tamil Nadu a few months back when Rahul Gandhi participated in a programme in a lady's college at Chennai and interacted with the students on politics. The actions of the Government of Tamil Nadu were criticized by many that it is an anti demonatic act. Yet the fact of the matter is the political regimes in Tamil Nadu in the past three decades carefully managed to see that there will not be any political socialization process among the youth more specifically the educated youth. It is also a fact that the same Dravidian parties came to limelight and power only through intense political socialization process that took place in the educational institutions with the active involvement of the teachers and students. Hence they know the power of the youth and that is why people who are in power are allergic towards such a kind of political socialization activities in the educational institutions.

The government has seen the wrath of the youth in the Jallikkattu agitation recently and it knows how it was difficult to manage and tackle the agitation. During the agitation what have been discussed by them are also known to the political parties. Hence, care was taken that there should not be any congregation or Assembly of youth in the form of agitation or a provocation for a struggle. It is also a known fact that how the youth are in a state of mind through social media against the state.

Questioning is fundamental core value of democracy but here in Tamil Nadu questioning is against the discipline of the organization and institution. Questing the authority is viewed as undermining the power of the authority. In such way, a culture has been created. Debate, discourse, argument, questioning and raising dissent voice in public are the core values of democracy but here these are all considered as anti establishment or negative thought or disturbance to orderly government. It is because of the poor understanding of the leaders about the value of democracy. Youth are with pent up feelings against the establishment. They are against the existing political order and system. It does not mean that it is against the ruling party alone. The anger of the youth could be seen only through social media. Now there is a debate going on against the existing political culture by brining the historic speech of Greta Thunberg of Sweedan in the UN conference. It was a five minutes speech which has shaken the whole world within a few days. The substance of the discourse in the social media is that Greta a young 16 years old girl hailing from an European country transformed herself as an environmental activist with research bent of mind questioned the world leaders with the full soul force without any fear. She had an intense obsession and a world vision and that made her to speak like this. It is persuasive, forceful speech drawing the attention of the whole world. She has emerged as a thought leader at this age to find out a way to save the planet. It reminded the obsession of M.K.Gandhi when he was returing from England to South Africa in 1909 to pour his ideas to show the alternative way by negating the violent economy came through Industrial revolution and Western civilization. He himself communicated to his friend Henry Polak even before he wrote it in the ship that something brewing in his mind and that should be communicated. It is nothing but inner illumination which made him to communicate, and hence M.K.Gandhi wrote the "Hind Swaraj". His thought came with a full soul force and hence he himself translated the Gujarati version into English as he felt that it was born out of obsession meant for the humanity and that is why treated it as a treatise without any correction in his life time.

Greta also did the same thing and she had a conviction that the new consciousness created by the leaders of the countries in the world without looking at the future generation and the future of the planet assiduously working for economic growth by inducing consumption which ultimately spoil the nature. Now she has been the subject of discourse in many social media fora. In this context we have to look at our demonatic practice. It moves away from the core values of democracy. It is to be understood that why our government is always not interested in cultivating democracy among the youth? It is a known fact that it would create formidable challenges to the present form of politics, governance and development. From the discourses emanated out of Greta Thunbug's argument in the UN conference, one has to infer that search is on for alternative governance, alternative development paradigm and alternative democracy. Substantially the youth have to be involved in all those discourses to find solution to all the ills of our modern democracy, globalized economy, development practices and modern governance.

46. Building a peoples movement for Water

The Ministry of Jal Shakti, Government of India is launching a massive scheme with a huge outlay of 3.60 lakh crores to provide protected water supply to 18 crore households by 2024 with the active involvement of the communities through Panchayati Raj institutions. It is not an easy task to enable the community to participate in the implementation of the new scheme Jal Jeevan Mission as the stakeholders, the people have been oriented to perceive that they are either beneficiaries of a government scheme or a petitioners to the government if the benefits are not reaching them. Never people have been conscientised to act as responsible and dignified citizens. Against this background the new scheme has been announced. Yet the Government of India has determined and committed to make this scheme reality as housing, toilets, electricity, cooking gas, health care, financial inclusion, social security, roads and broadband connectivity schemes implemented. The guidelines for implementation prepared by the Ministry gives hope that it would reach the masses as people have witnessed the water business, water market and water mafia and soar over the way in which the water issues are handled by the state governments so far.

The programme is conceived in such a manner to deliver water supply to the households on a regular basis in adequate quantity and of prescribed quality. It is not a dream but a reality as the government sets certain processes and procedures based on the past experience. There is already an initiative "Jal Shakti Abhiyan" an intensive campaign in water stressed districts to harmonise water conservation efforts of all the stakeholders. So far India has achieved only 20% in providing piped water supply to households. Hence government has to ensure 80% in the years to come before 2024. It is to be noted that in a country like India providing water supply to all households on a sustainable basis is not an ordinary task as in India 256 districts and 1592 blocks are declared as water stressed. Without the active cooperation of the state governments, local governments, communities, community based organizations, media and academic institutions, this scheme will not reach the intended goals.

To achieve the target, the Jal Shakti Ministry has prepared the guidelines to operationalise the scheme by providing all safeguards based on the experience in the past while implementing water supply schemes. The scheme adequately recognized the role of Panchayati Raj in implementing the scheme with the active participation of the people. It apparently gives a sense that it is a water supply scheme but in reality it is more than that. It adequately provide opportunity to plan for the water conservation activities to enable water supply on a sustainable basis. By using the Gram Panchayat Development plan including labour budgeting in MGNREGA, a comprehensive natural resource management plan can be evolved in every Gram Panchayat with an active support of an academic institutions through Unnath Bharat Abhiyan 2.0. A support agency can be created for that purpose to help every village panchayat to implement the scheme. A comprehensive village development plan has to be prepared in which activities can be included to desilt the water bodies available in the panchayats including the inlet and outlet channels to enable the water bodies to get adequate water during the rainy season. Massively water conservation activities have to be carried out through the scheme.

The whole exercise has to be done in such a way that water should be made everybody's business. Since huge money is pumped adequate safeguards are inbuilt in the operational part of the scheme. Money transfer can be tracked at anytime. It is interesting that total independence is being given to local bodies to fix levy for water supply. To do all the activities, people have to be mobilized sensitized, conscientised and enabled to participate in the scheme from planning to implementation and auditing socially the same. It is almost a peoples movement and it has to be created to achieve success in the scheme. It is to be noted that in the Kerala transformative process, three movements namely literacy movement, science movement and peoples plan campaign played a significant role in mobilizing the people of Kerala for the transformative activities. In the same way it has to take the shape of a movement for water. If any work takes sacredness in to it, it will achieve its goal in India. Hence such a sacredness has to be attached with this scheme as a movement. To do the above media has got a greater role in sensiting the people, NGO's have a role to play as a supportive agency to mobilize people, academic institutions have to play its role as resource agency to monitor the quality of water and the state government should play its implementation and monitoring role. Apart from the above, the available social capital in every village has to be used to build peoples movement at the grassroots. All have to play their due role synergistically to build a movement for water. It should be made as a sacred activity.

47. Can we look at J.C.Kumarappa Now?

"Man is the most insane species. He

Worships an invisible God and

Destroys a visible Nature. Unaware

That this Nature he's destroying is

This God he's worshiping"

Hubert Reeves

Canadian – French Astrophysicist

The material development and the human well being achieved through the state and market initiatives are remarkable. It was achieved through a process of industrialization, modernization and westernization. It is further accelerated through privatization, liberalization and globalization. It is unequivocally a market driven approach. The world is now entering into a fourth Industrial Revolution. From the first industrial revolution to the present the state was responsible for development and the market promised the state to enable the state and society to achieve development. But both state and market failed to live up to their promises and as a result many argue that both failed humanity. Both have not only failed but also caused huge damages to the ecology and environment. The world started realizing the loss of ecology and environment only in the beginning of 1970's. The UN had organized a conference at Stockholm in Sweden to deliberate on the issues of the human environment. The main theme of the conference is reconciling economic growth with environmental threat. Poverty has to be reduced, the environment has to be protected by achieving economic growth and the above should be the framework of development of the countries in the world. The conference emphasized the need for an approach to harmonize human actions with nature. Subsequently in 1980 the International Union for Conservation of nature prepared a report entitled "Sustainable Development" with an aim of conscientising the World leaders on the issues of environment. As a result in 1983 UN appointed an official independent commission under the chairmanship of G.H. Brundtland the former Prime Minister of Norway. The above commission went into the issues seriously and prepared a report. The report was submitted in 1987 under the title "our commission future". It emphasized that the three pillars of sustainable development namely, Economic Growth, Environmental protection and social equity have to work synergetically. Here the challenge for the leaders was how to harmonise prosperity with ecology.

At present no one country in the world can be cited as a model for emulation in this regard. This report has created a great awakening among a section of the intellectuals who were already influenced by M.K.Gandhi on this matter. Some incremental changes have been initiated in the global and national level and down below the nation there was no major initiative to change the framework of development. As a logical extension of the above, in 1992 Earth Summit was convened in Rio De Janeiro, Brazil. An action plan was prepared entitled "Agenda 21" in the above conference. When this initiative was on, simultaneously the world has moved into a new path of development which is called economic globalization which includes privatization and liberalization. This initiative instead of mitigating the ill effects of the development activities, accelerated the depletion of natural resources and annihilation of huge rare species on the earth.

In 2002 yet another conference was organized at Johannesburg South Africa on "Environment and Development". Globalization of the economy pushed further the fragile environment and ecology by projecting an argument that those who oppose the faster growth and economic development in the name of environmental degradation are anti development. But now a new report has been released by the World Economic Forum under New Nature Economy. It is prepared for presentation in the ensuing UN convention on Biological Diversity Cop 15 in October, 2020 in China. The first report brought to the world the serious crisis the world is going to face in the next ten years as a result of massive destruction of ecology and environment in the name of achieving double digit economic growth. There are certain areas in the Ecosystem coming closer to irreversible tipping points.

Market cannot move in the way it travelled as resources have been completely exhausted. The exponential economic growth at the cost of the rare natural resources has pushed human society on the brink of extinction. Disaster will emerge in any form and it would affect the whole of the human race. Of the living species in the world, human society forms 0.01% but it exploits 83% of the species living on the earth. The report adds that humanity has only ten years time to reorient its development path without causing much loss to the environment and ecology. The report indicates that humanity accelerates economic growth and destroys natural resources from ten to hundred fold. The new economy has changed the mode of production, consumption, land utilization, urbanization, population explosion, commerce, trade, governance and human relations. Basically human society lives on nature without knowing its relationship with nature and without knowing how to harmonise with nature. Hence it advocates a new economic framework has to be evolved and by which humanity has to establish a harmony with nature while it interacts with nature for its survival and development. Massive initiatives have to be taken in the new framework called "New Nature Economy". To move in this direction we have to reread the "Economy of permanence" by J.C.Kumarappa along with the framework of development advocated by Sri Aurobindo, Rabindranath Tagore. To build this New Nature Economy, we have adequate knowledge to evolve an alternative framework of development. It was advocated by M.K.Gandhi and it was appropriately phrased as "build a village movement" by J.C.Kumarappa. Hence it is time to build Green Economy and to reconstruct our rural areas so as to evolve a new model of development alternative to the present day exploitative development framework.

48. COVID -19 : The Emerging Leadership

Humanity has reached the present stage of material development through responding to the challenges given by the nature and other forces. Any adverse event whether it is a war or disaster both natural and human made, the event will produce new systems, institutions, practices, knowledge, politics, policies and leadership. In this process humanity will have to incur both material and human losses which are inevitable. The human society has witnessed this kind of events in the past with longer intervals. But now becomes a routine. It is natural that people will be leading life in a difficult situation only for a short period. But people who are in the helm of affairs to take care of the people and the governance system should not forget the lessons that humanity has learnt in the past adverse events. Societies and leaders who have used the learnt knowledge from the past events will minimize the human and material losses. The present epidemic COVID-19 has created unexpected miseries and difficulties to many of the so called developed societies. So also so in Indian society and the governments both the centre and states are facing the same.

At this juncture society needs a strong leader to manage the crisis. While looking at the world scenario one could easily gauge the leadership vaccum in the world. It is almost a deficit leadership and a leadership crisis. Neither the US nor the UK or any other western county could provide such a kind of leadership to manage the crisis. In this context while looking at India and its efforts to manage the crisis, India provides a new leadership to the whole world through Narendra Modi through his activities. He proved his leadership qualities at different levels in his political career by responding to the exceptionally highly complicated and difficult challenges through his inner strength consciously. In this process of managing this disaster he exhibits his exceptional leadership qualities by mobilizing the machinery and the people in a war footing to wage a war against this virus. His contact with the masses through his communication ability and convincing arguments are always unique. His leadership makes everyone to follow and move in line with the directives of his government. His messages and pronounced packages of relief have raised the hope and confidence among the people that the government will manage the crisis effectively. His sincere, committed and honest actions will produce expected outcome only if the state governments and the local governments work in tandem with the central government. As Narendra Modi emerges as leader at the national and international level the chief ministers of different regions can emerge as national leaders through their sincere actions in collaboration with the activities of the central government imaginatively based on their local experiences in the past.

Interestingly Kerala had demonstrated its ability to respond to the call of the people through their concerted actions innovatively by taking lessons from the past events. The new leadership was provided by non other than the chief minister Pranoy vijayan and his cabinet colleague Shylaja teacher. Since they have a strong local body system with effective local leadership involved in the process of relief by providing support system to all state government initiatives. Kerala has got rich experience in disaster management as they have witnessed natural disasters in the recent past. Further they have another unique advantage of using exceptionally skilled volunteers from both rural and urban areas. Moreover Keralites have got some civic sense in discharging the minimum citizenship responsibilities. With the above, Kerala may be emerging as a role model.

There is yet another model emerging from the south, the Tamilnadu. In the absence of strong mass leaders like M.Karunanidhi and J.Jayalalitha the present chief minister Edappadi K.Palanisamy is able to effectively manage the crisis by following the footsteps of his mentors. Tamilnadu is known for its committed and well functioning bureaucracy in delivering services to the people. It is a state known for its pro poor activities. By making use of the efficient bureaucracy and announcing series of relief measures to the people the chief minister is tackling the crisis by raising hope among he people. In such a way he has also demonstrated that he is an emerging strong governance leader in the region.

Yet a few things are lacking in the process of managing the crisis. As we are in a democracy people have to be prepared to face the crisis along with the government by creating awareness and sensitization. In this process local governments and the civil society organizations have to play a greater role in creating awareness among the people about the civic responsibilities to be discharged by the citizens of the country. This is lacking in the whole exercise. Further it is a responsibility of higher learning institutions and research institutions to provide skilled man power and knowledge support to the state government and the local government in tackling the crisis.

The indigenous medical practices which were in vogue for centuries in our societies have to be researched to prove that it is also a knowledge system to cater to the needs of the people. This could be done by the higher learning institutions and the stand alone research institutions in India. Yet another weak link in this process is lack of volunteerism among the educated youth baring Kerala to help both the state and local governments for their speedy and responsible actions. If all the weaknesses are effectively addressed our leaders and our country will emerge as a role model for tackling such a kind of disasters.

49. Do We Have Scientific Management of Household Data System in India?

Sound policy making depends on sound data management system. For precise policy making feeding of accurate and scientific data is most essential and imperative need. Faulty policies are the outcome of the incorrect feeding of data into the policy making mechanism. Many of the occasions while evaluating the policies, evaluators have pinpointed the inaccuracy of the data supplied to the policy or decision making system. Data collection, data validation and data management are problematic areas in India. In India various agencies and institutions are involved in collecting, collating and analyzing data. Only a few data sets are being fed into policy making process. Of the dataset, Government of India is relying on NSSO data for policy making process. Arguments are projected that scientific data collection is highly difficult job in Indian social setting especially for collecting household data. For many of the commissions and committees writing reports will be problematic as collecting relevant data for the task is highly tough job. Approximation is the only possible way because of the size of the country and population. Different types of data are being collected by adopting different tools, techniques and approaches by different agencies and individuals from World Bank to village panchayat. Collecting data relating to household is the problematic one and yet it is necessary for poverty reduction, risk reduction vulnerability mitigation and resilience building. Till date it is subjected to criticism because of its inaccuracy. In the recent interview given to a media the noble laureate who received noble prize for economics in this year made an observation while giving interview to the Indian television channel that the data provided by Indian government cannot be relied on. He said that the data projected by government on development are not very scientific and he will not rely on the data set. He made this observation based on his own experience in analyzing the institutional data in the past twenty years. Well being of people and development of the society soly relied on the sound welfare policies, decisions and programmes which have been evolved based on the household data set provided to the government by various agencies. Data are being collected by various agencies from International agency to individuals depending on their requirement. But they are being contested. Scholars believe only the NSSO data as they have got reliability. Even this was also contested. For meaningful decision making household data with accuracy are the need but they are not available at present.

Of the data set collecting data pertinent to household is a challenging task in India. In this regard, several attempts have been made since independence yet one could not find a reliable system in place at present to present a scientific household data set. Neither the households nor the enumerators have evinced real interest in getting and project a reliable household dataset. If anyone goes to any village for data collection, it is assumed by the respondents in the village that the data are meant for the government to evolve schemes. With this assumption the respondents give reply to the questions of the enumerators. They want to project themselves to the enumerators as poor. One cannot get the real data on poverty from the households. The enumerators never invent innovative data collection methods to get the accurate data from the households. The data enumerators use to inform the respondents that they are collecting the data to be passed on to the government for evolving suitable schemes to the poor. Many of the academic institutions do not have ethical committees to supervise data collection activities of the research project in the universities. At present, it is appropriate to fix a responsible institution for complete enumeration of household data. Since local bodies both urban and rural have been constitutionally created on a permanent basis, it is necessary to leave that responsibility of collecting household data to them by evolving a data sheet by the reputed research institutions. Periodically the data have to be updated. To justify my argument, I want to quote an exercise that happened in a Gram Sabha meeting of a Gram Panchayat. There was an exercise in a Gram Panchayat to finalize a list of poor households in the panchayat under BPL. It happened in Vadugampadi Gram Panchayat, Gujiliamparai block, Dindigul district. The Gram Sabha meeting of the Gram Panchayat to finalize the BPL list. The government has given a list containing 427 families. The entire list was read out in the meeting. Nearly 307 households' names have been removed from the list. They have added 97 families in the list. The Gram Sabha has finalized the list based on certain criteria. They fixed indicators for poverty. The family should not have own land for cultivation. They rely on only the wage earned by the head of the family. They do not have any pucca house. Likewise they have evolved seven indicators. All the Gram Sabha members have agreed to those criteria. Based on the above criteria they excluded certain families and included certain families. Name of the families which have been removed from the list in the presence of the family members in the Gram Sabha meetings. Household names which have been included in the absence of their family members in Gram Sabha. All these discourses were held in the presence of the observer (a government officer from the rural development). It was done in a scientific way. Only 217 families have been included in the list. Based on the above experience I have been pleading to entrust that responsibility to the local bodies to collect, validate and maintain household data. If that task is given to local body, it will be done meticulously. What we need is data collection through local bodies validate and maintains them through local bodies. At present, the 14th Finance Commission has given the responsibility of looking after the wellbeing of the community through preparing a perspective development plan. For a village perspective plan, data pertinent to household is necessary. The village panchayat has to enumerate the details of the households. They need tools for data collection. They need training and household support. In this country, we have more than 745 universities, 39000 colleges and 8 million students and 11000 research institutions and they are the biggest support agencies for the local bodies to enumerate and establish scientific data base for households in urban and rural areas.

50. Infinite Vision

If anyone says that s/he is joining politics with an aim of serving the society and people, no one will appreciate and believe the statement of the person is true because politics has been made in such a way that well-meaning and honest people cannot go nearer to political system. It is true that politics has been made not to attract honest and sincere person to serve the society. Yet people's aspiration to serve the society has not been diminished. Many are looking for ways and means to serve the poor and society. Many are doing such services silently without the notice of the public. Recently I have comeacrossed a new model which we call social entrepreneurship or social business to serve the poor. It is anchored in the market mode but serve the humanity in an exemplary manner. The best example for this model is Aravind Eye care system a leading community eye care system in the world. It was started at Madurai and spread across Tamil Nadu and now moving towards other states and other countries. It made history of sorts. What is the specialty and what is the uniqueness and how it is being organized and run are amazing and unbelievable. Yet it is the reality. It is possible in a most corrupt ridden politics, governance, administration and society. But it is being carried out in a most honest way. Health care problems are huge in the world and more specifically in the third world countries. It requires much attention from the state and the market. But to solve the health care problems of the poor neither the market nor the state have solutions as every issue requires huge resource. Currently barring a few countries, both the state and the market failed the poor in attending to their basic needs. Where is the solution for these problems? State has to do the service without cost and the market has to do the same with profit. The context requires a new model of service to help the poor. The Aravind Eye Care system has demonstrated a model whereby delivering service professionally and earn profit and help the poor by delivering the same service free of cost. Get money from the affordable and from that money do free service to the poor with the same quality of service as it has been done to the affordable.

It is not so simple. It needs a system, strategy, culture and values to sustain this model. Aravind Eye care system has developed all the above in its journey in the last four decades since its inception. It is a business model but it is a social business where service gets primacy and not profit. Profit comes not for any individual but to the hospital for service. It works on deeper spiritual values of the founder and the staff. The trusteeship and generosity of the rich and affordable who contribute for the service played greater role. The affordable need not pay huge sum for eye treatment in Aravind Eye care as they use to pay in private hospitals. They have to pay only less compared to other hospitals. Hence it is profitable for the rich also. People who are paying for the treatment they get from Aravind Eye care system without knowing, are also part of the service to the poor. They are both beneficiaries and contributors. For the success of the model volume plays its role. The volume fetch huge money and the same is responsible for fixing affordable cost.

Recently I had been to Aravind Eye care for a minor surgery in my eye. When I thanked the doctor for his service, he responded to me that Aravind Eye care hospital has to thank you for paying the amount for the treatment. "Because from the amount the hospital collect from the patients, the expenditure for the poor is met. Hence every patient who paid for his or her treatment is also contributing for the service of the poor" observed by the Doctor. There was a man behind the success of the model and its sustainability. It is the Divine Man as Sri.Aurobindo put it, Dr.G.Venkatasamy, a visionaly leader in social business. The vision evolved for this model by the founder Dr.G.Venkatasamy has firmly rooted on the spiritual values of Vivekananda, Sri Aurobindo and M.K.Gandhi. He was deeply influenced by all these spiritual Gurus. The family members who are responsible for running the system have been thoroughly internalized the value system evolved by the founder. In the same way the staff have also been oriented. The uniqueness lies in drawing the support staff from the rural areas that too from the poor socio economic background and oriented them in the culture and values of the Aravind Eye care system to suit the requirement of the new framework of service and more specifically to maintain a culture of service while serving two kinds of patients namely the paid and cost free. It is just like a Macnold model of business with a character of social business. When needless blindness has been eradicated through this model why not other issues like sanitation, diabetics, dental care can be tackled by perfecting the save model. This model has been studied by various business schools and a case study has been conducted by Harvard school of Business. It needs a public discourse. In India every state can organize three on four such hospitals by following the Aravind model.

51. Neo-Gandhians in Action

In the recent months I happened to meet a large number of youths hailing from most difficult conditions in the rural areas working with rustic folk in the remote rural areas with a hope to bring change in the life of the poor. They are unusual, determined, committed, passionate energetic with perspective and hope, working in the remote villages without expecting any reward and social recognition. They are not self-proclaimed Gandhians but practitioners of Gandhian way of life both in personal life and public activities. Since they are more relevant in the present context as models to be emulated, I suggested to a friend of mine to invite them while organizing a National Seminar on "Gandhi's Gram Swaraj: Theory and practice". He has readily agreed to invite them for the seminar to speak on the practice side of the Gram Swaraj. In a three day programme one day was devoted for practice and on that day, all the practitioners have come from all over Tamil Nadu and participated. It held in Gandhigram Rural Institute as part of 150th Birth Anniversary celebration of M.K.Gandhi, from 12th through 14th March 2019. First two days, the practitioners have put their stalls and listened to the lectures of the theoreticians. In the third day, the practitioners have been given a chance to speak. For the students, third day is the most important day as they have learnt the practice of Gandhism from the youth. One set of youth explained how they worked for strengthening Gram Sabha tirelessly for two years by bringing unity among the rustic folk beyond caste and political party affiliations. They explained how poor women have been educated to raise questions in the Gram Sabha meeting through a video film. Only five youth joined together to empower the poor and to bring them together to Gram Sabha to raise questions in the Gram Sabha by providing necessary information on the expenditure shown in the government website related to the activities carried out by the various departments of the government in the Panchayat areas. More than 700 members of Gram Sabha participated in the deliberations and the Gram Sabha meeting went on very well and the people mostly the poor achieved what they wanted to achieve on that day. The youth wanted to liberate the poor from the clutches of the state.

How social entrepreneur activities have been initiated to create plastic free and polythene free villages, have been explained succinctly by a team of youth in this seminar. They have explained that their business ventures are not to make profit but to serve the humanity and nature. Their profit is only for their sustenance and expansion. They plunged into action only by taking up the problems faced by the humanity. Followed by another set of youth shared their experience in organizing the farmers for organic cultivation and natural farming. They have explained that how with less money provide huge job opportunities in agriculture and to earn profit out of this new practice of farming. The farmers have explained their success stories. Yet another group spoke to the participants about their intervention in the villages through their IT. It enabled the poor to have access to get their entitlements and legitimate benefits from the Government. Some of the individuals working in the rural areas to organize schools where there is no school have shared their experience. It was a thrilling experience shared by a few youth groups. Of the individuals, no one is from an affluent family. They are from the ordinary rustic families. All the individuals are leading a very simple life as the poor as they want to work with the poor. Of the youth group members some of them came from Jallikkattu struggle with a determination to work in the rural areas for the upliftment of the ultra-poor. Having got fire in them, they have chosen the difficult path. Their path and perspective are Gandhian framework of development. They made it clear that they have learnt it only through the experience not through teaching by the conventional teachers in the Universities and colleges. They are Gandhians in action and not a conventional Gandhians. They have contextualized Gandhian ideas and hence they are called Neo-Gandhians. The third day activities of the seminar is really sensible contribution to the students coming from the rural areas and they have got rich benefits from the input given by the practitioners. Since they are practitioners and visionaries, they communicated in Tamil and thereby they have connected with the students emotionally and the student participants have richly benefited. After the whole deliberation on the day, mute question asked was, how to expand those activities to the other areas by following the above models. The youth group members made it very clear that opportunities are abundant to transform India by using the constitution, development rights given by the government, pro-poor schemes of both the centre and state governments. It requires only an unconventional leader who can transform herself or himself to transform the community. A fire has to be created in every individual that could be possible only through a training. This training cannot be given by any conventional training institutes. In our country we have different type of training institutes, but there is no leadership institution worthwhile to shape leaders. Even a few institutions in the name of leadership school, they train only business leaders' not transformational leaders. Now we need Gandhian Institutions to be made as Ashrams to train transformational leaders by adopting the methods and procedures followed by M.K. Gandhi to prepare leaders for freedom struggle.

52. Power of a Software and Youth

On October 2nd, Kambur, a village Panchayat in Madurai district in Tamil Nadu has witnessed a historic event in the form of Gram Sabha. More than 900 Gram Sabha members have reached the place where Gram Sabha was held. It started around 10.30 in the morning and it went up to 4.00 p.m. without having lunch break. Never the village Panchayat has witnessed such a big crowd in the Gram Sabha meetings in the past. It is also true many of the panchayats Gram Sabha meetings are becoming rituals. In this context, organising a Gram Sabha meeting with huge crowd without chaos and pandemonium is a strange event. It was a shock for the officials as they have to face the questions and demands of the people. What made the people to come to Gram Sabha meeting on that day is a question to many media representatives. Mobilization of people was not done by the officials of the Panchayats but it was done by a few dedicated and well informed youth of that village. They are not belonging to any political party or civil society organisation. They are the part of the village community. The youth group has used some information obtained through the software used by the Ministry of Panchayati Raj, Government of India. It is nothing but the income and expenditure statement of the panchayat. It sent a shock wave to all and people want to know the details of the spending by the panchayat and the officials in the village through various activities. The information relating to the spending of the governments departments and Panchayat have mobilised the people for Gram Sabha meeting. As M.K.Gandhi used salt to mobilize people emotionally to oppose British, the youth of the Kambur village have used the expenditure statement of the Panchayat to mobilize people. Having seen the statement of expenditure, people started asking, has the Panchayat really spent that money? The youth requested them to come and participate in Gram Sabha meeting and ask the questions to the officials responsible for panchayat administration. A few youth, who work in Middle East as labourers, used powerfully the whatsup to contact their friends and relatives and requested them to attend the Gram Sabha meeting. They in fact transfer some amount of money from their earning to youth to mobilize the people for Gram Sabha meeting. The youth group has used this opportunity to create awareness among the people about the importance of participation in Gram Sabha.

The team led by Mr. Selvarasu is highly matured and communicative with a perspective. Since they have witnessed heavy crowd in Gram Sabha with deep sense of anger after seeing the expenditure statement, the youth group members who mobilised them took responsibility to manage the crowd. The members of the team made it very clear that only through committed and peaceful action, people can achieve what they wanted to achieve. The team worked hard to convince the people that things could be possible only through peaceful means. Since they have leadership qualities, they were able to manage the people. Hence, they made it clear that everyone has to conduct in a responsible way while participating in the meeting. Secondly, they suggested to the members of Gram Sabha that while participating in the meeting, no one should look at issues from the perspective of caste or political affiliation. Village Panchayat is a little republic and not a kingdom. It is for all. It is inclusive. Hence, from the perspective of the wellbeing of all, questions, observations have to be made in the Gram Sabha and not from the perspective of the caste or political party. Further, they made it unequivocally that violence has no place in the Gram Sabha meeting. As a result, the Gram Sabha members conducted themselves in an orderly fashion and participated effectively in the meeting by raising questions, making observations on the activities of the Gram Panchayat. Members of Parliament and Legislative Assembly have to learn a lot from them. The members of the youth group have appealed to the members of Gram Sabha that while participating in the meeting and raising issues, they should not bring personalised allegations and they should raise only the issues. In such a way order has been achieved in the Gram Sabha meeting. Through their active, effective and peaceful participation, officials have been made accountable for all the expenditures. It was almost a social audit conducted by the people. Through their participation people have given a sense to the officials that people are awakened and there is no division in the community based on caste or political affiliation. More than that the decency and decorum followed in the meeting drew the attention of the media. While interacting with the members of the youth group, they informed that it is not the result of a few days' activities. The group worked with the villagers for the past two years. They informally visited all the seven hamlets met women groups, farmers, traditional panchayat leaders. To convince all the factions and to bring them together it took two years, they shared with us. Their objective is to strengthen the village panchayat by strengthening Gram Sabha. Their main aim is to build the social capital and through the entire responsibilities of transforming the village should be handed over to the people. To them, it is liberation from the yoke of the government. In this mobilization process, the youth group members involved a few women volunteers.

Representatives of different political parties have also been approached and they have been made to participate in the meeting of Gram Sabha. An orderly exercise, without emotion put the officials in a tight spot. They could not face the people and could not give reply. Glaring commissions and omissions have been noticed. The officials have committed to reply many of the questions in the next Gram sabha meeting. They have also committed to fulfil all the needs put forth in the Gram Sabha meetings. Once Gram Sabha was a ritual, now it becomes a vibrant village body meant for discourse and debate. It has been made a training ground for a deliberative democracy. People of the Kambur Village panchayat have crossed over the caste and political party affiliation and developed a community sense. It is the biggest achievement made in the Gram Sabha meeting. It is a model for other panchayats to build a peoples movement through panchayat and Gram Sabha.

53. Sanitation is not Constructing Toilets but Creating a Culture

Being an academic activist I have been visiting rural areas with a perspective in the past thirty years and I have been writing about the conditions of the rural populace both for journals and newspapers. While reporting about the transformative process of the rural areas and people, whether it is sanitation or livelihood or water supply, garbage cleaning or cleaning the streets, wherever people's consciousness has been changed through a process of conscientization one could find tremendous change. The changes and transformations are not driven by the external agencies but they are driven by the communities themselves. Someone to ignite the fire in the human spirit or consciousness. When I was a small boy, Sabapathy a Gandhian came to my house and taught me to create a toilet without expenditure. He sensitized me on the need of toilets and in unequivocal terms he explained the linkages between cleanliness and development. He brought the argument in a convincing way and thereby I was deeply impressed and convinced. But I was wondering how do we find money for that. It was a big question. Not only he explained the importance of the toilets but also explained to me that toilets could be created in zero cost. It puzzled me. He took me to his house. There was a toilet made out of coconut plantation waste. From our coconut plantation, we have coconut leaves. We have a large fencing in our farm house with different types of trees and from the trees a few poles can be created. With the above two a small fully fenced natural toilet can be created. In the toilet a small spade and packet of water have to be provided. When anyone goes with the spade a pit can be taken and in the pit the excreta can be put and water can be used for cleaning. He had created a model structure in his house. By following the model we have also created such facility in our house. We started using it and we had that toilet till we constructed a new house. This is the practice we have developed in the entire street. Every house in the entire street we have created toilets and the whole toilet arrangement can be shifted from one place to another place. Sabapathy played an important role in sensitizing the school going boys and girls. This kind of toilets had been created by us not by the elders. Our parents have also followed us as they need not walk a kilometer every day to attend natural calls. Later he asked us to clean our streets, surroundings of our houses. During those days he advocated that every house should have a small pit to dump wastes collected from the house. We had milch animals and bullocks for our farm operations. All wastes have been collected and dumped in the pit created for it. Huge quantity of compost manure we got from this process for our farmlands. Our parents were also happy as we did many works for the family. He educated us the value of the manual labour. The entire street we had toilets of our own. It was not made out of cement. It was made out of the waste material available in our areas. He created first a culture of sanitation in our place through sensitizing school going boys and girls. Sabapathy was a transformed individual and he was a selfless person. Every school going boy and girl used to love him. Because of his continuous work with the children a sanitation culture was created. Hence, we as young boys and girls created toilets. After this experience I never had such experience in the past among the youth.

Recently I went to a village to document the works of Sri Aurobindo society in a few villages in Villupuram district of Tamil Nadu as it worked for the transformation of the rural areas through the involvement of the communities. The document has been ultimately published in Delhi through a publisher entitled "Integral Rural Development" which brought a new thesis in rural transformation and development. Two individuals have worked with the community through the consciousness of the people. They acted through the consciousness of the school children first and moved towards their parents and through youth. Finally they have touched all segments of the village community. First they started with sensitizing the school going boys and girls on cleanliness and they created a culture for sanitation. Majority of the people in the village are Dalits. But it is a neat and clean village by constructing toilets and maintaining it neatly. The new thesis they have developed based on their experience in the villages is that villages are integral organic units functioning in their own pattern and they tend to change only when changes happen in their consciousness. Government wants to develop villages sectorally by implementing the schemes and programmes through the departments. They are not touching the consciousness of the people. The two individuals working on the consciousness of the people. In many villages government constructed toilets for the poor but they are not being used. But in this village all schemes have been used but consciously on their demands. Hence, a culture has been created first. Rests of the things are the works of the people. The two individuals are transformed individuals and they worked through the consciousness of the people. First by working with children, they have demonstrated the impact of the raising consciousness of the children to their parents and as a result parents started watching the transformation of their children's attitude, behavior and performance. The parents followed their children. As a result, the entire village has been sensitized and transformed. From the two stories what we infer is transformational leaders at the ground is the need of the hour as they change themselves and worked for the transformation of the communities. What we need to do is not toilet construction but creating a toilet culture. This could be possible only through transformational leaders. Now we have panchayat presidents in the Panchayati Raj system and they are all acting as political leaders not as transformational leaders. They have to be transformed into transformational leaders through a process of training. By doing so, a proper sanitary condition could be created in the rural areas by changing the attitude and behavior of the people. To perform the above all training institutions in the rural development department have to be changed into a new leadership school to conduct leadership training programme for the elected local body leaders.

Section III
Education

54. A New Rural Education Policy

Everyone looks at the draft New Education Policy (NEP) from his or her perspective and passes comments, criticisms observations and even condemnation. There are a few out rightly rejected the draft by saying that it is meant for privatization and commercialization of education. Perspective vary from individual to individual and organization to organization. I, as a teacher, researcher and outreach activist served in a Gandhian Institution well over two and half decades and worked with both centre and state governments for more than three decades in the domain of Rural Development, have gone through the document carefully in the backdrop of the Gandhian Framework of Education.

Education is fundamentally a process and by which human beings are shaped and transformed as better human beings for higher level activities. Human beings are transformational in character and they are having the resilience to evolve themselves as individuals with higher qualities and values. Hence people have to be transformed as evolving individuals and for which education has to play its crucial and significant role. Any educational exercise would change the human beings attitude, behaviour, skill, capacity and capability. Thus it is a man making process. It has to help the individuals to evolve themselves and at the same time it has to help the individuals to earn their livelihood. Thus education has to help the people to become active citizens and they should become independent in shaping their destiny by managing their affairs. If that purpose is being served through educational process, both the state and the society would be less burdened. In order to ensure the above, continuously the Indian state is trying scientifically from the dawn of independence.

But M.K.Gandhi specifically looked at India and observed that 80% of the people in India are in the rural areas and they are the real faces of India and hence transforming them is the new task of the new government. But it is not the task of state alone. The transformation task has to be done by the community itself through its volunteers. The volunteers have to be prepared and trained. To do that task a large number of institutions have to be created. These institutions have to work with the community for rural transformation. They are called rural institutes. Fundamentally they are different from conventional higher learning institutions. Rural community includes, the pastoral, the farming, the tribal, the craft, the fishing, and the trading communities, living with their skill, culture, knowledge, language, spiritual and livelihood practices. To transform them in the rural areas a new education framework had been evolved and advocated by M.K.Gandhi called "Naitalim" or New Education. It relied on the knowledge and skill base of the people well rooted in the Indian ethos of education.

After independence, instead of taking a new path in educating the masses in Gandhian framework of education, the new government followed the footsteps of the British colonial masters by giving a small space for experimenting the Gandhi's educational framework. As a result the whole educational system concentrating much on preparing students for urban industrial needs neglecting the rural masses and their transformational needs. Even M.K.Gandhi's educational framework has also been diluted over a period of time. The space provided for experimenting the educational process and procedures followed in the country in the past seven decades enabled the urbanities to exploit the rural masses. Hence the pastoral communities, the farming communities, and the tribal communities, the craft communities, the fishing communities in the rural areas are in deep crises. The Economic Globalization has intensified the rural crises and the village life is moving towards its natural death.

Against this background I look at the draft of the new education policy. Substantially it tries to address the problems in the existing framework of education meant for preparing youth for market and industry. But it does not make any attempt to address the issues of the rural masses through the new education policy. This document did not make any serious attempt to establish linkage between academia and the community for a meaningful outreach activities to be done in the rural areas by the students and teachers. Equally it did not spell out the framework to build citizenship among the students. Against this background I feel that the government has to evolve a new rural education policy and it has to be integrated in the education policy and that is the need of the hour.

55. A Significant Initiative of the UGC

On 29th November, the University Grants Commission has sent a circular with a document entitled "National curriculum framework and guidelines for fostering social responsibility and community engagement in Higher Education Institutions in India" to all the universities with a request to act on the document. It is basically a hard drive to exert pressure on the Higher Education Institutions in India to prepare a comprehensive plan to link the Institutions with the community through its teaching and research on a sustainable basis. This has been the aim of the Ministry of Human Resource Development from 2011 onwards and culminated in the form of a programme called Unna Bharat Abiyann. Now it becomes UBA 2.0 launched by the Government of India in 2018 in a more systematic way by developing a framework for the universities to reformulate their curriculum scientifically and more meaningfully to incorporate the outreach programmes more meaningfully to benefit both the community and the students. It is now made mandatory to all the Higher Education Institutions to incorporate the outreach service in their teaching learning and research programmes without any exception.

It is to be noted here that it is not new in India. At the dawn of Independence on the advice of M.K.Gandhi to work with the rural communities a large number of institutions had been created by the Gandhian activists and of them fourteen institutions had been recognized as Rural Institutes by the Government of India. But within a short span of time thirteen Rural Institutes had been merged with the mainstream Educational system which never insist outreach service as mandatory. There will be always reference about the outreach or community service in the policy documents of the Government of India ever since Radhakrishnan Committee Report released.

But never UGC insisted that it is mandatory to all the Higher Education Institutions to involve themselves in community service. There are stand alone activities through NSS units of the Higher Education Institutions. Of course there are a few institutions connected themselves with community service or community engagement out of their philosophical foundations. Barring a few institutions all the Higher Learning Institutions concentrated only in teaching and research. The teaching is meant for producing students for the job market and research for career development. No Institution in the country emerged as model for outreach in the seventy years as there was no pressure either from the funding agency or the stakeholders, the community. Yet there are passionate teachers in many institutions have a track record of connecting themselves with community through their community service activities. As a result what we have seen in the society is educated individuals without having a concern for the fellow citizens. Still 68% of the people in the rural areas in India. Suffering masses are mostly in the rural areas. In this context, the new initiative of the MHRD through UGC makes the Higher Education Institutions mandatory to reach out the rural communities through their systematic academic and research programmes. Higher Education Institutions have to do a massive exercise to prepare curriculum to incorporate the outreach programme in the teaching schedule. In the same way socially relevant research has to be designed with a view to find solutions to the problems of the rural areas. It requires a change of mind set among the teachers and a new orientation is also needed for the teachers. Through the report UGC has addressed all the structural and policy problems which have acted as hindrance so far to outreach activities in the Higher Learning Institutions. Further it has addressed the financial issues also. Now what is needed is every university has to internalize the document and conduct a workshop based on the document to incorporate the community engagement for outreach service in their respective curriculum in the subjects. It requires lot of thinking on the part of the teachers. Universities have to prepare areas for research based on the pressing problems faced by the rustic folk in the rural areas. It requires rural mindedness as M.K.Gandhi advocated. It is not only for the General Universities but also to professional Universities like Medical Universities, Technical Universities, Agricultural Universities and other universities. Equally it is important to prepare the communities in the rural areas, institutions and organizations working with the communities and the District Administration have to be prepared for a meaningful and impact making linkage between Higher Education Institutions and the communities. If it is done seriously the gap between book view and field view would be narrowed down. Students would be sensitive on the social issues. They will have concern for the fellow citizens. Many of the social issues would be addressed through the outreach programmes. The capacity of the teachers will be enhanced. Socially relevant research will be carried out to help the community to address the issues.

Academics and students will help the policy making through their research. Many of the rural development issues needs soft solutions. For instance toilets are being constructed by the Government but toilet culture cannot be created by the Government. It can be created only by changing the mindset and behaviour of the people and that can be done through the awareness programme with the outreach activities of the universities. It is the routine in our educational system to make even a serious event as a ritual. It is part of our culture. The Higher Learning Institutions should seriously internalize the document and take mission mode activities to fulfill the goals of the document. It requires serious debates within the Higher Learning Institutions and in the public domain to exert pressure on the teaching community to involve themselves seriously in this task.

56. Academic and Community Linkages

On 29th November 2019, the University Grants Commission has sent a circular with a document entitled "National curriculum framework and guidelines for fostering social responsibility and community engagement in Higher Education Institutions in India" to all the universities with a request to act on the document. It is basically a hard drive to exert pressure on the Higher Education Institutions in India to prepare a comprehensive plan to link the Institutions with the community through its teaching and research on a sustainable basis. This has been the aim of the Ministry of Human Resource Development from 2011 onwards and culminated in the form of a programme called "Unnath Bharath Abhiyan". Now it becomes UBA 2.0 launched by the Government of India in 2018 in a more systemic way by developing a framework for the universities to reformulate their curriculum scientifically and more meaningfully to incorporate the outreach programmes to benefit both the community and the students. It is now made mandatory to all the Higher Education Institutions to incorporate the outreach service in their teaching learning and research programmes without any exception.

It is to be noted here that it is not new in India. At the dawn of Independence on the advice of M.K.Gandhi to work with the rural communities a large number of institutions had been created by the Gandhian activists and of them fourteen institutions had been recognized as Rural Institutes by the Government of India. But within a short span of time thirteen Rural Institutes had been merged with the mainstream educational system which never insist outreach service as mandatory. There will be always reference about the outreach or community service in the policy documents of the Government of India ever since Radhakrishnan Committee Report released. But never UGC insisted that it is mandatory to all the Higher Education Institutions to involve themselves in community service. There are stand alone activities through NSS units of the Higher Education Institutions. Of course there are a few institutions connected themselves with community service or community engagement out of their philosophical foundations. Barring a few institutions all the Higher Learning Institutions concentrated only in teaching and research. The teaching is meant for producing students for the job market and research for career development. No Institution in the country emerged as model for outreach in the seventy years as there was no pressure either from the funding agency or the stakeholders, the community. As a result what we have seen in the society is educated individuals without having a concern for the fellow citizens. Yet there are passionate teachers in many institutions have a track record of connecting themselves with community through their community service activities. Despite fast urbanization 68% of the people still living in the rural areas. Suffering masses are mostly in the rural areas. In this context, the new initiative of the MHRD through UGC makes the higher education institutions mandatory to reach out to the rural communities through their systematic academic and research programmes is timely and meaningful. Higher education institutions have to do a massive exercise to prepare curriculum to incorporate the outreach programme in the teaching learning schedule. In the same way socially relevant research has to be designed with a view to find solutions to the problems of the rural areas. It requires a change of mind set among the teachers and a new orientation is also needed for the teachers. Through the report UGC has addressed all the structural and policy problems which have acted as hindrance so far to outreach activities in the higher learning institutions. Further it has addressed the financial issues also. Now what is needed is every university has to internalize the document and conduct a workshop based on the document to incorporate the community engagement for outreach service in their respective curriculum in the subjects. It requires lot of thinking on the part of the teachers. Universities have to prepare areas for research based on the pressing problems faced by the rustic folk in the rural areas. It requires rural mindedness as M.K.Gandhi advocated. It is not only for the general universities but also to professional universities like Medical Universities, Technical Universities, Agricultural Universities and other universities. Equally it is important to prepare the communities in the rural areas, institutions and organizations working with the communities and the District Administration have to be prepared for a meaningful and impact making linkage between higher education institutions and the communities. If it is done seriously the gap between book view and field view would be narrowed down. Students would be sensitive on the social issues. They will have concern for the fellow citizens. Many of the social issues would be addressed through the outreach programmes. The capacity of the teachers will be enhanced. Socially relevant research will be carried out to help the community to address the issues.

Academics and students will have to help the policy making community through their research. Many of the rural development issues need soft solutions and for which higher learning institutions have to work. For instance toilets are being constructed by the Government but toilet culture cannot be created by the Government. It can be created only by changing the mindset and behaviour of the people and that can be done through the awareness programme with the outreach activities of the universities. The higher learning institutions should seriously internalize the document and take mission mode activities to fulfill the goals of the document. It requires serious debates within the Higher Learning Institutions and in the public domain to bring clarity on the process of implementation of the new programme.

57. Missing Rural Higher Education in the Draft Input for New Education Policy

Seventy years of intensive modernization, westernization and urbanization, have brought only a peripheral change in the rural India where 68 per cent of Indian population lives amidst a mix of poverty, backwardness and deprivation. The impact of rural development initiatives through a slew of project and schemes is to be seen in patches of development in the semi-rural areas only. For majority of Indian villages development and modernity is like a mirage in the tradition bound society. Village life in India lies somewhere in between the ideal village of M.K. Gandhi and the casteist village described by B.R. Ambedkar. Transforming rural India remains the biggest challenge before the policy-makers, bureaucracy, educational institutions and civil society even after implementing more than 2000 rural development programmes since Independence. Lack of proper attention to the educational needs of this vast segment of rural population can be seen as one of the reasons for this deficit in desired development. Rural development can be made sustainable and pervasive only by supporting it with institutions dedicated to rural socio-economic, cultural, development aspirations and livelihood related needs. One wonders how a model of rural development can thrive without institutions specializing in rural planning, management, technologies and agricultural economics.

It was M.K. Gandhi who envisioned a new educational paradigm to transform India. He spoke about various approaches to transform India and creation of a new educational paradigm which still remains significant and relevant for its suitability to Indian society. The first education commission after Independence under the leadership of Dr. Radhakrishnan had given due attention to the educational paradigm of M.K. Gandhi and it devoted a chapter in its report on the need to create rural universities. This chapter had significant inputs from Dr. Arthur E. Morgan and Dr. Tigert, members in the University Commission of Education 1948.

Basically, the concept of rural universities proposes an opportunity for transformational leaders to work with people in the rural areas without ruling over them. Its conceptualization integrates the three experiences and experiments of Danish People's College Denmark, the land-grant model of

American Agricultural and Technical Education and Gandhi's model of *Nai Talim* experimented in India for about 25 years. Within a short span of time yet another committee was constituted under the leadership of K.L. Srimali in the year 1954 and it was called committee on Higher Education for Rural Areas. While constituting the committee two important assignments were given to the committee through its terms of reference. One, how to take forward the experiments of rural higher education that was being conducted in a number of Gandhian institutions and secondly, to suggest ways and means through which existing conventional universities can make useful contribution to the rural areas by solving the problems of the rural communities. Basically the rural institutes were meant to break the development barrier between rural and urban population, and enable the narrowing down of the gap between culture and work, between humanities and science and technology, and between the practice and ideals. Essentially rural institutes have to focus upon planning for the development of the region. These institutions are expected to produce transformational leaders to change the communities and the rural scenario. Their core function is to link the higher education to communities and societal aspirations.

The chapter twenty three of the Second Five Year Plan of the Government of India a reference was made under the heading "Rural Higher Education" with a note mentioning that rural institutes are intended to perform a variety of functions for the rural community. Time and again it has been reiterated that the rural institutes are meant for a comprehensive educational program integrating with research and extension activities. These have been visualized as a combination of local culture and training centre and apart from the above these institutions have to work as centres for development planning in rural areas. The Ministry proposed to establish ten rural institutes during the Second Five Year Plan period with the investment of rupees two crore. These institutes were not meant to be altogether new entities. Leading centers working on these lines had been selected for this purpose. To coordinate the activities and functions of the rural institutes the central government had constituted a Council for Rural Higher Education. Subsequently a few more institutions were added to the list. And at one time a total of fourteen rural institutes were functioning in various regions. Following the rural institute model, there have been several other experiments in the country. While evolving a new education policy in the year

1986 some aspects of rural higher education were included in the policy. Even at that point of time neither the government made a thorough analysis of the functioning of the rural institutes nor it explored possibilities in this direction. On the other hand, in place of a new framework for rural higher education, it advocated for extension activities. For this advocacy the report got sufficient input from those institutes which had been carrying out rural higher education activities.

In the meanwhile, mainstream education framework has not accommodated these new experiments and as a result almost all barring one institute, merged with the mainstream educational framework. Since it was convenient for the teachers who worked in the rural institutes, they also have accepted to toe the line without raising any question. But it was a loss for the rural community. However, during the tenure of P.V. Narasimha Rao as Prime Minister, an initiative was taken to revive the rural higher education in India in order to meet the challenges of globalization. A National Council for Rural Institute was created with a mandate to further the activities of the rural institutes contextually. Under the agency of the National Council for Rural Institute, Hyderabad, a comprehensive study was undertaken to trace the achievements, failures and needs of the rural institute in India.

The comprehensive study was undertaken by Dr. J. Karunakaran, former Vice-Chancellor of Gandhigram Rural Institute. He brought out a volume entitled "Liberating Education for a Knowledge Society: Lessons from Nai-Talim and Rural Institute Experiments". However, the initiative of P.V. Narasimha Rao could not move further and now the National Council for Rural Institute is dormant and defunct due to lack of financial and institutional support from the successive governments at the Centre. The comprehensive study undertaken by Dr. Karunakaran came out with a strong proposal for creating regional development university to meet the challenges of globalization for the rural areas. The new regional development university is envisaged to work with the community by extending knowledge, skill and approach to make use of the opportunities of globalization and to avoid the threats of globalization. It was a well thought out proposal to create such universities. He has given a blueprint for the regional development university as rural-urban continuum needs support from this kind of a new university. Further, the newly proposed regional institutes are highly relevant to support the activities of the rural and urban local bodies to evolve development plans as per the mandate based on the recommendations of the Fourteenth Finance Commission of Government of India, as resource agencies. While developing such a plan for village development in the context of climate change, disaster preparedness and green growth, the regional development universities' role is inevitable. Against this background, the draft new education policy has neither talked about extension nor about the rural higher education. It can be observed as a conspicuous omission in the report. It needs to be deliberated. Further, our policy community is very vociferous in making declarations that India is going to establish world class IITs, world class IIMs, world class central universities, etc. But there is no such declaration for creating world class rural institutes meant for rural transformation. By creating such regional development institutes, the hitherto unaddressed issues of extension or outreach activities of the higher learning institutes will be addressed.

58. Extension: A Missing Dimension in Indian Higher Education

Higher education in India is passing through a difficult phase at present in the absence of a well defined contextualized policy and actionable framework though it has demonstrated its capacity in achieving growth quantitatively since independence and more particularly in the last two decades. Economic globalization has accelerated the speed of growth of the higher learning institutions in India. Yet crises afflicted the system. Constellation of factors are responsible for the present state of affairs in higher education in India and of which globalization led manpower production is a major one and it drives the whole process to achieve profit and prosperity. Totally it neglects the humanizing function of education. As a result, an exploitative culture has been nurtured and perpetuated in the education system from elementary to higher learning which ultimately has changed the thought process of all the stakeholders of education. In the formative years of independence the teachers advocated 'serve and scarifies' to the students. Contextually it can be modified to "serve and prosper". But in reality students have gained impressions from the practice that "serve to explicit" as they are being exploited. Knowledge gained in the educational process is to serve the human society without exploiting the people but the reality is otherwise. A dominant thought and discourse have been set in motion in the functioning of the regulatory and funding bodies to focus on employability, skilling, quality, ranking, accreditation, academic accountability and auditing, standardization and internationalization in the context of manpower production for industry. Many of the attributes mentioned above are drawn from the north and west to drive the higher education system to produce quality manpower for the labour market in India and the world. It is a known fact from policy maker to practitioner in the realm of higher education that the disparities and differences that exist in Indian society reflect among the higher learning institutions in terms of availability of infrastructure facilities and quality teachers. As we find graded social structure, we find graded higher learning institutions from third rate institutions to the first rate premier institutions. The conditions have been further worsened by perpetuating corrupt practices in the higher learning institutions by the political class which is being swallowed by the intellectual middle class without any resistance as they are not much affected by it. In the market driven approach, crony business class along with crooked politicians have started capitalizing the weaknesses of governance by investing huge money in higher education as new opportunity emerges out of globalization to fetch profit. By creating education factory for manpower production which incidentally paid rich dividend fully to the investors and partially to a few segments of students' community leaving large segments of the students to the unemployable category despite warning signals given by employers to the higher learning institutions. In this process one can see the marginalization of public funded institutions that too institutions in the rural areas and difficult terrain. As a result, one could see a trend in the higher learning institutions among the students and teachers that profit driven business approach is dominating in their thought. Concern for poor, nature, marginalized, oppressed and pressing social issues are absent both among the students and teachers as they are driven by the new economic Tsunami and consumerism.

The task before any government at present in higher education is huge and difficult as the size of higher education institutions, their conditions and the nature of problems have grown many times since independence and variations in terms of facilities are wider as between Africa and America. Higher education in India is undergoing transformation with much complication. It seems that the trend in India in higher education is that it adds more problems to the existing. But indications we see in the outcome does not seem any positive for majority of the people in the society. Hence, we have to consciously discuss and decisively act on issues. Even in difficult times one can find opportunity to achieve better things. Hence, even today the difficulties what we see in higher education can be turned into opportunities and through which transformation could be achieved in the society as we have more than 745 universities, 39000 colleges, and 11000 research institutions with 80,00000 students in the institutions. It is not a small strength. It is a huge number which can transform India within a decade on many basic aspects of human life. It is a critical mass which has to be used to achieve critical development in the society. For a meaningful engagement of the critical mass we need to have a comprehensive policy for higher education. In the new policy an important aspect, the outreach activities of the higher learning institutions has to be integrated. It could be possible only through a meaningful engagement of the teachers and the students in social reconstruction activities by evolving a scientific outreach policy for higher learning institutions. Basically higher learning institution has to perform three functions. They are research, academic (teaching) and outreach (extension). In India, only a fraction of higher learning institutions are performing two major functions research and teaching and majority are only performing the teaching function. Very rarely higher learning institutions perform all the three functions. Higher learning institutions can excel in their performance only when all the three functions are performed integrally. Quality can be achieved in higher education by linking all the three functions integrally. Further they should be in learning mode.

Government of India is contemplating a higher education policy. Conventionally intellectuals and bureaucrats concentrate much on teaching and research in higher learning institutions but they tend to ignore the extension dimension which has got rich potential to transform our society without adding much cost to higher education. Each and every department or academic discipline in higher learning institutions can contribute directly to the community to transform the society. It needs only a policy, an approach, a system and a framework of action. In India beyond NSS and Agriculture, no institution has consistently developed perspectives, approaches, tools, technologies of extension in the higher learning institutions. The regulatory bodies of higher education have not paid much attention on this subject and hence in the evaluation process of the institutions and teachers rigrous attributes of extension have not been evolved and incorporated. As a result, extension becomes a discretionary function and not an obligatory function of the teachers and the institutions. Academic institutions whether they are conventional arts and science or medical or engineering or agriculture and others, can extend the available extendables from the respective institutions to the community. It requires only a coordinating agency in each and every institution to carryout extension activities. It may be a centre or a Department exclusively for outreach activities. Even if an awareness is created about cleanliness, sanitation, water supply, skill, available opportunity in government schemes for poverty reduction and prosperity, communities and the rustic folk in particular can be transformed. In the higher learning institutions, there are many extendables and they may be in the form of mere ideas, information, skill, knowledge and technology. They could be shared with the community systematically, perspectively and they are to be followed up on a sustainable basis. All the activities could be designed in such a way that they are integral part of the educational activities of the higher learning institutions. While outreach programmes are carried out at the community level everyone will get substantial benefits. Students and teachers are also gaining benefits as communities. Against this background, a policy perspective is needed for extension activities of higher learning institutions in India. By doing so, the university system can be transformed into peoples university.

59. How to Connect Community?

"Community Connect" was the article published in Millennium post on 22nd January, 2020 provoked many to raise a question to me to explain how to do Unnath Bharath Abiyan 2.0 and hence this write up. Academic World has been oriented to write and speak in intellectual language and not in people's language. To reach anything to the masses, one has to write or speak in people's language and for which academic writings have to be simplified through peoples language. Teachers in higher learning institutions have to be conscious of the social realities of the rustic folk in the rural areas. The moment they become conscious, and concern for the rural poor, they will speak the language of the people and lead a life of the ordinary citizens living in the rural areas. To carry out the Unnath Bharath Abiyan (UBA

2.0) a teacher has to think of what available with them to share with the poor living everywhere. They may be ideas, knowledge, skills, products and applications and they can be shared with the community. It requires only concern and not a formal order from the university. It is not a charity but a responsibility. It needs only passion, commitment and concern not direction from the above. Here is a story about the activities of a Department in a higher learning institution. Ours is a Department conventionally named Political Science and Development Administration in a Gandhian Educational Institution (Gandhigram Rural Institute – Deemed to be University, fully funded by Government of India) and we are not offering a conventional programme in Political Science but we offer only an innovative post graduate programme termed "Development Administration" meant for preparing middle level managers for development agencies. It is a five year integrated Sandwitch programme with more field component. The Department after passing the conformity legislation to the 73rd Constitutional Amendment in Tamil Nadu an awareness programme has been conducted in the rural areas with the help of the students. When we conducted such programme in the rural areas we have involved the local civil society and community based organizations. Media both print and electronic had given a wide coverage for our activities and thereby we reached out not only to the masses but also to the policy community and political class. After the conduct of local body election in 1996 we have created a separate unit 'Rajiv Gandhi chair for Panchayati Raj studies' in the Department to carryout multiple activities to strengthen the rural local government. In Rajiv Gandhi chair we have prepared modules for conducting training programmes to the newly elected representatives of the people. Since the Rajiv Gandhi chair equipped itself professionally to conduct training programme government and various other agencies have entrusted the responsibility of training the pacnhayat leaders. As a result the Rajiv Gandhi chair has conducted capacity building exercise for 8000 Gram Panchayat leaders and of them 4000 are Dalit and women. Preparing participatory planning is the mandated activity of the panchayats as per the constitutional Amendment the Rajiv Gandhi chair initiated micro plan in 73 Gram Panchayats in five districts with the cooperation of the District Administration. There are nine category of elected representatives are in three tier system of the Panchayati Raj and for them reading materials have been prepared and published. For Gram Panchayat leaders and the officials an administrative manual has been prepared and published. This was the first of its kind in India. Till to-day many of the states do not have administrative manual for panchayats.

In Tamil Nadu District Collector has a role to play in Panchayati Raj activities as Inspector of panchayats. Hence a separate administrative manual has been prepared by the Rajiv Gandhi chair and gave it to all the District Collectors. Having seen the administrative manuals, the Ministry of Panchayati Raj, Government of India wanted a generic administrative manual, we have helped the Kerala Institute of Local Administration to prepare such a manual by following our administrative manual and it has been submitted to the Ministry of Panchayati Raj. Having seen the active academic and outreach activism in the field, the Ford Foundation has entrusted the responsibility of conducting a study on the impact of economic globalization in the livelihood of the poor in Tamil Nadu. Based on the study a training module has been prepared and conducted training for the local body leaders as to how effectively utilize the opportunity comes out of globalization for the poor and to avoid threats of globalization. Yet another assignment given by Action Aid to to the Rajiv Gandhi chair to conduct a study on 'Disaster Management' in Orissa and Gujaraj and prepared training module based on the experience of these states. By using the modules training has been conducted for the local body leaders drawn from coastal areas on "Disaster preparedness and Disaster Management". Yet another agency the UNDP through the state planning commission asked the Rajiv Gandhi chair to prepare District Human Development Report (DHDR) for two districts in Tamil Nadu.

To scale up our Panchayati Raj activities we brought out a supplement with a Varnacular news paper on every Monday titled "Panchayat Malar". This was carried out for an year. Like this "good governance through local governance" an All India Radio programme was conducted for six months through out Tamil Nadu.

Periodically panchayat leaders summit has been arranged and the problems of the panchayati leaders have been sorted out by the intervention of the local body Minister and higher officials. Women Elected Representatives Federation has been formed and it has been facilitated by us for its activities. A specific government order has been obtained from the Government of Tamil Nadu to help the women leaders by the District officials for the smooth functioning of panchayats and effective delivery of services to the community.

While implementing the poverty reduction project in Tamil Nadu the Raji Gandhi chair has been asked to train the managers of the project on the new approach "Community Driven Development". It is an intensive training for the project officers for a month and it was conducted effectively in the filed and not in the class room.

The Rajiv Gandhi chair activities were assisted by the World Bank, UNDP, UNICEF, the Ford Foundation, Population Foundation of India, Rajiv Gandhi Foundation, State Planning Commission, Ministry of Panchayati Raj, the Hunger project, and a few other agencies. Having seen the activities of the Rajiv Gandhi chair five members of parliament have contributed from MPLAD fund to construct a separate building for Rajiv Gandhi Chair. A member of Parliament has helped the Department from his MPLAD fund to create a computer Lab for our training and students use. Even while entrusting the work of preparation of "Devolution Report" to the Institute of Social Sciences Mumbai, by the Ministry of Panchayati Raj, Government of India it has been advised to keep one Panchayati Raj expert as an adviser and hence I have been asked to guide the devolution report preparation work. Here it is to be noted that in all our activities our students have been involved and they benefitted immensely. Village stay, and field activities are mandatory for our students. All our experiences are documented in different books published by us through reputed publishers. Seeing the competency of the Department, the UGC has sectioned Special Assistance (SAP) programme for our Department. All these activities are carried out by our Department over a period of time with the active participation of the faculty members, Research Scholars and students with the support of the administration. When a small Department with six staff members in a small University is able to do this kind of activities the conventional Departments in conventional Universities with huge human power with teachers and students coupled with infrastructure facilities can do much more work more professionally than us.

60. Interface between Higher Learning Institutions and Communities

It is an axiomatic truth that higher the usage of science and technology by the communities, higher will be the quality of life. Equally higher the practice of democracy at the community level higher will be the dignity of life. To enhance the quality of life and to achieve dignity of life for the citizen education has to play a key role and educational institutions have to contribute substantially. Educational institutions have to work for producing quality human power needed to industry, agriculture and service sector through its teaching programmes. By producing knowledge through its research and by disseminating knowledge to the stakeholders through outreach or extension programmes the higher learning institutions have to work for improving the overall economy and polity of the society and the country. In the last six decades the educational system in India has been geared up to move in expansion mode leaving the quality unattended. It is always a natural corollary that while expansion takes place at a faster speed, quality will be the casuality. In India, the universities are offering academic programs, but they are carrying out research not with the intensity as they exhibit in teaching. Thus the higher learning institutions do research a little and offer teaching programmes, massively with the aim of producing more number of students. As a result, we find there is a mismatch between the reality and the capacity, skill and capability of the candidates passing out from the academic programmes of the higher learning institutions. Many do not realize the importance of the link between research and teaching academic programmes. There is yet another dimension which is totally missing in higher learning institutions which will also enhance the quality of the products coming out from the academic institutions is outreach activities. It is nothing but connecting academic institutions directly with the community through their services in the form of information, idea, skill and knowledge for enhancing the quality of life of the people. The higher learning institutions have not developed a scientific framework for outreach activities and hence there is no systematic outreach programme at present for the students of the higher learning institutions in India. The outreach programme is not to serve the community alone, but to enhance their systematic understanding of the society and to inculcate the value of working with the community with concern. Recently the president of India has made a fervent plea that every higher learning institution has to work with people in four or five villages for the transformation of the communities while he participated in the convocation of Agricultural University, Punjab. He made such a plea with an objective that our higher learning institutions will engage the community through their support services to enable the rural communities to lead a decent dignified human life.

The higher learning institutions are having enormous extendables in the form of knowledge, skill, ideas and information which are useful for the transformation of the rural society. All the above can be directly transferred to the community for the benefits of the people. But due to non availability of institutional mechanism to transfer the above benefits to community from the universities, they are not being used fully. Teaching and research in the university system will get strengthened and made useful only when the universities connect themselves with the community. It has been brought to the notice of the policy makers by different committees since independence. Even the Nayudamma committee, while reviewing the IITs made a strong recommendation that IITs have to carry out outreach programmes for the benefit of the rustic folk but they have forgotten conveniently. At the dawn of independence fourteen rural institutes have been created to carry out extension activities in Gandhian perspective for rural transformation. Barring one all have merged in mainstream education. Agriculture universities had extension activities and they have also left those activities to Krishi Vigyan Kendra (KVK). NSS is the only unit from the academic institutions has contact with a community and that too not an organic and systematic way. Thus extension or outreach is considered as unwanted and unstipulated work for the academics. Teaching and research can be done within four walls of the university, but for outreach activities the teachers and the students have to go to the community. It is always felt that working with the community is not an easy task. Hence, neither policy makers or academics thought of the interface between the university and the community. Both teaching and research can be done systematically within the premises of the institution. But outreach programmes cannot be done as teaching and research. Outreach has to be carried out in accordance with the requirements and settings of the communities which are not under the control of the university system. Many of the academics do not know the advantage they can gain out of their engagement with the community. It is not a service. It is a kind of learning to make the academic programme socially relevant. Only a few civil society organizations have continuously impressed upon the central government and the University Grant Commission to make extension as part of the core responsibility of the higher learning institutions. This advocacy was also based on the experience in the US and the west. In response to the continuous persuasion, the University Grant Commission has launched a scheme called "Centre for Fostering Social Responsibility and Community Engagement (CFSRCE)" in select universities. Its main objective is to promote partnership between university and community to develop knowledge for improving the quality of life. It is a kind of learning called experiential learning. Variety of activities has been indicated for universities to engage communities for the benefit of both. There is yet another breakthrough has been achieved in this regard. While ranking of the universities in India based on the performance, one major component for evaluation has been incorporated is an outreach or an extension of the university on par with teaching and research. This has been a neglected aspect for a long. Now it is being part of the evaluation. It gains currency. But it is not known to the academics.

Though this new initiative is being appreciated, the argument which I want to advance here is that every university can do such a kind of community engagement either in the rural or in urban areas and thereby a meaningful relationship could be fostered between higher learning institutions and the community. Already we had some experiments in a few higher learning institutions. We can systematically advance such activities for the benefit of the students, teachers and the communities. When the academic community engages themselves in community work on socially relevant critical issues of development large number of social issues of the communities will be addressed very easily without looking for government support. While doing so socially relevant issues could be identified for research. When they do socially relevant research in the universities they can do policy advocacy more relevant to the development of the communities. In this exercise both community and the institutions can get benefits. Apart from the above two, students passing out from the academic institutions will have adequate skill and capacity on the relevant issues of development. Policy community will also gain much from this kind of exercises. By moving with the community for a meaningful exercises community can be nurtured democratic practices and the academics will learn to listen to the poor. By doing these exercises communities will be engaged in the democratization process. By doing these activities at the community level with the active involvement of the teachers and the students, social responsibility could be cultivated as a value in each one of the staff and students involved in this work. What they need in the university is a center to coordinate the academia from different departments to organize community activities. It is possible with the existing infrastructure and staff as we have community colleges, Adult and continuing education, lifelong learning and extension departments in the university system itself with different mandates. All the units can be used for outreach programmes. These centers can link with Gram Panchayat or a municipality or a division in corporation for outreach activities. Hence, it is high time to realize the value of extension and it can be incorporated in the new education policy.

61. Make the Higher Learning Institutions as People's Institutions

The present government has unequivocally demonstrated that it will follow a different paradigm of governance in which cooperative federalism will be the guiding principle, and thereby much responsibilities and autonomy will be given to state governments for achieving development through an effective way of planning and decision making. All the development activities will be done through a synergetic action between state and local governments and for which adequate resources will be given to both the state government and local governments. This message has been unequivocally given through two major decisions namely abolition of central planning commission and approval of the fourteenth finance commissions report on resource sharing. All within the neoliberal framework of development. There is no ambiguity or vacillation in making its stand on governance and development. The above paradigm is visible through the central government's decision to create Niti Ayog, proclaiming that the central government will involve in policy making and not in preparing schemes and programmes for the states and local bodies. The federal government unambiguously states that it will follow neoliberal policies but all safety nets have to be created for the poor only by the state governments and local bodies as they are closer to people at operational point.

When the central planning commission was abolished, the centre government has indicated that the local bodies and state governments have to initiate the planning process from below. Huge united resources come to state governments and local governments to carry out activities as they plan with the active participation of all sections of the society and more particularly the poor, marginalised and vulnerable groups. Till date high intellectual activities had been done at the central planning commission, central finance commissions and the ministries of the Government of India, whereas at the state and local governments levels out and out all governance and development activities had been carried out only by the bureaucrats and lower level bureaucracy respectively. Both governments considered themselves as only implementing agencies of the schemes of the central government. Barring a few state governments, many of the state governments do not have adequate resources to evolve schemes and programmes for development. The efficiency level of such lower level bureaucracy is always being questioned as they lack professionalism at the ground. There is always a gap between the central government decision making process and the state and local government implementation process. People who are involved in implementation of schemes are poor in professional competencies as there is no adequate professional training institutions offering training and capacity building organically. Further the institutional structure, design and manpower at the grassroots are always inadequate, less facilities and less professionals at the grassroots level as compared to the central government functionaries. In the above given context, people expectation from the government is increasing geometrically as political parties practice competitive populism for electoral politics. Apart from the above, the life led by people is not based on science and technology but based on cultural practices. Governance at grassroots is not based on rule of law and provisions of the constitution but on the basis of practices of the community. Many of the occasions we see conflict between community practices and constitutional provisions. In the above backdrop, the new paradigm of governance has to operate. It has been noticed while evaluating the effective resource utilization by using power both the local bodies and state governments, they are being criticized by the central government on most of the occasions by citing the evaluation reports and audit reports. Why the state and local governments deviate from the well established financial framework of norms? The reasons are many. Of them the closeness of the government to people, proliferation of rules and regulations by the central government schemes and programmes by the state and local bodies without giving flexibility to accommodate regional variations, poor professionalism of personnel and competitive populism practiced by the political parties for electoral prospects are primary.

But the present context is complex. The state governments have to reorient themselves fastly to cope with the expectation of the centre in reshaping the governance process to get advantage of the new paradigm of governance of the central government. The new context, envisages the state governments and local governments to act fastly, professionally, organically and transparently and they have to work with the active participation of people and work on the demand of the people to achieve better outcome out of economic growth. To transform the process of governance and development, institutions at the ground has to be strengthened, professionally equipped and for which the state and local governments can involve the higher learning institutions in this country. As they have grown phenomenally, they can involve themselves in a systematic way in the process of social transformation activities. 722 universities, 39000 colleges, 11000 research institutions, 8000000 students are the real source of strength and they can be involved in preparing data base, micro level planning and implementation process. Even if all the institutions are not involved, at least 400 higher learning institutions fully funded by the Government can be involved in this process as these institutions have 500 social science departments with 250000 teachers. Apart from the above 200 social science research institutes funded by the Central Government of India and state governments are in India and they can be involved in micro level research studies and micro level planning.

From awareness creation to skill building and knowledge sharing, higher learning institutions have to interact with the community organically. By doing so, the state and local bodies can act professionally. To make the governance process effective, people will be mobilized for achieving development and deepening of democracy. By doing so, the linkage between higher learning institutions and the communities becomes a movement. The interface between the society and higher learning institutions will be meaningful and mutually beneficial, if they work organically on a sustainable basis. Apart from the above, the quality of education will be enhanced. Like the linkage between industry and technical education, linkage between higher learning social science institutions and society will enhance the quality of higher education which will be productive and creative. Both community and the higher learning institution will find ways for engagement. Their engagement will make every university or every higher learning institutions will become people's university. In the process of engaging the academic community in outreach activities, students will be sensitized on the social issues. They will develop concern for the community. Academics and students will realize their social responsibility. It will serve not only the students but also to the entire society directly or indirectly. Academic programmes and research programmes will be more socially relevant while interacting with each other. It needs only a framework and it can be evolved by the University Grants Commission.

62. Research and Policy Advocacies in Higher Learning Institutions

Recently I was invited to participate in a public vivo-voce examination of a candidate from social science faculty in a university wherein the candidate has to defend his Ph. D thesis. As the title of the thesis is very interesting and more relevant to my specialization, I have agreed to participate with the expectation that the scholar would throw more lights on the issues as it is an empirical study. I have participated in the programme for about two and half hours. When the candidate made a presentation I was curious to see the policy advocacy section of the presentation as the subject of the thesis is - "Evaluating a Centrally Sponsored Rural Development Scheme in Tamil Nadu". It is to be noted here that now the scheme taken up for investigation in the research is not in operation as it met with several failures. But an improved version of the scheme with a new name is in operation. I thought that though the scholar has evaluated an old scheme, its policy advocacy will be of much use to the present scheme also. From that perspective I consciously listening to the presentation. The scholar suggested a few recommendations for effective implementation of the present scheme and outlined a few areas for further research. While listening to the presentation, I found the scholar linking the relationship between the scheme selected for evaluation and the empowerment of the beneficiaries of the scheme. I was tempted to ask a question as to how effectively the scholar controlled the impact factors of the other schemes of rural development on the beneficiaries who are recipient of benefits from multiple schemes as Government of Tamil Nadu operates volley of schemes for the poor and more particularly the poor women. He replied that he has not taken any effort to control the influence of other schemes on the respondents who are the beneficiaries of the scheme under evaluation. I further asked how come you make all these suggestions to make course correction in the scheme without making a comprehensive analysis of data covering different regions of the country. He replied that he has created this section as it as necessary for thesis with the limited analysis of data collected from a few districts. He further said that he has not taken into account the variations of the regions. From the above experience one can easily understand the status and seriousness of research in the university system today. To write a report for a Ph.D degree they select samples in a few districts and analyse the data with some statistical tools. The results of the analysis are being explained in a general way without the background of the theoretical underpinnings. They derive results and bring conclusion more broadly. Based on the above the scholars write policy implications and further areas for research. These aspects are conventionally followed in the framework of Ph.D thesis in the Indian universities. At present the scholars in social science take up some studies pertinent to rural development schemes and evaluate the impact of the schemes and forwhich they collect data from one or two districts. After analyzing the data, they tend to generalize the results as if he or she has covered the entire India.

Any research in social science will help either policy community or the community at large. To make it to happen rigorous analysis is needed and logical explanations have to be given to the results of the analysis of data. While collecting data proper sampling technique has to be adopted. At all levels from problem formulation to arriving at conclusion, scientific rigour has to be maintained. If the findings, conclusions and policy implications of the scientific studies are properly communicated to the end users namely policy community or community in general many of the pitfalls in the rural development schemes could be avoided and the schemes could be implemented in an effective way. More particularly policies will be evolved more professionally by using the input drawn from research reports. But the trend in the university system is that policy implication of the study is not the concern of the scholars and even if there is a section in the research report after getting the degree nobody to bother about the research reports.

When a scheme of the central government is evaluated, samples have to be taken from different states for analysis. Without covering many of the states, if a scholar makes policy recommendations based on his or her studies in one district or one state, it will not be useful for policy makers. In India, we find more number of micro studies covering a district or a few districts or a state. Beyond a state scholars never move due to paucity of resources. But they make policy recommendations. Ofcourse they are not reaching the policy community as most of the theses are in the shelf's of the universities. If some are published some time they may reach the policy corridors. Only a few scholars, not at the doctoral level, have the courage to reach out to the policy community with the policy note. The higher learning institutions produce heavy load of documents from Ph.D scheme. But policy documents are not emerging out of research documents proportionate to the volume of work carried out in the higher learning institutions.

In my academic experience I have evaluated 96 Ph.D thesis and of them only 10% of the thesis brought out some relevant policy recommendations. In 90% of the Ph.D thesis, there is a section meant for policy recommendation and effectively nothing worthwhile discussed in this section. While evaluating those documents one can easily draw out a proposition that our scholars never look at the research issues from the perspective of the utility of the findings or conclusions. Their botheration is completing the task and getting a degree. If it is a sponsored project, submitting a project report to funding agency and beyond that no botheration. Many of the government departments and funding agencies keep tons and tons of reports on many socially relevant issues and on the other hand policy makers are looking for input for policy making or midcourse correction in the implementation of a development scheme or programme. Huge investments have been made to conduct studies but nothing comes out from the academic corridors to policy corridors. Research substantially helps the scholar to acquire Ph.D and the teacher to get promotion in the higher learning institutions. Ofcourse occasionally knowledge creation takes place. But it does not reach out to the needy. Because there is no mandate for the researchers either from the research institute or from the funding agency that the researchers have to submit one policy note or administration note to the appropriate authority from their research output. The researchers are not evincing keen interest in preparing policy note from the research reports. It is also a problem in India that our research scholars are not adequately trained to prepare policy note. Preparing policy note requires orientation and skill. This has to be addressed seriously by the research institutes and the funding agencies. In this regard, the regulatory authority of the higher learning institutions namely the UGC has to take serious steps by directing the higher learning institutions to take note of these lacunae and to act accordingly to prepare policy note from the research reports.

63. Standoff between HRD Minister and Drafting Committee Chairman

The drafting committee to draft the new education policy under the leadership T.S.R. Subramanian submitted its report to the HRD Ministry, Government of India recently and sparked a controversy because of the opinion expressed publicly by T.S.R. Subramanian and thereafter discourse started on the opinion expressed by the chairman of the committee T.S.R. Subramanian. The crux of the matter is that he expressed and asked the Ministry of HRD to put the report in the public domain to get opinion from all quarters. On this matter, he has written a letter to the Minister of HRD also. Promptly the HRD Minister Smriti Irani has given a fitting reply that it is only a draft and on which the opinions of the state governments have to be obtained and only after seeking their opinion, the draft will come to public domain. Here, one important aspect has to be understood by everyone. The entire report was not prepared by this committee. This committee has consolidated the input of the public and other stakeholders and drafted the report. Coordination was done by the Ministry for drawing and consolidating the input. It is not Dr. Radhakrishnan or Dr. Yashpal or Kothari committee report prepared by intellectuals on a top down basis. This committee has only done the job of drafting the report. The HRD Minister's statement on this issue of putting it in the website of the Ministry carry a strong message that the HRD Ministry wants to take into account the views of the state governments on the draft policy of the Government of India on education.

The HRD Ministry wants to keep the state governments in good humour as they are the implementing agencies of the policy. It does not want to impose its ideas on the state governments. The Ministry wants to have the state governments on board on this issue as their support is crucial for its implementation. Here, it is to be noted that education was in the state list and subsequently it has been transferred to concurrent list. By taking a decision at the centre, it can convey its decision to state government and the state governments have to be implemented. Since it is in concurrent list once decision is taken by the central government it has got all legitimacy of a decision to be implemented by all. Everyone knows education in the past one decade is in a mess in the name of expansion without a clear cut policy. Now the new government wants to clean up many of the unattended things in education sector and for which it strives to bring out a policy.

The Prime Minister of India Narendra Modi has been reiterating that his governance framework will adhere to the basic values of cooperative federalism and by which he will take the views of the state governments along with the centre for better governance and delivery of service to the people. In this regard, the argument projected by the Minister of HRD is logical and sensible. This time the policy is not directed from the above and it is being evolved from below. A massive consultative process took place with stakeholders. No doubt it is historic in nature.

It is appropriate that the seeking the views of the states are more important than mere publishing the report. The report or policy should not be for the sake of adding one more point for the achievements of the government. Policy should have resilience for implementation. Further, the state governments cannot be treated as if they are subordinates. They are to be treated as equal partners. Then only the state governments will commit themselves to implement the policy of the central government. If the new education policy enacted in the 80's is evaluated now one can easily argue that many of the aspects mentioned in the earlier policy have not been implemented in letter and spirit in the educational sector. Many educationalists lamented that many of the fine aspects of the new education policy had not been operationalised. It is to be noted that at present one has to read the tone and tenor of the letters written by many Chief Ministers of the states to the present Prime Minister of India Narendra Modi on various aspects. Against this background, one has to look at the draft of the new policy. Fine documents can be prepared with the active involvements of a few intellectuals. There is no dearth of reports or policies in our country. The problem we face in India is the translation of policies into action. Best policy is one which is actionable and capable to produce expected results at the quickest possible time.

Here, it is an example to be remembered that with a brutal majority in Parliament, Rajiv Gandhi brought an excellent Constitutional Amendment to establish local government in India but he could not do so as it was opposed by regional and national political parties as it was the state subject. Further, state governments felt that without devolving powers from the centre to the state governments making the state governments to devolve powers to local bodies is basically weakening the state. Hence, it was defeated in Rajya Sabha. No doubt, it was a best draft for the creation of a strong local government in India but failed to deliver. Later a minority government under the leadership of P.V. Narasimha Rao brought the same constitutional amendment and got it passed unanimously in the parliament and Panchayati Raj was created in India on a sustainable basis. He gave instruction to the officials to prepare a document which can be implementable. Major objections raised by the state governments were removed in the draft submitted to parliament by Rajiv Gandhi and subsequently the draft was placed before the parliament for its approval. Now a system is in place for governance at grassroots. What was not possible in Rajiv Gandhi period was possible in P.V. Narasimha Rao period? Instead of preparing a fine intellectual document, a workable draft is the need of the hour as state governments have to accept it as they are the implementing agencies. We have seen the reactions of the state governments on NEET issue as how the state governments have exerted pressure on the central government to stop the process of conducting the test. Hence, the line taken by the HRD Minister is pragmatic in nature. It is highly a matured strategic decision to keep the state governments in good humour. Pragmatic decisions will get good results and ideal arguments can be appreciated at a media platform not in the society. It has been captured subtly by the HRD Minister Smriti Irani while reacting to the observations of T.R.S. Subramanian.

64. Where are the World Class Rural Institutes in India?

Transforming Rural India by enabling the people who live in the villages to lead a decent, dignified human life is a very big challenge to both the central and state governments even after implementing plethora of schemes and programmes since independence. Sanitation, livelihood, poverty reduction, vulnerability reduction, empowerment, sustaining productive rural economy are still challenging tasks for the governments due various factors and ofwhich the neglect of rural higher education advocated by M.K.Gandhi and Rabindranath Tagore is one and significant.

It was M.K. Gandhi who envisioned a new educational paradigm to transform India. He evolved various approaches to transform rural India and ofwhich creation of a new educational paradigm still remains significant and relevant for solving many of the problems in rural society. The first education commission after Independence under the leadership of Dr. Radhakrishnan had given due attention to the educational paradigm of M.K. Gandhi and it devoted a chapter in its report on the need to create rural universities. This chapter had significant inputs from Dr. Arthur E. Morgan and Dr. Tigert, members in the University Commission of Education 1948.

Basically, the rural university or rural institute was basically conceived to prepare transformational leaders to work with people in the rural areas to transform the community without ruling over them. Its conceptualization integrates the three experiences and experiments of Danish People's College Denmark, the land-grant model of American Agricultural and Technical Education and Gandhi's model of *Nai Talim* experimented in India for about 25 years. Within a short span of time yet another committee was constituted under the leadership of K.L. Srimali in the year 1954 and it was called committee on "Higher Education for Rural Areas". While constituting the committee two important assignments were given to the committee through its terms of reference. One, how to take forward the experiments of rural higher education that was being conducted in a number of Gandhian institutions and secondly, to suggest ways and means through which existing conventional universities can make useful contribution to the rural areas by solving the problems of the rural communities. Basically the rural institutes were meant to break the development barrier between rural and urban population, and enable the narrowing down of the gap between culture and work, between humanities and science and technology, and between the practice and ideals. Essentially rural institutes have to focus upon planning for the development of the region. These institutions are expected to produce transformational leaders to change the communities and the rural scenario. Their core function is to link the higher education to communities and societal aspirations.

In the Second Five Year Plan of the Government of India a reference was made under the heading "Rural Higher Education" with a note mentioning that rural institutes are intended to perform a variety of functions for the rural community. Time and again it has been reiterated that the rural institutes are meant for a comprehensive educational programme integrating with research and extension activities. These have been visualized as a combination of local culture and training centre and apart from the above these institutions have to work as centres for development planning in rural areas. The Ministry of education proposed to establish ten rural institutes during the Second Five Year Plan period with the investment of rupees two crore. These institutes were not meant to be altogether new entities. Leading centers working on the lines of *Nai Talim* had been selected for this purpose. To coordinate the activities and functions of the rural institutes the central government had constituted a Council for Rural Higher Education. Subsequently a few more institutions were added to the list. And at one time a total of fourteen rural institutes were functioning in various regions. Following the rural institute model, there have been several other experiments in the country. While evolving a new education policy in the year 1986 some aspects of rural higher education were included in the policy. Even at that point of time neither the government made a thorough analysis of the functioning of the rural institutes nor it examined the possibilities to move in new direction. On the other hand, in place of a new framework for rural higher education, it advocated only for extension or outreach activities.

In the course of years, mainstream educational framework has not accommodated these new experiments and as a result thirteen rural institutes, merged with the mainstream educational framework abandoning the Rural Institute experiments. Since it was convenient for the teachers of the Rural Institutes, they also have accepted to toe the line of the mainstream educational pattern without raising any question. But it was a loss for the rural community. However, during the tenure of P.V. Narasimha Rao as Prime Minister, an initiative was under taken to revive the rural higher education in India in order to meet the challenges of globalization. A National Council for Rural Institute was created with a mandate to further the activities of the rural institutes contextually. Under the agency of the National Council for Rural Institute, Hyderabad, a comprehensive study was undertaken to trace the achievements, failures and needs of the rural institute in India.

The comprehensive study was undertaken by Dr. J. Karunakaran, former Vice-Chancellor of Gandhigram Rural Institute. He brought out a volume entitled "Liberating Education for a Knowledge Society: Lessons from Nai-Talim and Rural Institute Experiments". However, the initiative of P.V. Narasimha Rao could not move further and now the National Council for Rural Institute is dormant and defunct due to lack of financial and institutional support from the successive governments at the Centre. The comprehensive study undertaken by Dr. Karunakaran came out with a strong proposal for creating regional development university to meet the challenges of globalization for the rural areas. The new regional development university is envisaged to work with the community by extending knowledge, skill and approach to make use of the opportunities of globalization and to avoid the threats of globalization. It was a well thought out proposal to create such universities. He has given a blueprint for the regional development university as rural-urban continuum needs support from this kind of a new university. Further, the newly proposed regional institutes are highly relevant to support the activities of the rural and urban local bodies to evolve development plans as per the mandate based on the recommendations of the Fourteenth Finance Commission of Government of India, as resource agencies. While developing such a plan for village development in the context of climate change, disaster preparedness and green growth, the regional development universities' role is inevitable. Against this background, the draft new education policy has neither talked about extension nor about the rural higher education. It can be observed as a conspicuous omission in the report. It needs to be deliberated. Further, our policy community is very vociferous in making declarations that India has been establishing world class IITs, world class IIMs, and world class central universities, but there is no such declaration for creating world class rural institutes meant for rural transformation.

65. Where we are in skilling our youth to the world of work?

Recently I was invited to be part of a book launch function in Indian Institute of Management, Bangalore as a contributor of a chapter in the edited volume "India: Preparation for the world of work- Education system and school to work Transition" edited by Prof. Mathias Pilz from Cologne University, Germany and published by Springer. The book was released by Consul General of Germany Jorn Rohde. It is a book on how the educational institutions in India from schools to higher learning institutions prepare students to the world of work. It is an issue and challenge to Indian academics, researchers and policy makers. But it was brought out by a German Publication, edited by a Professor working in Cologne University, Germany and released by Consul General of Germany. Why Germany evinced keen interest in skilling our youth in India? What made them to focus on Indian educational issues? are the curious questions one would raise. If I give a little background of it, it is easy to understand the background of the issues and the contributions of Germany to both academics and policy community in facing the challenges in converting the youth to the world of work as workforce in India.

The edited volume is the outcome of an International Conference held in Germany in 2014. When I was in Cologne University as visiting professor for a semester in 2011, I had a meeting with Prof. Mathias Pilz who is considered as a specialist on vocational education to explore the possibility of sensitizing Indian academics and policy communities in India on the issue of skilling our youth for the world of work as we found enormous work opportunity for our youth in India and abroad in the context of globalization. I was tempted to deliberate on this issue after visiting several vocational schools in Germany and it was also facilitated by prof. Mathias Pilz. I found a total struggle in the educational process in Germany to prepare the students for the world of work. After visiting the schools I had several meetings with many academics and I wrote several popular articles in Tamil Newspapers to sensitize policy community and opinion makers. Because our politicians made rhetoric that India is going to achieve demographic dividends by skilling 500 million youth in India. While seeing the reality at the ground as an Indian to make the dream a reality I felt that we have to go a long way to achieve the desired goal. But we have to bring all seriousness among the policy community, opinion makers and academics on this issue and hence, I wanted to do something and on this objective I broached this idea with Prof. Mathias Pilz. In order to evoke enthusiasm from the German partners I informed them that Germany can contribute substantially to India in helping our educational and training institutions to prepare our youth to the world of work. By doing so both countries can get benefits out of it. In this regard, Prof. Mathias Pilz took initiative in organizing an International Conference in Germany. A team of academics and researchers presented papers based on their research in the conference. In the sidelines of the conference we had a deliberation to move forward on this issue. Finally we have agreed to bring out a volume based on our contributions in the conference. It was decided to publish the book through a reputed publisher. Springer came forward to publish the volume and it was supported by DAAD, Germany for publication. As a result, it is now ready to be placed in the market. Having seen the importance of the issue the same DAAD, Germany subsidized the price 50% to the Indians with a aim of reaching out to every policy maker and every academics who teaches and researches on the issue of skilling youth in India. When the book was released the Consul General Jorn Rhode made a few observations about the book and the context which are so important at this juncture. He said that there is a close correlation between the efficiency in building the skill among the youth and their employability. He indicated the fact that wherever the skill education is effective and efficient, unemployment rate is very low. He cited the examples from many of the countries in the world. He further said that there is a close correlation between the skilled jobs and the quality of life. Higher the professionalism, higher will be the salary of the workforce and in the same way higher will be standard of living and quality of life. In order to transform the workforce in unorganized sector in India, these observations are more relevant. Following the remarks of the Consul General, the editor of this book Prof. Mathias Pilz made some remarks which are also highly relevant to India. He said that skilling 500 million is not an easy job. It is a movement by itself. It is a movement for professionalization. This process will happen properly only when hard core academics to do research on those issues and guide the policy community and the academic communities who are involved in skilling the youth. He further said that he hardly found academics in India evincing keen interest on this issue on a sustainable basis. Very few are doing quality research on this issue. Even to edit this book he found difficulty in searching for scholars in India who are specializing on vocational education. Country of this size need more scholars and institutions to do research on vocational education and training to guide properly the policy makers and bureaucracy and academics to achieve demographic dividends by using the new opportunity.

66. A New Report for Policy Makers on Higher Education

Last year a German publisher brought out an anthology entitled "India: Preparation for the world of work: Education System and School to Work Transition" edited by a Cologne University Business School Professor Mathias Pilz with the active support of the academics of India and other countries who participated in an International Conference, with an objective of mapping up the issues connected with labour market and the higher learning institutions in skilling the youth. Given the nature and scope of the book, DAAD of Germany has given a concession to the publishing company to sell the book with 50% of the price. The book has captured the key issues of skilling youth and the problems associated with it. The above book is a significant contribution in the given context. Several key recommendations have been made and of which one is key and very important that the approach of the government to make the students employable, an integrated and coordinated efforts should be made among the departments and institutions involved in educational administration.

Now a new report entitled "Responding to Massivefication: Differentiation in Post Secondary education Worldwide" by Philip G. Altbach, Liz Reisberg and Hans De wit sponsored by the Hamburg Transnational University Leaders Council published in 2017 which brings new insights in the higher learning process in India. No doubt it is a global report it has covered Australia, Brazil, Chile, Egypt, France, Germany, Ghana, Great Britain, India, Japan, Russia and the United States. The report has to be validated in a validation workshop to be held in Hamburg Transnational University Leaders Council to analyse and evaluate the post secondary system in the world. This report is essentially to conscientise the leaders of policy making communities both in the centre and state governments and educational institutions on the challenges faced by the higher learning institutions. In this report one chapter deals with India. In that chapter, it is indicated that despite massivefication of higher secondary education in India, the whole country faces a problem of mismatch between the demand in the labour market and the labour supply to the market through the higher learning institutions. The requirements are at two levels. First the increasing sophisticated global knowledge economy requires world class higher learning institutions to produce quality students to involve them in the process of knowledge production and do active quality applied research to meet the market requirements. No doubt India is fast growing economy and populous country with young population. In India 35 million students are in post secondary education which is second in the world. Despite its successful economic growth story, India still continues to be a low middle income economy. The problem which India faces in employment and income growth is due to poor skill profile of its people. It is increasingly felt and observed based on the research findings that youth have not been prepared in post secondary education to meet the diverse needs of the changing economy and society. India is not only a populous country but also a country with diverse behaviour and practices based on the cultural conditions. Indian society is known through 4600 communities, 1720 languages and of which 30 are spoken by over one million people. India has 63840 higher learning institutions from industrial training institutions to institute of national importance including universities and colleges. India had 20 universities 496 colleges and 215000 students at the dawn of Independence. But now we have 757 universities, 38056 colleges and 11922 independent research institutions with 33.3 million students and grass enrolment ration of 27.4% excluding enrolment in distance education. In the growth of post secondary education, private sector played an important role.

At present 77% of the institutions are private and they engage 64.6% of the students. In the last 25 years private sector played an important role. In this context, research survey found out a few faultlines to draw the attention of the policy makers. As the sector grows speedily and in scale there will be volley of problems in any society. Not only scale and speed but also private players involved in the sector brought series of challenges to policy makers. They are to be addressed very effectively and quickly to avoid compounded problems. The report listed out the challenges as faultlines. They are: 1, Mismatch between the demand from labour market and supply from the educational institutions; 2, A formal vocational education and training system is small and weak and it is underdeveloped; 3, There is no awareness on the part of the stakeholders on the contextual importance of skill education in the country to the growing need of skill workforce; 4, There is no serious scientific attempt in projecting the kind of skill required currently in the labour market and in foreseeable future. As a result, one could witness oversupply and undersupply of personnels from the higher learning institutions to the labour market. It is still pathetic to see a mismatch that half of Indian labour force is in Agriculture and significant labour demand is in informal sector. This is not corrected despite initiatives from the 11th Five year plan period. It is indicated in the report that research capacity of the academic system is weak and limited. The higher education system lacks quality culture in academic and research programmes. While analyzing the key issues of the post secondary education in India in a comparative perspective, the report has listed out all the weaknesses in the system. The report has indicated that the current issues afflicted with the post secondary education have to be tackled through an integrated policy approach with the joint efforts of both the state governments and the central government. It requires a holistic systems approach to respond to the challenges of the educational system and the labour market. Better policies, higher funding, level of governance, effective efficient regulations and fair accreditations are to be in place urgently to take advantage of the labour market opportunity. The most critical issue the demand supply mismatch should be addressed systematically through school and collegiate education by incorporating skill based courses. Integrating smaller institutions to operate at scale to deliver products professionally to the labour market is the need of the hour. Institutional reforms are imperative for promotion of autonomy, quality and a performance culture. For a better coordinated and coherent approach, the report suggests a single ministry to deal with post secondary education. Both the professor Mathias Pilz's edited volume and the new report on post secondary education have suggested menu of activities to act upon by the policy makers in India. The question here is whether the centre and the state governments are sensitive to act fastly and build a movement for it. But we hear the bold statements of the Prime Minister on 'Skill India'. Yet action at the ground is not so sound as the noise of the Prime Minister as we hear from the reports. The report is a wakeup call.

67. Creating Human Rights Culture in Schools

On 30th August, 2016 I was asked to deliver a lecture on "Creating Human Rights Culture" to the teachers of 250 High Schools drawn from 15 districts of Tamil Nadu sponsored by the Human Rights Education Foundation based at Madurai with the approval of the Government of Tamil Nadu with an objective of orienting the teachers to help the Human Rights clubs of the students to be created in 250 schools in Tamil Nadu. This initiative is based on the experience we gained in the pilot districts on this subject. No doubt that it is a progressive step to prepare the younger generations to understand the values of rights, liberty, and fraternity. It is a preventive step. All along the Human Rights Foundation worked on the incidence of violation of Human Rights and to seek remedy for the violations. It is a pity that in India constitution grants equality, it is only the community denies equality. We have to go a long way to establish a just human society. In a feudal society like India deepening democracy and democratizing the society is a challenging task. It is always swimming against the current. High inequality that to social inequality in a hierarchical society always work against democratization and deepening of democracy. But in India since independence people are struggling to create a new social order through democratizing the society with the support of the constitution of India. It is to be kept in mind that all the social practices are not guided by the constitutional principles but by community norms and values which are drawn from manusmitri. Thus social democracy gained importance as it will alone strengthen the democratic government for its functioning. Core values of democracy namely equality, liberty, freedom, fraternity, fairness, justice, respecting dissent voice are mere dreams and visions as Indian society is chocked in oppression and marginalization. But social groups are slowly moving with the support of the state initiatives towards achieving the core values of democracy through institutions. Despite all initiatives, mechanisms, institutions and processes, one would find more of violations of human rights either in the family or in the organisations or in the institutions or in the communities. No doubt, Indian society is democratic institutionally but behaviourally it is not as rights violation becomes part and practice of the society. Even political democracy is afflicted with the issues of the Indian society. In this context, initiatives like this will be of immense use to transform the younger generations to be made sensitive towards democracy and human rights. To sensitize the students, teachers have to be prepared and they are to be made committed on this task as they have to do the work voluntarily out of the educational framework mandated to them in the schools. Here the Government of Tamil Nadu has to be appreciated for its willingness to allow the schools to such a kind of orientation and training. By influencing the teachers and students in the schools through creating Human Rights clubs we expect a new culture among the youth on democracy in the years to come. The human rights clubs are not the clubs to impart human rights education, it is a process through which they learn and realize the potentials of democracy to solve the problems of human society. It develops deliberative capacity, debating skill, argumentative skill and problem solving ability. It is learnt from the pilot experience that the students move from the zone of fear to the zone of joy by moving closer to the teachers and develop arguments with other students through the human rights club. A new activity with a passion and a sense of commitment has been initiated in the public schools. The students have to be oriented to run the club. Proper modules have been evolved to guide this programme in the schools. When the students are involved in the club activities it would bring awareness among the students about the implications of equality. The students would realize the value of equality, gender equality and responsibility. Beyond the above this deliberative culture developed by the students through the human rights club in the school with the help of the teachers shapes and moulds the character of the students. It is equivalent to that of creating citizenship culture. They will be socially conscious and sensitive on rights and responsibilities. It starts with rights but ends with responsibility.

Some of the teachers who were part of the process in the pilot districts shared their experiences in the programme. They have underlined one important aspect that they have noticed among the students is that the students are conscious about their responsibilities and they are concerned about the rights of others after their involvement in human rights club activities. They called it a citizenship training for the students. It is inferred from the sharing of the teachers who assisted the clubs in the schools that this process inculcates more responsibilities on the part of the students.

After listening to the teachers I made some observations. "Now education becomes a commodity and it becomes a tradable commodity. We teachers become instruments of production of products to the market. Hence, a new business opportunity has been created by the government in the context of globalization. The entrepreneurs found in education huge business potentials. It becomes an industry and students are becoming marketable products. Success of an educational institution is assessed based on the quantum of students produced for job markets. Value of education lies in transformation of the individuals and the society towards human growth and not mere economic growth. Human growth is an end and economic growth is a means. But now end becomes means. We basically teachers belong to middle class known for catalyst role. We have to play the role of a catalyst. Once middle class acted as catalyst force to bring positive changes in the society. But now they are away from the responsibility as they involved themselves in production of marketable goods. Preparing the students through education is for higher level activities meant for evolution of human being from one to another level. When the students are prepared socially conscious and responsible citizens, human society will bring wonders with the active participation of the citizens. Thus the role of the teachers is important in bringing out the inner talent of the students through the clubs. To do this we have to walk extra mile and work beyond our normal time. We should be part of our transformation history". Human rights activists and officials from the school education department of Government of Tamil Nadu spoke about the role of the teachers in democratizing the society through this human rights clubs.

68. Neglect of Social Science

It is an axiomatic truth that education will enable the people to lead a decent and dignified scientific human life based on the knowledge acquired through education. It will bring understanding of the problems of the human society by the people and it will pave way for finding solution to the problems of the humanity by using the knowledge created by education. Now education becomes a universal movement. It has grown leaps and bounds. It produced unfathomable level of knowledge yet humanity is in deep trouble. The produced knowledge has helped a few segments to achieve prosperity to the unimaginable level and made bulk of the population to lead life in poverty and distress. It is due to the changing goal and objective of education. Once it was considered as means to transform the society and through which people have to lead a happy and meaningful life. But now it has acquired a new meaning. It is for achieving material prosperity through market mechanism, students are considered as marketable goods to be sold in the job market. Hence it helps only few segments. Why it helps a few and it does not help many.

No doubt the educational process brought unfathomable transformation in the human society through science and technology. All the infrastructure facilities what we have seen are the products of education. In the same measure humanity witnesses plethora of problems and miseries. The miseries and worries are not only affected the society which are in ignorance but they have affected the most educated societies also. As a result, one can easily conclude that education is not a solution but a means to find solution. In reality today education plays an unlimited role in producing knowledge and knowledge is being used for solving problems and creating problems. It depends on what type of education one acquires. When knowledge is used for a limited purpose, it will end in creating problems in the human society. To make the knowledge useful to the society, the knowledgeable have to be conscientised on the broader role of the knowledge created through a process of education. Now education has been commodified as an instrument to make profit and prosperity and hence professional education has been given a new thrust. Nothing wrong in giving importance to professional education provided the professional education tend to solve the problem in the human society. Contrary to expectation, it makes the leaner to be more aggressive in earning unfathomable money by using super specialization and by leaving the social responsibility of solving the problem of the society. Because these professional courses have completely neglected the human aspects as subject of humanities are not taught in the professional courses. By doing so the professionals are not conscious of the social realities and their social responsibilities. It is a fallacy in the educational system today. This can be solved only by teaching minimum number of social science courses to the students who are pursuing professional courses. In this sense, any science subject is a social science, as it has to be useful to the humanity. If knowledge created through education is not useful to the society or harm the society it cannot be considered as knowledge. Hence, in order to make use of the science to the society social sciences are essential to be thought to all the students. Social sciences are reflecting the social realities and the knowledge created through science has to help the society to find solution to the problems. It will take place only when students are oriented to look at the issues from the perspective of the people that too the people who are in poverty and distress. Hence, science and technology and social science are inseparable. They are to be taught together. But in the modern world, humanity has developed aspiration to accountable wealth, knowledge utility has been narrowed down to make profit individual centric without looking into the broader utility. As a result, despite higher level of attainment of knowledge, humanity is confronting plethora of problems which led to major segments of humanity is in suffering. How to overcome this problem today? To with in start education process of the society, social sciences should be taught to all the students in respective of their courses. Every student while acquiring knowledge, he or she should relate it to the human problems. When a student is pursuing medicine or engineering or astrophysics or chemistry or any subject, he or she should undergo one course on social science. It is imperative to make the knowledgeable more human with empathy in reality today social sciences are neglected and excluded subjects. Social science courses are branded as nonutility courses. It is done by the State itself. As a result, more knowledge, more wealth, more profit, more comfort but full of miseries and worries. Rich are not in peace, poor are in hungry. Knowledge created for the humanity has been used for limited ends and hence the broader utility is neglected.

If knowledge is to be used for all, knowledgeable have to be sensitized on the broader objective of knowledge. That could be possible only through teaching social science to science and technology students. Social science will make the person to grow in full form externally and internally. Social science will make the person cultured. The culture will make the individual useful to the larger human collectivities. Today's education makes more experts not culturally rich individuals. Unless the educated are prepared or oriented to understand the humanity's problems and their role in solving the problems of the humanity, education is missing its objective. Hence, it is imperative to make the higher learners sensitive on the problems of the humanity. It could be possible only through social science teaching in engineering and medical colleges. It is the need of the hour to create socially concerned professionals.

69. Research Capacity in VET in India

A team of researchers in Germany and India under the leadership of Prof. Matthias Pilz, from Cologne University, Germany involved in research in Vocational Education and Training in India in the past six to seven years with the financial support of DAAD, Germany. Scholars from Tamil Nadu Agriculture University, Indira Gandhi National Open University, Indian Institute of Management, Bangalore, Indian Institute of Technology, Mumbai, Gandhigram Rural Institute – Deemed University, Tamil Nadu and a few other institutions joined together for conducting research in the area of Vocational Education and Training in India. Within the short span of time the scholars have met two times in Germany and two times in India through organizing conferences. There are scholars from other countries like Switzerland, Austria, China, England have also extended support to the team by going through the research documents prepared by the team and offering valuable constructive suggestions to move forward in research and policy advocacy. Despite our size and strength of higher education, it is a known fact that the capacity of research in Skill education is poor, sketchy, unidirectional and in the nascent stage. But our requirement is huge. We need higher research capacity but our effort in this direction is minimal. Whenever our policy community visits Germany, it gives slew of promises and they are being published in the media also. But the ground reality is that no systematic effort is on to support research on the issues of Vocational Education and Training. In order to sensitize the stakeholders in India, an anthology "India: Preparation for the World of Work Education System and School to Work Transition" consisting of research papers prepared by the team has been published by a German Publishing Company (Springer). The German Government has given 50% subsidy to Indian educational institutions as the price of the book is exorbitant. They have also formed a small academic association called Indian Academy for Vocational Education and Training Research Studies. All are serious minded, committed and passionate researchers evinced keen interest in Vocational Education and Training Studies. With the limited funding from Germany the scholars have done state specific and sector specific studies and they are being supervised and coordinated by Prof. Matthias Pilz from Cologne University. He involved a large number of young researchers in those projects and invited them to the conferences in Germany and India when he organised in both countries.

Recently he organised a conference in New Delhi on "The Past and the Future of research in the field of school to work transition, skill formation and vocational education and training in India" on 24th and 25th October, 2017, a number of papers prepared out of the project done with the support of DAAD, have been presented and discussed. Till date, for all funds has been provided by the German Government for all the activities. But now after seeing the declarations and announcements made by the Indian Government, the funding agencies in Germany made it very clear that for Indian scholars, Government of India has to provide and for the scholars in Germany, DAAD and other funding agencies in Germany would support. In the two day conference, a special session devoted for funding research for Indian scholars. In the same way, yet another session devoted its attention on future research. They have identified the areas and opportunities. Finally, a fine declaration document has been prepared and signed by the academics involved in the research project in the past seven years. It is prepared to draw the attention of the policy community.

Declaration

Declaration on research between India and Germany in the field of skills development and vocational education and training New Delhi, October 2017

Current situation:

Over the past eight years, the signatory researchers have acquired wide-ranging experience of joint research projects, sharing expertise and learning from each other. They have successfully conducted a wide range of research projects and disseminated the findings to the interested public. The German Academic Exchange Service (DAAD) 'New Passage to India' funding stream set up by the German Federal Ministry of Education and Research (BMBF) have been essential to this fruitful activity.

In this context, India's substantial need for academic expertise in the area of skills development and vocational education and training (VET) has become evident. VET is increasingly crucial to the country's social and economic development.

We therefore believe research is needed in all areas of VET in India, including pre-vocational education in schools, formal vocational education and training, college and polytechnic courses, and non-formal and informal learning. Such research should also focus on studying the experience of other countries like Germany, to understand the best practices and evaluate which of those practices can help Indian VET system to progress faster and create visible impact.

This anchors the relevance of academic research into VET firmly in an international context. For example, the importance of VET and academic cooperation was reflected in the UNESCO Kuala Lumpur Declaration of 2015 (Asia-Pacific Conference on Education and Training: Quality Education and Skills Development for Sustainable Future).

We are therefore outlining our vision and what will be needed to achieve it and addressing relevant stakeholders in politics, the private sector and society:

Vision:

The signatory scholars' vision for the future of VET research is to:

- Strengthen the development of a research infrastructure in India, predominantly at university level, that meets the highest international quality standards.

- Step up recruitment of future generations of researchers into vocational education and training in India. We envisage a joint Indian-German training scheme for PhD students forming the basis for this strategy.

- Seek stronger cooperation between India and Germany at university level (including academic institutes) with a view to initiating and conducting joint research projects. The networks built will help to ensure quality and sustainability, with a focus on mutual learning by both countries.

- Develop possible research priorities in a number of areas, including curriculum development, implementation research, research into teaching and learning, teaching development, workplace learning, media and technology, school development and quality, school management, school-to-work transition, social policy, training economics, etc.

- Build networks in India with relevant stakeholders in the field of skills formation and VET, including the formal and informal economy, schools, state and private educational institutions, NGOs, and administrative and ministerial bodies.

What needs to be done:

Certain conditions and enablers need to be put in place to translate this vision into reality:

- Existing cooperation arrangements between Indian and German researchers need to be deepened and widened. We need to approach interested researchers in both countries with a proven track record and invite them to collaborate.

- It is impossible to plan research activities without appropriate budgets, so the provision of funding by the relevant state bodies on both sides is essential. The German-funded project 'New Passage to India' has been very successful and may therefore serve as a role model, but the model requires a stronger research component.

- Efforts are needed to smoothen the formal and administrative processes. This applies, inter alia, to the administrative management of research programmes, the provision of official authorisations required, etc.

- The political side in both countries seeks a shift in focus. The focus so far has been on support for promoting technology; in future, this will shift to a combination of research into technology and research into VET to implement technology effectively. For implementing technical innovation at operational level successfully and sustainably, India must have a very well trained workforce at an intermediate skills level.

- Activities will be closely linked to the cooperation activities of the Indo-German Joint Working Group on Skill Development and Vocational Education and Training.

Expected results:

If these aspects can be addressed, the signatories agree that significant added value can be created both for India and for Germany:

- A new high-quality research network will emerge and have long-term influence.

- Research by both Germany and India into VET will acquire international visibility and enjoy an enhanced reputation. The developments outlined above may also serve as a role model for other countries.

- The provision of wide-ranging and academically robust data and findings on VET and skill development in India will be broadened substantially and will underpin decision-making by training policy-makers. Indian, German and international companies will also have access to a set of essential information about employees' skills.

- Prior assessment and post-hoc evaluation of VET activities can be achieved through academically robust support programmes, enhancing the spirit and purpose of state-level innovations in vocational training.

- The quality of VET in India will be improved to better tackle the skills gap, which is the only way to solve India's economic and social challenges in the long term.

- Finally, research cooperation will also help to deepen cultural exchange and understanding between India and Germany.

70. Tasks for the New HRD Minister

The interview given by the new Human Resource Development Minister Javatekar to India Today T.V. channel on 22nd night 7.30 raises hope among academics that education will be freed from politics and ideologies. Higher learning institutions can enjoy freedom and autonomy for their academic and research pursuits. He mentioned that his concentration will be on maintaining quality in education as higher education has been expanded in geometric proportion in India. It is understandable that during any massive expansion which happens within a short span of time will have to face the problem of quality. In the world of work, enormous opportunities are available for skilled youth, but we find more of unemployment problems due to unemployability of the youth passing out from the educational institutions. This crisis is due to quality of education. Addressing this issue is not a small managerial problem. It requires a comprehensive plan of action with a sense of commitment and fire at all levels from governance to practice in the educational institutions. In the meanwhile he observed that accessibility, affordability and accountability are also the focus of his attention in the years to come.

The same statements have been given during UPA regime by the then HRD Minister also. The same statements have appeared in all UGC documents. These are all ceremonious declarations as convocation address. What comes out from the Ministry and the UGC is only a framework. It is to be translated into action. To do it all stakeholders in this process have to be conscientised. The present Minister has only three years at his disposal and within the period the targets and tasks have to be achieved. In the course of his response to the questions of Karan Tapar, he said that he always likes rebels in the academic institutions who are the real agents of innovation and change. Even while selecting the heads of many higher learning institutions and bodies, he will follow the due process and there won't be any insertion of ideologues of any category left or right into the institutions. Acclaimed intellectuals will be appointed for all those positions without bias and controversy. He maintained an argument throughout that he will keep education as a subject of all since it affects everyone. It has no ideology. It has to work for transformation of the society.

While looking at the points made in the interview one can presume, that he has agenda and he has a road map. But the ground has got disturbed. Because in the recent years the private played a major role in expanding the higher learning institutions. It is to be noted that the individuals who involved in expansion of higher education are not the traditional philanthropist as TATA or missionaries. They are money lenders and politicians who have entered into this job for making money. Terming them is not a small task. The governments have not prepared to invest in public institutions for expansion. They have only disturbed the institutions. The UGC is being disturbed and in turn it disturbed the higher learning institutions. Deemed universities are most disturbed institutions. Varieties of Deemed Universities have been promoted and they are in deep trouble. Yet another issue is the Deemed Universities very few in numbers roughly seven are fully funded by the MHRD through the UGC. They have been created for specific purposes. But the UGC has insisted to follow the regulations it has brought it. The new regulation has been brought in by the UGC in 2010 to regulate the private institutions and all the special purpose deemed universities have been asked to follow the new one. The special purpose deemed universities by following the regulations have lost the special purposes. They have been converted into third rate arts and science colleges.

In the meanwhile, nobody knows the decision of the government on the report submitted to the Ministry about the functioning of the UGC. Everyone in higher learning institutions is interested to know what is the fate of the UGC? Till now it is working as a post office. Whatever orders the HRD passes and it will be transmitted to the universities and colleges. The colleges and universities are taking directions and acted on the basis of the directions given by the UGC. But now it wants to implement the orders of the HRD. Many of the bottlenecks in the higher learning institutions are created only because of the gap that exists between the Ministry and the UGC from the perspective of perceptions on certain directions. It started from UPA-I while contextualizing and conceptualizing higher education in India in order to take advantage of the positive impact of globalization. Prime Minister office had a different perspective, HRD Ministry had yet another perspective and UGC contradicted the above two. Because of the differing perceptions, the country could not get a policy direction. As a result, education becomes a subject for free ride.

It is to be remembered that education is in current list which creates a lot of confusion as per the observation of many of the state governments. All regulatory bodies which are meant to regulate the system started functioning without having any perspective and commitment by using their autonomy. Globalization has brought different kinds of stakeholders to higher education sector for the expansion to meet the labour market requirements. Higher education has been moved towards market mode from service. As a result, profit drives everyone. All unscrupulous cronies have entered into higher education by investing huge capital mostly in unlawful ways and thereby the higher education has been privatized. Finally, it has come to mean that education becomes a commodity or a business for making profit. It becomes an industry that too unlawful industry from admission to appointment the institutions have adopted illegal means. Because there is no other way to do it. To regularize the illegality at present, it has been officially made a business or an industry where one can invest and get profit in education.

Vyabam in Madhya Pradesh and SRM University controversy over capitation fee collection illegally in Tamil Nadu are the tips of the iceberg. Education is converted into a tradable commodity. Foreign universities are coming only for that purpose. Now the Minister is touching only the broader issues and not the core issue. The core issue is, he has to define what is education. What is the real meaning of education? It is for what. It is for money making or for producing marketable students for industry or for increasing economic growth. Now it gives a sense that it is working for increasing the opportunity to earn more money. Education has to work for transformation of the society. It is for higher level activities of the human being. It has to work for the community and society and not for the educated alone. It should not be looked at investment return framework. It has to work for human evolution and human growth. If it is so how to fund higher education is the question. Unless the funding is regulated higher education will produce negative impact on the society. The present day education teaches effectively how to exploit the society. In the educational process, students have not acquired the values needed to serve the humanity. The students are losing the human values. Dehumanization takes place in the educational institutions in the name of education. If it is real education, the students when they are going out from the academic institutions, they have to go with self dignity, self confidence, finest human values to serve the society with empathy and sympathy. The educated are the agents of transformation. The students are going out from the higher learning institutions with certificates and skills and not with human values. This exploitative educational system has to be reversed and for which the Minister has to work. Education has to be humanized. Through the process of education young boys and girls wherever they are in the portals of higher learning institutions, they are to be humanized. The task is not so simple. It is herculean task. It requires a team, perspective, commitment, strategy and support from the central government, state governments, institutions and the public along with opinion makers at every level. Will it be possible for him to do the change? We hope he will and he can. Wait.

71. Third Dimension is missing in the Draft Input Policy Document

Higher education has got three dimensions namely research, teaching and extension or outreach. If all the three dimensional activities are integrated with each other, quality output and outcome the society will get out of educational process in the higher learning institutions. Substantially higher learning institutions in India are concentrating in teaching and less number of institutions are performing both research and teaching. Only a very few institutions are performing all the three functions. But even among a few institutions oflate extension is fading away as there is no encouragement from the regulatory institutions. But till date one cannot find a perfect model of extension which is to be followed as a framework in all higher learning institutions. Because of the lack of encouragement for the extension activities. While evaluating the higher learning institutions by the NAAC, due waitage is being given for the extension component. Absolutely the extension dimension of the higher learning institution has not been allowed to progress and expand in the functional domain rather it has been made stagnant or diminish without receiving needed attention. Against this background, the present document for the preparation of a new education policy is being looked at.

The context requires a new social orientation for our students and teachers to make them socially responsible and responsive individuals and this orientation could be given only through a systematic extension and outreach programme. But this new input draft report of the new education policy is unequivocally silent on extension activities in higher learning institutions.

Dr. Radhakrishnan committee report has devoted substantial attention on extension. Exclusively on an experimental basis, the committee suggested to create rural institutes in India to promote outreach in rural higher learning institutions. Based on the recommendations of Dr. Radhakrishnan committee report fourteen rural institutions have been created. Of the fourteen, thirteen have been integrated with mainstream university system and the remaining one is Gandhigram Rural Institute. This institute is also moving towards the mainstream and mainstream university. Subsequently the new education policy evolved in 1986 also highlighted some of the aspects of extension and recognized the importance of extension. For the above recognition for extension in the policy, the Gandhigram Rural Institute has contributed to some extent by sharing its experiences with the committee. But afterwards absolutely there is no follow up. Nothing has been translated from the policy to practice. Ofcourse on a project mode Adult and Continuing Education and later Life Long Learning Departments and centers have been created in the university system by the UGC and they became yet another institutional entities came into being meant for specific and targeted activities. But they are not mandated to carryout systemic extension work and bywhich entire staff and students of the university are taken to communities for extension work.

In terms of institutional strength India is in the second in the world which has got more than 750 universities, more than 39000 colleges, 11000 research institutions with 80,000 students. With this strength can't we attack the illiteracy? 208 million illiterates are in our country. If we have a proper extension system and process in our universities this problem could be tackled within a year. Next year we can declare India is totally a literate country. In the same way for clean India we fix target to build toilets to make India clean. The problem lies not in toilet construction, it lies in toilet culture. Toilet culture could be created by changing the attitude and behavior of the people. Attitude and behavior could be changed through awareness creation and sensitization of the communities through a process of campaign and training. This could be achieved through extension. By creating a meaningful extension system, processes and activities linking with curriculum our academic programmes could be more meaningful and socially relevant. When extension component is integrated with the curriculum, the students' employability will be increased. Then one could see the visible impact of higher learning institutions in the communities. Today higher learning institutions have no organic linkages with the communities. While going through the new input policy document and subsequently the reactions and responses of the political class and intellectual class, missing of this vital aspect extension is noticed. Hence, I want to bring it to the policy community the importance of extension in higher learning institutions by this write up.

Informally the committed teachers are working with civil society organisations to reach out the community. It is being done only a minority of the teachers in the higher learning institutions. Ofcourse in a few universities, teachers are in the Department of Extension to teach this subject. They teach extension education. Beyond that they could not move. They are also not interested in making it as a system for the whole institutions to take the students and staff to the community work. Because there is no mandate on the part of the institutions, teachers and the students to do extension activities and earn credit for promotion to the teachers and degree for the students. Hence, outreach programme should be made compulsory. In this context, creating a community college should not be equated with community outreach. It is totally different as system and process. What could be done now in the policy document?

We need a segment in the New Education Policy document to deal with extension or outreach component meant for higher learning institutions. A clear cut operational mechanism has to be spelt out to involve both teachers and students in outreach activities. While giving promotion to the teachers, substantial evaluation has to be untaken as to what extent teachers have contributed for the community through his or her outreach activities. While grading the universities, higher score has to be given to outreach activities in the evaluation process. This kind of activities will enable the institutions of higher learning to make the teachers and students socially responsible, responsive and conscious which will transform the society in the years to come.

72. **Where is Science, Technology and Market support structure for our Farmers?**

When I was standing in front of a farm in our institute in a fine evening along with a friend of mine from IRMA, Anand, Gujarat a foreign national came in a motor bike and reached very near to us. He asked us 'where is the way to reach Sarvodaya Colony?'. We told him that you have come in the wrong road and you have to take a different road to reach your destination. Since it was in the evening in the foothill of Sirumalai hills, small farmers brought their goats from Sirumalai hill to their houses which obstructed the movement of vehicles in the road. Hence, he has to stay for a while in the place where we were. During that time we asked him about his origin and purpose of his visit. He informed us that he is from Switzerland and he came here to learn yoga. He used to come to India once in a year and stay in anyone of the Guest Houses owned by people from Germany, Paris, Switzerland and Belgium. These Guest Houses are in the foothills of the Western Ghats. Since expenditure for their stay is cheaper, they used to come annually and stay there for a month or two. The foreigners are doing various kinds of activities. But the specialty of our interaction with him lies in his observations about the rural life led by rustic folk.

When we asked him about his background, he briefly told us that he is a small farmer with three milch animals leading a decent human life with all basic necessities. "He enjoys life and he is happy with what he has" he said. Annually he takes a break for a month and comes to India and stays in anyone of the Guest Houses maintained by the westerners. He told us that in India many of the people in the rural areas are having adequate resources to earn reasonable good income and they can lead a decent and dignified human life. But they lead life with poverty and penury despite adequate resources are with them. He also indicated that the life led by the rustic folk in the villages is not human life. They are not leading a decent and dignified human life. They live in sub human conditions. This life is not due to lack of resources. It is due to inadequate use of science and technology. Life without science and technology is full of tragedy and poverty. Life of the people is not guided by science, technology and the constitution in India. Their life is based the inherited community practices. After making this observation about the rural life in India he started narrating his life in his country. He has not even half an acre land. He cultivates some vegetables in his land. He has three milch animals and he prepares milk products by using simple technologies.

He sells pasteurized milk, butter, cheese in the local markets with a brand "home made". Apart from the above he sells honey also. All are homemade. Weekend homemade bread his wife prepares and they are also sold in the local market. The brand is "homemade". With this he earns adequate income from these sales and he leads happy life. He told that even poor families in the rural areas, by maintaining a few milch animal goats and chicken they can earn reasonably a good amount of money. But their life in India becomes difficult in the rural areas as their work and labour is exploited by many. He observed that it is a huge country and 68% of the people in the rural areas and people in the rural areas relying on both Agriculture and animal husbandry for their livelihood. If a little bit of education to use technology is imparted and provided with some technologies which are available in the market, the poor in the rural areas can earn huge profit through producing value added products from milk and animals.

He further informed that this can be easily provided by the agricultural and rural development universities in India. But in India, the universities are far away from communities and they act as silos. Neither they provide ideas nor knowledge or practices or technologies to the rural communities. It is a tragedy that opportunities are in India to transform the rural communities but they are not used properly. It needs enabling conditions. That could be provided by the higher learning institutions. People who owned a few milch animals by using separator, cheese and butter can be prepared and skimmed milk can also be prepared and sold in the local markets instead of selling milk directly to the vendors. Now in India everywhere we find super markets and they can be used very effectively. Apart from the above, meat and chicken flesh can be prepared and sold through local markets. For this rural entrepreneurs education is needed.

Apart from this, social education has to be imparted to the rural populace to lead a scientific decent, dignified human life. By educating them in hygiene and sanitation, their expenditure on medical care could be reduced and for which two important activities are needed. They are: a, hot water has to be taken as kerelites and b, toilet culture has to be created. By doing both rural people life style can be changed. This could be done only through social education. This kind of education is needed for the rural people. This could be given easily by the rural development universities and agriculture universities in India. As a farmer, he looked at the life of the rural rustic folk from his own perspective and expressed his remarks about rural life. Within fifteen minutes he has explained to us everything about rural transformation that is to be done in India. Rural life has not been transformed through science and technology and the technology which has reached the rural communities have enabled the poor to be exploited. Sanitation has not reached the poor but cell phone has reached the poor. Taking clean drinking water has not reached the rural areas but coco-cola reached the poor. Thus, what rural India needs today is education for livelihood and life through social education. All the above observations have been made by him. It was just like a class room lecture. Sun set was about to take place, he left and he made us to think whether our higher learning institutions have the perspective or commitment or skill or capacity to link up with the rural communities to transform them. It is a million dollar question.

73. Where we are heading towards in Higher Education in India

The All India Vice-Chancellors conference held in Hyderabad Osmania University on "Higher Education in India: Perspectives on Faculty, Funding and Freedom" on 27th and 28th April, 2017 brought to light the appalling conditions of the public funded institutions in India by the Vice-Chancellors through their presentations. While hearing the speeches of the speakers one would easily gauge the helplessness of the Vice-Chancellors in rejuvenating and contextualizing the higher learning institutions by responding to the challenges posited by the market and the society. Expected leadership was not forthcoming from them as they were always in the side of the problems not as part of solutions. It is a well recognized fact that higher education has become accessible to masses at present. Once it was for the elites and now it is meant for the masses. In the massification process it is only the public funded universities are the worst affected as they are being regulated by the regulatory bodies. As a result, the private agencies have moved into education sector to make profit. This process has resulted in conversion of education into a tradable commodity. The education which is being imparted now in higher learning institution is not inculcating either values or self confidence. The unchecked commercial growth of private higher learning institutions has further weakened the public funded institutions. The required number of staff to those universities has not been sanctioned by the regulatory and government agencies and the universities are not allowed to fill up the existing vacancies also. As a result, universities are facing shortage of faculty. Quality of the faculty recruited for higher learning institution is yet another serious issue highlighted by the Vice-Chancellors in the conference. They lamented that with the help of guest faculty courses are being run in the universities and it has affected much the quality of teaching. Technology has come to rescue the system if it is handled properly and yet handling technology for the benefit of the students is a problematic one. In this context, one could not find right mix to enhance the quality of teaching. There is yet another serious issue highlighted by the Vice-Chancellors in this conference is the resource sharing among the public funded institutions. While distributing the resources one would find discrimination between central and state universities. It has been emphatically indicated in their presentations that 86% of the resources are allocated to central universities but 86% of the students are passing out from the state universities by utilizing 14% of the total grant. This inequality persists for a long period. Poor investment of the state governments in higher learning institutions is yet another issue figured in the discussion. Politicization of the state universities has been done by the state governments and the political parties. This was viewed seriously in the discussion by the Vice-Chancellors. The topic chosen for discussion reflects the conditions of the higher learning institutions. Inadequate resources to higher learning institutions and the universities are not allowed to fill up the existing vacancies have figured in the presentations repeatedly. Along with the above two, they emphasized the need of autonomy for the universities for their functioning.

Yet another issue the quality of the graduates coming out from the institutions has also been focused in the discussion. It is stated that 78% of the graduates passing out from the higher learning institutions are unemployable and unless this issue is being seriously addressed, there is no meaning in deliberations in higher decision making bodies, lamented by many in the deliberations. The above statement is repeatedly made by the Vice-Chancellors by quoting the statements of the employers in various sectors. They have admitted that it is a slur on the part of higher learning institutions. It has been pointed out that there is no proper eco-system in the higher learning institutions to have a proper teaching learning process as we find in the west. Creativity and innovations cannot be achieved in the higher learning institutions in the existing framework of the higher education. In India, in our higher learning institutions what is to be done in the classroom has been done in home and what has to be done at home has been done in the classroom and thereby whole system is operated mechanically and not organically. Universities are meant for adventurous activities but the conditions will not allow the students to make such adventurous activities. A major shift is needed in teaching learning in higher learning institution in the present context. But, it is not happening as functioning of higher learning institutions are severely controlled by the regulatory institutions. While listening to the presentation, one will come to a conclusion that our higher learning institutions are in decline in every aspect.

To respond to all the points, the member of Niti Ayog, Dr. Vijaykumar Saraswath has lamented that our higher learning institutions has not only attracted the foreign students but also not prevented the Indian students to go abroad for higher studies. Because, original research is not being done in Indian academic institutions to retain our students in India and to attract the foreign students. Basically, it is due to weak leadership in the academic institutions. They are neither visionary, nor knowledgeable. Equally, the leader of higher learning institutions lack high academic standard and moral turpitude. Indian higher learning institutions are not involved in innovation or in application of the knowledge in finding solution. Higher learning institutions have not created proper eco-system for innovation. Our researches are additive and repetitive. Our university system has not attracted the professionals. A course correction is needed urgently in the Indian higher education system. Unless it is done urgently we are not only wasting valuable time but also huge resource. It is interesting to listen a story in the course of presentation that in a convocation of a university, the Chief Guest made an observation after seeing the long list of Ph. D awardees. 500 Ph.D degrees have been awarded in a university in a year. The Chief Guest openly asked the young graduates, how many of the thesis car give concrete solution to the existing problem of the society. Not even a single individual responded positively. Such a disconnect exists between the society and the academic contributions in the higher learning institutions. Yet another issue, the academic social responsibility is also being discussed as UGC has got a scheme called "University Social Responsibility" with an allocation of Rs. 2.5 crores. All weaknesses affecting the higher learning institutions have been discussed barring the poor quality of leadership of the higher learning institutions. The Vice-Chancellors need money to spend, to fill up post and non interference in their functioning. There were a few hard-hitting speeches about the academic accountability in the conference. From the speeches, one can conclude that neither the central government nor the state governments took serious interest in saving the higher education from further deterioration. After listening the discussions, lectures and deliberations as an observer I make the following suggestions:

1. Indian universities need visionaries and not managers to lead the institutions. Hence, without giving consideration to party affiliation or caste affiliation and to monetary consideration reputed academics have to be appointed as Vice-Chancellors. They should have high integrity and moral stature.

2. Make the higher learning institutions to perform teaching, research and outreach or extension as mandatory duties and equal weitage has to be given to all the three components while evaluating the performance of the university and teachers.

3. Fix problems and the social issues for research in higher learning institutions and allocate funds only to those problems. It should be made essential that socially relevant research have to be carried out.

4. Examination system has to be delinked from the university and it is to be conducted by an independent agency.

5. Education as a subject has to be listed in state list and it should be the responsibility of the state. The present crisis in higher learning institutions is due to its placement in concurrent list.

6. Funding for higher learning institution has to be rationalized. The present pattern of funding will create mere cleavages in the higher learning institutions.

7. At the earliest Education Policy has to be evolved and put in place.

While hearing speeches of the Vice-Chancellors, one can come to a conclusion that the present day leaders in universities could not provide leadership and unable to mobilize resources apart from the government. They could not enthuse the academics. It seems that they are caught in the web of regulations.

Section IV
Panchayati Raj Institutions

74. Believe People and their Powers

A Gram Panchayat president from Tuticorin district (Mr.Prapanjan, President of Thirukalur Gram panchayat) has silently mobilized the youth from the same village and issued identity card and asked them to help the villagers to get the needed materials from the nearby town to keep the people inside the house. The youth have been trained to do the work with care and sense of dedication. He has also personally supervised whether anybody is in need of food and he takes steps to provide the same. He has created needed awareness among the people about the pandemic and at the same time he has built the confidence among the people that the village panchayat would provide regular water supply and enable the public distribution system shops to provided the food material to all without any omission. He has also raised hope among the people that people are safe from the disease as long as people are continued in their houses during the lockdown period. There is no panicky among the people as there is a person with power along with a group of youth to take care of them. What messages given by the Prime Minister and the Chief Minister have reached the rustic folk. This is the leadership.

"Leadership is not position but a responsibility to be discharged with a sense of concern and commitment" observed by Rudolph W. Giuliani, two time Mayor of New York who faced the crises emanated out of the twin tower blast on September 11, 2001. In his book "Leadership", he narrated how he faced the crisis with the active participation of the functionaries and people. A leader has to give hope and build confidence among the people that we will emerge victoriously more powerfully than we were in the past. In this book he explained the role of leadership and the power of the local body in tackling unusual crisis.

Humanity reaches the present stage of material development through responding to the challenges given by various forces and of which nature is one. Any adverse event whether it is a war or a disaster both natural or human made, the event will produce new systems, institutions, practices, knowledge, skills, politics, policies and leadership. In that process loss both material and human will be inevitable and the humanity has seen that loses over a period of time. People while seeing the new developments after the disastrous event they tend to forget the past. But people who are in the helms of affairs to take care of the people and the system should not forget the lessons that humanity has learnt in the past disastrous events. Societies and leaders who have used the accumulated knowledge will minimize the loss and save the people. The present epidemic has created untold misery to many of the so called developed societies. During any crisis what people need is a strong leader to raise hope and give confidence to the people. In the present crisis people are in need of a strong leader in the world to overcome the crisis. The world events today have unequivocally brought to the notice that the world is in deep leadership crisis. Total deficit of leadership is being witnessed in the current scenario. Leadership is needed at different levels from global to local. Whatever have been taken at New Delhi and the State capital have to reach the people without any transmission loss. The messages have to reach the people in the same tone and tenor as exhibited by the national leaders and the provincial leaders to fight against the virus. Messages are louder at Delhi and at state capital but at the grassroots they are feeble. It needs more people at the ground with authority, power and resources to work closely with people as their leaders.

We have such a kind of institutional system is at the grassroots legally. They are panchayats, municipalities and municipal corporations. These institutions have to be used very effectively and keeping them in the governance and administrative loop. In India it seems that it is missing. The Prime Minister in his messages he has to emphasize the critical role of local bodies in disaster mitigation and preparedness work. They are the bridges to reach out to the people. In the same way the Chief Minister has to involve the local body leaders in all disaster preparedness and mitigation work. Unfortunately it has not been done in India barring a few states and more prominently Kerala. No doubt the Revenue Department has to play an important role as per Disaster Management Act. But supportive role has to be effectively done by the local bodies.

Kerala has done this work more effectively than any other state by involving the local bodies in the disaster mitigation work. Kerala state has walked extra mile by involving volunteers in the activities after skilling them. Since they had rich experience in the past, the state has used the past experience more effectively than many other states. In almost all the states the mitigation works have been done by the officials and volunteers from civil society organizations. We could see the members of the Legislative Assembly and Members of the Parliament are distributing food packets to the needy. These are all adhoism and not systematic work. These activities can be done by the local bodies.

If a local body is involved it will be more effective as known persons are on the job and exactly reaching out to the needy. Realistic information about the conditions of the people could be obtained only from the local institutions. Local leaders are responsible and responsive to the people as they are elected representatives who have to go to the people again to seek their support for re election. By involving the local institutions in the crises management a battalion of leaders will emerge with outstanding capacity, capability and skill which is an endowment for the politics of the country. Crises provide challenge to the people who are heading the institutions and the challenges are being responded by the leaders through their innovative strategies and ideas. Leaders are always be better groomed only during crisis. To overcome the pandemic crisis the local institutions and local leaders can play an exceptional role. In order to overcome all these weaknesses in our governance and administrative system for an efficient delivery of services a responsive, responsible and a representative governance system has been created through the 73rd and 74th Amendments to the constitution of India and thereby local governments both rural and urban are in part IX and IX A of the constitution of India. It is created for fixing an institution responsible and responsive to the people locally. But it is missing to-day in the governance loop in managing the present crisis. If the local bodies are involved by the central and state governments with a true spirit of recognizing people's power managing the present crisis will be much easier.

75. **Belittling a Constitutional Body**

Of the three constitutional institutions namely the State Election Commission District Planning Committee, and State Finance Commission, the State Election Commission is the only body active but it is also belittled by many of the State Governments through their delayed discharging of their responsibilities. This I have noticed when I participated in the conclave of State Election Commissioners at National Institute of Rural Development and Panchayati Raj on 9th and 10th of January 2020, Hyderabad. The problems are so serious yet the State Election Commissioners are able to conduct the elections by facing plethora of problems. The panelists and experts have made presentations on the problems faced by the State Election Commissions in conducting free and fair elections to local bodies in Indian states. Almost all the State Election Commissions have been facing problems as most of the State Governments reluctant to have local bodies elections in time. There are a few exceptions like Kerala. The State Governments create road blocks to delay the conduct of elections by using their powers by procrastinating the completion of their responsibilities of redrawing the wards, effecting rotation of offices and fixing reservation of seats.

Many of the occasions State Governments did not cooperate with the State Election Commissions to the conduct of election to the local bodies. The State Governments do it covertly. The State Election Commissions cannot criticize the State Governments as it would harm the whole process of the conduct of the elections. In many of the states local body elections are being conducted as pressure has been exerted on the State Election Commissions by the judiciary. It is learnt from the presentations of the State Election Commissioners that State Election Commission find more clarity in the judgements of the Supreme court rather than the directions of the High Courts. Article 83 of the Constitution of India is meant for conduct of election to state legislature and the parliament. This article does not say that it is mandatory on the part of Election Commission of India and yet it takes place regularly. But Article 243 of the same Constitution of India says that it is mandatory that election has to be conducted for local bodies every five year and the whole process of election will be over before the expiry of the term of the office. Yet local body elections are not being conducted regularly. There is yet another instrument "Peoples representatives Act 1951" can be used for the conduct of the local body election as local bodies are integrated into part IX and IXA of the Constitution of India. Despite the availability of all those instruments for the support of the State Election Commissions, elections are not conducted in time. Periodically the State Election Commissioners use to meet but they were not serious about articulating the problems of the State Election Commissions. But the National Institute of Rural Development and Panchayati Raj and the State Election Commission of Telengana took serious note of the problems afflicted with the State Election Commissions and organized a conclave of State Election Commissioners. While deliberating on the issues it has been argued that the State Governments have retained many of the responsibilities of the State Election Commission which are to be completed in time to conduct the election to local bodies in time. State Governments rarely complete the works of fixing rotation, reservation and delimitation of wards. Unless the above tasks are completed in time the State Election Commissions cannot conduct the election in time. If all the above works are vested with delimitation commission one can expect the election to local bodies would be conducted in time. The State Election Commissions have been created in such a way that they have to be at the mercy of the state governments for finance to run the whole machinery and carryout the mandated responsibilities.

It is a pity that there is no public pressure for the conduct of free and fair elections in time. Neither the central government nor the political parties or the media show concern on the serious issue of the regular conduct of election to local bodies. What is the way out to resolve this serious problem. By bringing an amendment to the constitution of India the State Election Commissions can be integrated with Election Commission of India. Otherwise through yet another amendment the State Election Commissions should be given the responsibility of fixing reservation, rotation and redrawing of the wards. While doing so enough care has to be taken to ensure regular flow of funds to the State Election Commissions to discharge the mandated responsibilities. Further the State Election Commissioners have to be appointed through a collegium consisting of Chief Minister, Chief Justice of the High Court of the state and the opposition leader of the State Legislative Assembly. The issue has to be properly analysed by looking at Article 83, Article 243 and peoples representative Act 1951. Unless otherwise, the local government becomes a laughing stock. It is a serious issue which needs the attention of the central government opinion makers, media and the research institutions. Central government role does not end with amending the constitution to create new local bodies. It's responsibilities lies in implementing the same letter and spirit and it is the need of the hour and it has to see whether enacted legislations are properly implemented.

76. Training Policy for Grassroots Leaders

Keeping India together and maintaining democracy in India continuously with a break of two years and introducing constitutionally mandated governance at local level with three million representatives have drawn the attention of the exponents of democracy in the world and made them to look at the paradoxes of transformations that take place in India. For many of the incorrigible optimists, India has done many revolutions contrary to the expectations of the established theories. But to some others, they are in rhetorics and not in practice. Both are realities if we look at the transformative process of India like the arguments of B.R.Amedkar and M.K.Gandhi on village swaraj. The enactment of the 73rd Constitutional Amendment provided enormous scope for deepening of democracy and democratization at the community level. It is to be critically evaluated as to what extent it has impacted in the democratic practices of the communities. India being a land of diversities, it is unfair to make sweeping generalization on the life, livelihood and socio cultural practices of the Indian societies. Since the 73rd Amendment to the Constitution of India is applicable to Indian society, it is imperative to make some general observations about the impact of democratic decentralization based on the studies conducted by various research agencies.

But pan Indian evaluative studies on decentralization have come with remarkable conclusions that a, despite many hurdles and barriers rural local governance institutions have delivered services more effectively than the bureaucratic raj; b, corruption has been reduced in quantum but the number of people involved in corruption has increased; c, percapita bribe is more than percapita tax; d, local bodies have been transformed into an errant boy of the central government and state governments to implement their schemes and programmes; e, poor and marginalised groups have started asserting themselves and claim their rights on development despite barriers and obstacles. With the above conclusion, they posited a question that despite all the barriers the local rural governance institutions have delivered goods and eased out frustration of the poor, why the state governments are not evincing keen interest in strengthening the rural local governance institutions? If they are to be strengthened what are the steps to be taken and who has to take such decisions? are the daunting questions linking in the minds of the hardcore academic community today.

Before making any policy suggestion one has to look at the task to be performed in the society through the rural local bodies. It has to work for economic development and social justice and they are to be performed through a participatory process of governance and development. Here, it is to be recognized that our communities follow the age old community practices in regulating the affairs of the community but not the provisions of the constitution. At the community level there has been always a clash between community practices and constitutional provisions. First time the communities are brought under democratic governance with the participation of the people through the constitutional amendment. In the same way the local governments have to work for economic development and to achieve social justice. It is to be recognized here that both the centre and state governments could not achieve to the level of the target fixed by them despite their programmes, schemes and strategies along with huge outlays. Against this background one has to visualize the task of new local bodies. To achieve the above task at the grassroots a new leadership is an imperative. In this country electing a leader is not a difficult task but shaping the leaders is very difficult. There is no consciousness on the part of the national leaders that the leaders at the grassroots are to be shaped and oriented to perform development administration and development politics. There is no training culture in our political system as there is no training policy in India to train our Members of Parliament, Members of Legislature and Members of Local Bodies. The tasks assigned to the local body leaders are tremendous and hence to fulfill the tasks, we require transformational leaders. Are they going to be born? They are in local bodies as elected representatives and they are to be informed that they should become transformational leaders. One cannot be a leader once he or she is elected unless he or she is trained. How could we transform the elected representatives as transformational leaders? It is through a process of training. It could be done through the training institutions. Do we have such a kind of training institutions? Yes, we have training institutions but not to train transformational leaders. The existing training institutions are not creative leadership schools. They train only managers for micro institutions. First the training institutions have to be transformed into 'Leadership Schools'. How these schools have to be created? These schools have to be created as 'Ashrams' of Mahatma Gandhi. Because the new local bodies are here not to follow the style of our MPs and MLAs. They have to work for total transformation of the rural areas. It is a new socio economic reconstruction of the villages. It is a Neo-Gandhian constructive programme. Hence, the leadership country wants for grassroots action is unique and they are to be groomed as Mahatma Gandhi groomed workers for constructive programme. To conduct such a training programme, all the existing training institutions have to be liberated from the shackles of the state bureaucracy and they have to be placed under the autonomous governing boards headed by strong transformed leaders. They should be independent. They should take a new avatar. For all the training programmes Government of India is giving resources. So a training policy could be evolved to training grassroots leaders for governance and development at community level. Budgeted resource allocation should be in place regularly.

77. Can Government make the noise into voice?

Feedback from the Students

Students are drawn from the different socio economic settings for participation in the focus group discussion on the issues of Governance.

Effective governance could be seen from the behaviour of the people who are in power. There is correlation between behavior and performance. Those who are leading a simple life with minimum living conditions can understand the conditions of the poor. Performance lies not on sound words in simple actions. What poor wants from the governments? They need rations through public distribution system. They need water, they need shelter, and they need basic health facilities. Apart from the above, they need simple livelihood options. People who are in helm of affairs should be responsive and responsible. Poor are always making noise, and the government consider them as petitioner. They are not treated as responsible and honourable citizens. Majority in our society live without dignity. Restoring dignity is most important duty of the government. In our country those who are in power are most honourable and respectable. But poor are dishonourable but they are honourable only during election. In this country poor are only abiding and adhering to laws. Others only violate. Violation becomes a culture. To arrest violation of laws and regulation one has to go to court. Unless people behavior is changed this violation will continue. When the noises of the poor people are respected it becomes voice. Poor will feel that they are considered when government looks after the basic needs of the poor that is the accountable government.

Poverty and deprivation are the root cause of violence. Their issues and problems are not addressed but police and army are being strengthened. Development of the poor gets less attention as they can be ruled. It is a pity that in our country people are ruled and not governed. If they are governed, people will get their due respect from the governing class.

Effectiveness of the government could be seen only in the condition created for the people to lead a decent and dignified human life with peace and joy. In our rural society culture based norms are guiding the people for their life. Science and technology have to guide but not in practice.Now rule of law is only in discourse. We find everywhere ruling party oral direction as ruling party laws.

In a democratic country, if the cost of politics is very high, possibility of corruption is more. Today's politics we have to spend a lot and for election Parties and candidates have to spend huge money. Where from money comes? is a question. People are not giving money to political parties. Political parties are spending huge money. They collect money from the industrial houses and monetarily powerful people. When they get money from them for whom the governing class will work. Work for the people who support them monetarily to mange party and election. Corruption has afflicted politics and now it has involved public. Everyone in part of it what is the need of the hour? It is reduction of cost of politics

A maid servant working in four houses said that a good government is one which keeps the prices of essentials commodities for food well within the earnings of the poor. When the poor are unwell they should get treatment in nearest hospital without making payment. To educate the kids of the poor, they should not spend much. Along with the above every able bodied men and women get employment opportunity in their vicinity commeasure with their skills. The entire struggle of the poor is to manage the above. If a poor get what all are the facilities required , he or she does not bother about how many times prime minister goes to foreign countries. It is pity that in India poor have to struggle for their livelihood. In this context where poor will find time to think about politics excepting going to the booth to cast their vote.

78. Elusive Development and Distress in the Rural Areas of Tamil Nadu

Recently I have visited a village (my own native T. Melakkadu, Pattukottai Taluk) in Thanjavur district after a gap of ten years. The visit was aimed at mapping up the transformation happened in the village in the past one decade. To my surprise, I could find concrete houses small, medium and big ranging value from five lakh to one crore rupees. Most of the houses I found cars in the porticoes. In all the streets I have seen black top roads and some of the lanes are completely cemented. Around the houses compound walls have been erected by replacing live fencing with plants. After visiting the main villages, I have gone interior villages where I found all the water tanks (forty six) are empty and there is no trace of water stored in the tanks. The connecting channels both inlet and outlets have been disappeared. I have reached the paddy field, and it was a shock for me that there was no trace of cultivation of the land in the near past. Six thousand acres of cultivable lands have not been cultivated as there was no water either from channels connected with Cauvery water channels, or from the lakhs which store water during rainy season. In the paddy field after harvest one can see cattle gracing in the field. But very rare to find cattles in the village. No milch animals either in the houses or in the paddy field. No birds rearing in the houses. All the channels carry water to the paddy field dried up and not cleaned. They are all with full of obstructing weeds. After visiting the paddy field I have reached the market place where I found mini malls and not a conventional grocery shops but of reliance model of super and hyper market where one can get all products as one gets in Delhi, Bangalore, Mumbai and Chennai. Packets milk available and sold in the mall. Meat stalls with all kinds of birds with mutton being sold on all days. Never we had the practice of taking non-vegetarian food everyday in our village in the past. There are vegetables in plenty not the local variety available in the store. I could not see the old village full of green, streets with trees on the two sides. I could not see the local birds either in the houses or on the trees. There were no birds chipping in the evening and morning. I have seen the riddles in the village. To me it is a paradox. To find out the truth I met a few opinion makers and informed individuals in the village at the market place. Being a native of that village having visited village after a long gap, it was a surprise for many and everyone evinced keen interest in meeting me and interacting with me. I started my argument with the richness what I found in the village in the form of palatial buildings, higher end cars in the bungalows and blacktop roads, the responses came spontaneously from the opinion makers that it is nothing but cosmetics. People from the main village long back felt that through agriculture one cannot earn much and develop and hence they tried to migrate to Towns, Cities, Middle East and western countries. People who migrated to nearest town established some business ventures. People who migrated to Chennai established big business ventures. Others who migrated to foreign countries to work as skilled workers and by doing all kinds of works, they have created this asset in this village through these hard earnings. Most of the family members are not in the houses constructed in the village. These bungalows with cars are the symbols of their achievements. All others in the villages who could not migrate are facing volley of challenges. No doubt village has been changed and transformed but not developed to lead a decent dignified, happy human life with needed basic minimum facilities. Since the progressive formers realized the future of agriculture is bleak they migrated from the village in search of profitable livelihood. Since they abandoned forming and migrated to cities and foreign countries, all the maintenance works of the water bodies have been abandoned. Since water supply was given by the local bodies, interest in maintenance of the water bodies has been declined. As a result, water bodies have been encroached. Inlet and outlets channels to water bodies have also been encroached. When farm practice has been declined, people abandoned growing cattle both rich and the poor. People with skill and money have migrated and established alternative livelihood. The poor stagnated in the village. But the arrival of MGNREGA was timely and poor have got livelihood. But the life of poor has also been affected as they have stopped growing milch animals in the houses. Because, they could not find feed for the animals from agriculture. Now even poor have to purchase water in the rural areas. But public have picked up the urban living practices as they have been cultivated by the market. Living in rural areas for the people who are in Government jobs, doing business here and elsewhere, politicians, is enjoyable and cost of living is not cheap as in the past. One has to pay for everything. But for the poor it is torturous. People have to struggle if they are poor as there are no adequate basic provisions in the ration shop, inadequate drinking water supply to the poor. Poor had adequate firewood collected from the village commons. But now they are purchasing firewood. All common properties have been encroached by the party men and influential individuals. For all physical ailments the poor have to pay in the hospitals for treatments. All public schools are meant for poor. Since they are meant for poor, the quality is poor. Since the poor has developed aspiration to become rich, they also spent money to put their wards in private schools. Poor have to lead a life with full of stress and constraints.

The MGNREGA wages have not been distributed in time. This year Tamil Nadu has witnessed 65% deficit rainfall. As a result, the poor could not find enough work to earn their livelihood. Hence, in Tamil Nadu the hundred days work has been increased to one hundred and fifty days which was also approved by the Government of India. At present, there is no elected local body in place to respond to the call of the people for their minimum needs. Life in the rural areas is not comfortable as we expect. They lead life with stress. The distress is growing. As a result, discontent is growing against the state. Against this background, rural areas threatened with the methane and hydro-carbon projects. Tamil Nadu is the fast urbanizing state. Nearly 50% of the population is in the urban areas. Beyond certain level urban areas cannot cater to the needs of the migrant population. To solve many of the rural problems an alternative paradigm of rural development is needed. A study sponsored by the Ford Foundation came with the conclusion that globalization of economy has helped only the rich and the upper middleclass and not the poor. The study was done by me and the findings have been published through two books. This rural paradox is the result of industrialization, modernization, westernization and globalization along with weak decentralization and democratization. Our policy makers and political pundits have not been sensitive to look at the rural problems properly and perspectively as 68% of the people are in the rural areas in India. M.K. Gandhi having realized this scenario hundred years ago suggested a new education for India to transform villages in India. Not even a single university in India to find solution to the problems faced by the people in the rural areas. The need of the hour is a world class rural institute to transform rural areas in India.

79. Where is Local Government in the Fight against Corona

Even the highest body in the world like WHO can take a decision to fight against the pandemic corona in a most efficient way. But the results could be achieved only through committed local actions by the local bodies with the active involvement of the stakeholders. It requires appropriate policy sets at the national and regional levels. Synergetic actions are needed among the institutions appropriately from the International to local levels. Throughout the world the institutions and organizations involved in the fight against corona established partnership with the local bodies and carried out their activities. In the recent news letter of the Swedish International Centre for Local Democracy carries the stories about the excellent role performed by the local bodies in the fight against corona in some of the African countries. In India media has highlighted the achievements of Kerala state in fighting against corona by involving the local bodies and self help group women along with huge volunteers drawn from both urban and rural areas. To some extent Odisha too followed the model of Kerala in involving the local bodies in tackling the crisis. Barring the above, state governments are not interested in involving the local bodies in the fight against Corona. Yet the central government has transferred panchayats Rs.200292.2 crores under 14th finance commission allocation and Rs.257597.96 crores under MGNREGA (100 days work) alone for its activities.

Then why the other state governments have not evinced keen interest in involving the local bodies in managing the present crisis despite the presence of local governments. It is pertinent to ask why the Prime Minister of India or the Ministry of Panchayati Raj has not sent directives to states to make use of local bodies as partners to tackle the crises by using their powers and resources. But at the same time the Prime Minister on 24th April in connection with panchayat day celebration he interacted with elected representatives of the local bodies and asked them to work for the creation of 'Gram Swaraj' as envisioned by Mahatma Gandhi. Had the local bodies in all the states involved in the crisis management as done by Kerala the impact would have been different one. Kerala's achievements in managing the pandemic corona have drawn the attention of the world. Of course, in many places all over India the local body leaders on their own acted as volunteers as they have not received any directives from the state governments. This kind of voluntarism has indicated the huge leadership potentials are available at the ground. One could understand the reasons for the reluctance of many of the state governments in involving the local bodies in managing COVID19 if anyone goes through the sixth volume of the second Administrative Reform Commission reports and the report of the Mani Shankar Aiyar committee. Both reports have indicated the potentials of the local bodies and the reluctance of both governments in strengthening the Panchayati Raj system.

While investigating the reasons for the reluctance of the governments in empowering the local bodies a few scholars argue that in India the design of decentralization is a faulty one and hence it will not enthuse the state governments to decentralize powers from their pool to local bodies. The central government has not devolved any of its powers to the state governments. Nor even given back the powers taken away from the state but state governments have been asked to devolve powers to the local bodies. Logically speaking power has to move from centre to state and state to local bodies. It is not happening in India.

Interestingly the Ministry of Panchayati Raj had a Cabinet Minister with a budgetary support of Rs.8000 crores at once during the UPA regime to strengthen the Panchayati Raj activities. But when NDA came to power in 2014, it had been reduced to Rs. 90 crores in budgetary allocation for the Ministry of Panchayati Raj in 2015. In such a way the importance of the subject has been reduced at the central level. Why this kind of lukewarm attitude towards decentralization of powers? There is a reason behind it and it was explained long back by Jayaprakash Narayan in 1965 itself in the conference organized by the All India Panchayat Parishad at Bangalore. He stated that "everyone will talk about Gram Swaraj and decentralization of powers in India especially people who are in helm of affairs both in the state and the centre. In reality they know that it is very difficult as the power brokers will not allow power to reach the poor and the rustic folk. The power brokers know that the majority in India are poor and they are to be ruled only through state apparatus and they should not be empowered and hence empowering people in India is a herculean task. If it is to be done it should be through a peoples movement not through any legislation". The above observation holds good even to-day.

Yet panchayats are functioning not as an institution of self governance but an agency of the centre and the state governments. A state like Tamil Nadu gets Rs.3600 crore under Central Finance Commission allocation for panchayat institutions and around Rs.5000 crores spent on MGNREGA in the rural areas and yet another Rs. 5000 crores from the State Finance Commission allocation. They are being spent as institutions of spending. But the accountability at the ground is very minimum. It is very difficult to get data on spending at grassroots. Every finance commission both central and state found it very difficult to make recommendations based on the reliable data set. Yet the Central Finance Commissions continuously gave sufficient allocation of resources to the panchayats with a hope that they would deliver services to the people. It is the right time to raise a fundamental question why the state governments are reluctant to devolve powers and why the centre is also not exerting pressure on the state governments to devolve the powers appropriate to them despite the huge flow of funds to the panchayats.. The local bodies are not mere spending institutions. It is high time to take it to the constitutional bench of the supreme court to spell out the constitutionality of the bodies in terms of its standing as an institution of self governance.

liance